H. G. WELLS: DISCOVERER OF THE FUTURE

THE INFLUENCE OF SCIENCE ON HIS THOUGHT

Roslynn D. Haynes

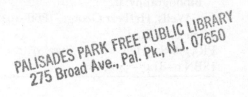
New York University Press · New York *and* London

Library of Congress Cataloging in Publication Data

Haynes, Roslynn D.
  H. G. Wells, discoverer of the future.
  (The Gotham library of the New York University Press)
  Bibliography: p.
  1. Wells, Herbert George, 1866–1946 – Knowledge –
Science. I. Title.
PR5778.S35H28   823'.9'12   79–67177
ISBN 0–8147–3403–0

Printed in Great Britain

For Raymond, Nicola and Rowena
and for my parents

Contents

Preface

As a scientist who defected to the literary camp I have long been struck by the profound effect that scientific developments had on the literature of the nineteenth century, and the lamentable lack of such cross-fertilisation in the twentieth.

H. G. Wells was the last great literary figure to have been so strongly influenced by science. Not only did contemporary theories contribute ideas to his books, but he, in turn, predicted so many consequences of current scientific knowledge that he had the misfortune to be hailed as a prophet. His scientific romances, short stories, novels, blueprints for utopia, his history of the world and encyclopaedic textbooks of biology, sociology and economics, made him the most widely read author in the language, and secured him the respect of even Roosevelt and Stalin.

But if a prophet can be said to be without honour in his own country, he is even more bereft of it in the next generation, and Wells is no exception. The reprisals taken by the generation following him have been severe. In their zeal to show how gullible their fathers were, critics have reduced Wells's scientific romances to the status of imaginative fairy tales which merely pretend to authenticity by a scattering of scientific terms. The utopian and sociological novels have fared still worse. They do not win even the minor award for imaginative merit, but are rejected on grounds of both form and content.

Whatever the immediate outcome of the controversy between Wells and Henry James about the novel form, James succeeded in the long term in converting the more influential critics to his own artistic criteria, which could not accommodate Wells's writings. In addition, since the 1930s, utopias have become universally suspect, for it is assumed that they are all merely cowardly fronts for a brave new world, or a 1984 concentration camp.

It is the purpose of this book to trace the actual extent of the scientific influence on Wells's thought, not only as it appears in the scientific romances, but in the character novels and utopian works as well.

As a result of this influence, Wells *was* a prophet, not merely in the popular sense of having predicted space travel, processed food and the Common Market, but in the wider sense of being able to think in a completely new way about the future – to be, as it were, at home in the future. Such a way of thinking freed him, as he immediately realised, from much of the seemingly iron-bound determinism under which nineteenth-century novelists had laboured; it provided a new perspective from which to view man in his personal and social relationships.

Any balanced assessment of Wells's contribution to literature must take account of his sins against the canons of form, but it should not neglect his enthusiastic attempts to break the mind-forged manacles of the present.

December 1978   R.D.H.

Acknowledgments

It is a great pleasure to be able to thank Dr Peter Keating of the University of Edinburgh for the stimulating discussion and helpful comments which accompanied the preliminary stages of this book.

Throughout all stages of its gestation I have been blessed with the encouragement and enthusiastic support of my parents and two daughters, and especially of my husband, who has in addition contributed everything from exhaustive discussions on relativity to exhausting bouts of household management.

The author and publishers wish to thank the Executors of the Estate of H. G. Wells and Professor G. P. Wells for permission to quote from the works of H. G. Wells.

Introduction

H. G. Wells was one of the first professional writers of fiction to have had a formal scientific education and the first for whom the role of science in society was a primary question, for in his case this qualification was no mere optional extra – the icing, as it were, on the literary cake; on the contrary it formed perhaps the basic ingredient in the strange and diverse mixture of his thought. Before he enrolled as a science student Wells's only literary output was fourteen copies of 'The Up Park Alarmist', a mock daily newspaper written, as he later said, 'on what was properly kitchen paper', for the amusement of the 'below stairs' staff and satirising the trivia of Up Park, the stately home where his mother was housekeeper. It was a measure of the environment in which he had grown up that even this insignificant performance was regarded as a cause for some pride on the part of Wells and, one suspects, for trepidation at such daring on the part of his mother. Yet after, and very largely because of, his years at the South Kensington Normal School for Science, Wells became the most prolific author of any stature in his generation, and certainly the most widely read of his contemporaries. His influence on the younger writers of his day was immense, firstly as a model for emulation in their revolution against the establishment, and subsequently as a tradition against whom it seemed to them obligatory to react. George Orwell, who was by no means uncritical of Wells's philosophy, wrote in 1941:

> Thinking people who were born about the beginning of the century are in some sense Wells's own creation. How much influence any writer has, and especially a 'popular' writer whose work takes effect quickly, is questionable, but I doubt whether anyone who was writing books between 1900 and 1920, at any rate in the English language, influenced the young so much. The minds of all of us, and therefore the physical world, would be perceptively different if Wells had never existed.[1]

1

and Scott Fitzgerald recorded the effect on him of the 'gloriously intoxicated efforts of H. G. Wells to fit the key of romantic symmetry into the elusive lock of truth'. Yet it is one of the quirks of literary criticism that, although Wells was originally hailed in vastly exaggerated and eulogistic terms as a scientific prophet, the reaction against this aspect of his work soon set in. Wells has now become, for most critics and biographers, the forerunner of the 'doomsday syndrome' or the writer of fairy-tale fantasies which, despite their veneer of scientific terms, are fundamentally anti-scientific.

It is not the purpose of this book to duplicate the biographical material which has already been extensively documented in several autobiographical novels, in a spate of biographies and, perhaps most interestingly, in Wells's own *Experiment in Autobiography*, but rather to attempt to right what seems a gross imbalance by assessing the degree to which Wells's years as a science student affected his subsequent way of thinking and hence his writing. This influence is not confined to the scientific romances, although it is most obvious there; it extends to the utopian writings, to the sociological novels and treatises, and it underlies even Wells's style of writing and his approach to characterisation. Indeed it is scarcely possible to overestimate the extent to which his scientific training changed and moulded his life and thought. It affected not only the way he approached the novel's traditional themes of personal relationships and the social order, and the view-point from which he assessed traditional values, but also the scope of his interests and the issues which he judged appropriate for inclusion.

In 1912, Wells delivered what was in effect a manifesto of his intention to enlarge the scope of the novel, asserting the right of novelists to 'have all life within the scope of the novel'. Inevitably he did not succeed in including 'all life' within his compass but it cannot be doubted that Wells did indeed expand the scope of the novel in several important respects. The broadest and ultimately the most far-reaching effect of his work was the introduction into literature of a new awareness of the future. This arose out of Wells's scientific consciousness and particularly out of his interest in evolutionary theory, which is essentially forward-looking and glances backwards only for comparison and reference. In this respect, his writing embodied a genuinely new set of assumptions, the literary correlatives of the new attitudes to science emerging early in the twentieth century. Indeed, in so far as Wells was already writing of the new climate of thought and feeling before the turn of the century, he actually anticipated it, and may be said, in the light of his wide reading public, to have fostered it.

It is a familiar statistic that 90 per cent of all those who, since the beginning of recorded history, could be called scientists are still alive, but such a statement implies something fundamental about the general attitudes of a large proportion of educated minds today. The most striking difference between them and the attitudes of the preceding centuries is the vastly decreased reliance on the past, on history, on precedent, as ends in themselves, and a corresponding awareness of the future as the necessary and largely predictable outcome of the present. For the humanist, on the other hand, most things today come *after*. George Steiner comments that:

> Language, musical notation . . . even the most radical of modern visual forms, carry with them the overburdening luggage of the past. Language, in particular, has its past literature, past achievements, and past dreams. The greatest of our twentieth-century artists are masters of the pastiche: Joyce, Picasso, Stravinsky. . . . The statement that there will not be in the English language, ever, a writer as great as Shakespeare is, in terms of the semantics of the future tense, an odd paradox. It is the kind of statement one should have no grounds to make, linguistically, psychologically. Yet in the moment that we do make it, it carries a real weight of conviction.[2]

Classical literature had customarily looked back to a Golden Age and nineteenth-century Romanticism revived and expounded the belief that everything was at its best and purest at the time of its origins, implying that any apparent progress could, by definition, be only a deterioration. For the scientist on the other hand the future is, by simple definition, in advance of the present, just as a schoolchild of today uses concepts and arguments of which Newton and Gauss were unaware. It is this latter attitude which underlies all Wells's work, even *The Outline of History* for, unlike any previous history, it was written not out of interest in the past, but for its relevance to the future. Wells, despite his unquestionable literary ability, had imbibed a future-oriented turn of mind rather than the characteristically literary turn of mind which values and absorbs tradition. His 'Discovery of the Future' was indeed a genuine discovery, for both author and readers, in that, after the publication of *Anticipations*, prophecy came to be seen as an organised and methodical activity rather than mere guesswork, and the future as being capable of manipulation by non-magical means.

This belief in the knowableness, the innate 'reasonableness' of the future is of course a necessary prerequisite for science fiction but it also had several other important consequences in Wells's writings. Firstly, there is a sense of courage to live for the future because we need no longer be helpless pawns of circumstance but may confidently embark on a course of action to influence the future for good by fostering the best possible development of society and ultimately of the human race. This spirit of adventuring into the future underlay Wells's belief in the aesthetics of the machine age, both attitudes being in total opposition to the prevailing spirit of the nineties. Pre-eminently in his writings, Wells captured the exhilaration of living in a modern, mechanised world, a sense of delight in change and development free from any sense of hankering for the past.

Again, although Wells succeeded to a long tradition of utopian literature, he also unwittingly fathered a new trend which repudiated the whole concept of sociological progress, for the major anti-utopias of the twentieth century were conceived either in reaction against Wells's utopias with their extensive technology or as an extension of his picture of the future in *The Sleeper* and 'A Story of the Days to Come'. Even the former anti-utopias are modelled in considerable detail on Wells's concepts, since they all have in common the description of claustrophobic states where conditioning ensures obedience, where freedom is eliminated, individuality destroyed, and all memories of the past rigorously erased; where men are artificially isolated from 'Nature' and where science and technology are used not to enrich the quality of the individual's life but to enforce obedience and control its slaves even at the subconscious level. These later works are all continuations of Wells's own imagination. Hillegas comments, 'It is doubtful that without Wells, the anti-utopian phenomenon would ever have taken the shape it has,' and of *The Time Machine* in particular:

> In imaginative qualities it excels the later anti-utopias, such as even, *We*, *Brave New World*, being both more successful in domesticating the incredible and more poetic in its conception. Its coherence and power explain why it not only contributed

numerous details and images to the twentieth-century anti-
utopias, but made available to the literary consciousness a new
form (science fiction) and suggested one use for this form (the
attack on Utopia).[3]

Thus, in a real sense, Wells instigated many of the twentieth-
century 'traditions' about the future. Zamyatin's *We*, for example,
is set in a superstate of the twenty-sixth century, a giant city roofed
with glass and cut off from the surrounding country by a wall of glass
which isolates the citizens from nature and provides a completely
artificial environment, a situation almost identical with that which
Wells described in *The Sleeper* with its glass-domed roof. The citizens
of *We* wear identical blue-grey uniforms equivalent in every way to
the blue canvas of the Labour Exchange Co. in 'A Story of the Days
to Come'.

It was Zamyatin also who pointed out that Wells's scientific
romances are the urban fairy tales of our century, with trees, beasts
and the earth being replaced by smoke-stacks, automobiles and
asphalt roads. Zamyatin considers that these fairy tales attain the
status of myth which is 'always, visibly or invisibly, bound with
religion . . . and the religion of today's city is exact science'.[4] It is in
this role of myth-maker that Wells becomes important to the
development of the novel in yet another sense – that of relating
much of modern fiction and particularly science fiction, to the
mainstream of literature. Thus in many of his scientific romances
Wells relates his fantasies either metaphorically or allegorically to
the real world or, alternatively, expands a realistic situation to a
cosmic plane. Possibly no other writer has matched Wells's grasp of
space-time or related it so vividly to the world of immediate
experience.

When considering Wells's ability to write about science it has
been customary to discuss only the scientific romances, but while
these earlier works embody some of Wells's best and most original
writing, they by no means exhaust the measure of his scientific
thought. His increasing preoccupation with sociological interests
arose largely from his stress upon the relevance of scientific
principles to anyone attempting to participate fully in modern
Western society. However, despite Wells's considerable contribution as a sociologist, both of his own time and, through the
'prophecies', of our contemporary scene, it is not within the scope of
this book to consider all the diverse sociological aspects of his work,

but only those emerging as the result of his scientific development. I have therefore traced through the scientific romances and the novels, as well as through the more doctrinaire works of his Fabian and later years, five areas in which Wells endeavoured to work out for himself, and later to propagandise, the role of science in society. There will inevitably be some overlap between these areas both because his ideas about science were all closely related to evolutionary theory, and also because he progressively built up in his mind a synthetic view of an ideal society in which all aspects of social functioning were regarded as part of an organic and integrated approach to life.

The most obvious impact of science on society was of course through technology which was quickly seen to raise problems as well as benefits. Wells believed that these problems could be solved, but only through a clear-sighted appreciation of the intrinsic differences between science and technology, and an awareness of the necessity for intelligent control over the progress of technology. Such a programme, in turn, raised questions about the form of government most appropriate to cope with this comparatively new and specialised issue, and the theoretical ideals towards which it was desirable to channel the increasing power of technology. These considerations form the basis of Wells's utopian works, both fictional and non-fictional; hence any discussion of his scientific thought must include also some assessment of the social novels, and the several non-fictional treatises on social reform.

Wells's markedly synthetic way of thinking imparted to his work an extraordinary unity and a philosophical dimension rarely accorded to the themes he chose to consider; ultimately, each entity is seen, at least implicitly, in relation to every other. This being the pattern of his own thought, Wells naturally stressed the importance of order and unity in all aspects of life. Waste and disorder became increasingly abhorrent to him, whether in the mundane details of everyday life, in lazy inaccurate thinking, or in the panorama of waste and disorganisation which characterised the social sphere, and these issues feature largely in his work.

At a more theoretical level, science, and particularly biology, raised for Wells the perennial problem of determinism and free will, a question over which he toiled until he found a solution satisfying within his own particular terms of reference. Discussions of the problem appear explicitly in several of his works, both fictional and non-fictional, and are also implicit both in his approach to characterisation and in his concept of the role of the individual in society. Thus any analysis of these latter must begin with Wells's views about determinism. The apparent paradox involved in his formulations of free will and determinism is present in another aspect of his work. Despite his stress on the power of the scientific method and its relevance to all areas of experience, Wells was also led, through his very preoccupation with science, to embrace a quasi-mystical approach to life and to the universe; hence his attempts to demonstrate the compatibility of mysticism with experimental method and to trace a mythical dimension and significance in the basic principles of science, are of particular interest.

Besides this all-pervasive influence on his abstract thought, Wells's scientific training radically affected his approach to characterisation, both in his general view of the individual and in his preoccupation with the figure of the scientist – a character previously rare in literature and never before treated in psychological depth. In most cases Wells was able to realise such a character for his readers as capably as he presented scientific principles for the intellectual consideration and entertainment of a reading public which had had little if any background knowledge of science. His methods and techniques are therefore of particular interest in a generation which has intended to accept unquestioningly allegations of the immense difficulty, if not the impossibility, of adequate conversation between the 'two cultures'.

Lastly, it seems clear that Wells's style of writing, which was intimately associated with his approach to aesthetics and to art in general, and which brought him into sharp conflict both with the literary giants of his own time and with form critics to the present day, was the direct, perhaps inevitable, result of his scientific training. Belief in an ultimate truth which may be discovered by diligent research and experimental pursuit renders all lesser truths in science of transitory value. Any hypothesis may be overturned and disproved by a single contrary fact, and the history of science is strewn with discredited theories which pass unmourned by scientists. Every scientific postulate has a tentative quality and certainty is, by definition, unachievable, for a theory may be disproved, but strictly it can never be proved. It is almost certainly this sense of transitoriness which underlies Wells's much quoted reply to Henry James's criticism of his style:

I am a journalist. I refuse to play the 'artist'. If sometimes I am an artist it is a freak of the gods. I am journalist all the time and what I write *goes now* – and will presently die.[5]

This book examines what lasting contribution the scientific aspects of Wells's thought and writing may have made to literature, and thus assesses whether the value of his work is as transitory as he himself declared.

Part I

Wells's Scientific Background. Scientist or Visionary?

1 The Conversion to Science

The third son of a cricket-playing shopkeeper and a lády's maid, Herbert George Wells spent his childhood between the dreary squalor and inefficiency of his parents' china-shop home in Bromley, Kent, and the equally dreary and inefficient private school to which his mother sent him because she had class aspirations which excluded the educationally superior but socially less prestigious National School. This travesty of education was rudely aborted when Wells was fourteen, at which tender age he was thrust out into the inhospitable world of small business as a draper's assistant at the emporium of Messrs Rodgers and Denyer, Windsor. However it was soon apparent that despite his mother's habitual attitude of ingrained servility towards her social betters, and her fixation concerning the draper's trade as the dignified and proper calling for her sons, Wells was not of a similar mind. Messrs Rodgers and Denyer found him to be sadly lacking in both servility and the requisite cash in the till, although this latter deficiency was apparently the result of inattention rather than intention. Two other apprenticeships followed, for Mrs Wells was indefatigable in soliciting opportunities for her boys, but Wells displayed no greater talents or gratitude for these later openings and was finally, as a last resort, permitted to fill in time as an usher at the nearby Midhurst Grammar School.

Byatt, the master of the school, was, by virtue of his university degree, eligible to organise evening classes in any of thirty-odd science subjects and to reap financial rewards from the Education Department for his students' examination successes. Finding Wells a veritable sponge for soaking up facts, Byatt organised a number of spurious 'classes' for his star student, that is to say, he procured the relevant textbooks and left Wells to absorb their contents. At the end of the year, Wells obligingly procured A 1s in his subjects, but Byatt's triumph was a Pyrrhic one and his financial reward short-lived, for Wells's results earned him a teacher-training scholarship to the Normal School of Science, South Kensington, to study biology under Huxley. Set beside such an alternative, the position of usher in a grammar school paled into insignificance, and Byatt's supplementary income was not to be repeated on this scale.

This was the turning-point in Wells's life. In intensity its effect was nothing less than that of a religious conversion. It was as though, by the grace of the Education Department and through the miracle of science, he had been saved from the darkness of confusion and baptised into the light of reason and truth, to become an acolyte under the high priest of science, Thomas Henry Huxley.

Ironically, Wells's devoutly Evangelical mother was at least temporarily mollified by Huxley's ecclesiastical-sounding title. Having heard that the professor was an irreligious man, she had been doubtful about her none-too-pious son's taking up his scholarship, but on learning that Huxley was Dean of the School, she was reconciled and perhaps even hopeful of Bertie's conversion.[1]

In order to understand why science, particularly biology, and the personality of Huxley, to whom he spoke only once in his life, should have had such an enormous influence on Wells, it is necessary to look briefly at the progress of biology and the reputation of Huxley just prior to this.

Biology itself had but recently undergone a revolution, one which profoundly affected not only the scientific fraternity but, to an extraordinary degree, the general public as well. The nineteenth century had begun in a state of complacency, assured of the concepts which it had inherited from the Renaissance and which the history of science had hitherto confirmed as virtually unassailable. Within the bastions of science itself the knowledge of physics was, until the mid-nineteenth century, so vastly in advance of biology that theories about living things relied heavily on analogy with the laws of Newtonian physics, and hence a mechanistic interpretation of life was almost inevitable. This was particularly apparent in the two major assumptions of each discipline – the existence of an ultimate basic entity, and the equating of purpose with design. Physics had its fixed ultimate entity – the atom – and biology held doggedly to the sanctity of its unit – the species. The great biological classifier, Linnaeus, had concluded that there were as many species 'as the different forms which the infinite Being created in the beginning', these species being traditionally arranged, by biologists and moralists alike, in ascending order of complexity, in a *scala naturae*. But by the nineteenth century there was considerable difficulty in accommodating on the 'ladder' the increasing number of discovered forms which seemed to fall awkwardly between classifications and hence to require ever more closely-spaced 'rungs'.

The other major assumption of biologists of the period was the teleological one – that all organisms had been created for a specific purpose, like the components of a watch, for Paley's famous analogy – characteristically a mechanical one – of the universe to a watch, made and set going by an omnipotent Watchmaker, inspired physicists and biologists no less than theologians to dwell upon the adaptations of nature as evidence of God's benevolent plan.[2] Indeed, Paley's *Natural Theology* and the *Bridgewater Treatises* of 1838 stand as witness of the lengths to which teleologists would cheerfully go in confounding utility and adaptation with purpose.

Both these assumptions – the fixity of species and the argument of purpose from design – Darwin's theory immediately and irrevocably destroyed. But its effect was by no means chiefly negative, for Darwin's alternative scheme – the progressive evolution of organisms by the mechanism of natural selection acting upon chance variations – proved to be singularly fertile in biology as a whole. In the concluding chapter of *The Origin of Species*, he predicted that evolutionary theory would open the way for progress in the understanding of systematics, ecology ('natural history'), genetics, geographic distribution, psychology and anthropology, and in all these fields it did indeed stimulate new developments. Hence, despite its initially disruptive effect, the theory of evolution soon became a distinctly unifying concept. Huxley wrote in the *Contemporary Review* of November 1871:

> The gradual lapse of time has now separated us by more than a decade from the date of publication of the *Origin of Species* – and whatever may be thought or said about Mr Darwin's doctrines, or the manner in which he has propounded them, this much is certain, that, in a dozen years, the *Origin of Species* has worked as complete a revolution in biological science as the *Principia* did in astronomy – and it has done so because, in the words of Helmholtz, it contains 'an essentially new creative thought'.[3]

This comparison between Darwin and Newton was no mere extravagance. Newton had provided a meaningful interpretation of a mass of otherwise unrelated data about the physical universe, and

Darwin performed a similar service for biology by giving it a theme and a unifying philosophy.

Darwin himself was by nature a retiring man, and while he spared none of his sensibilities when grappling with ideas in the solitude of his study, his was scarcely the disposition to engage in the acrimonious public debates which followed the publication of his work and which were frequently more akin to battles than to academic discussions. In these contests it was Thomas Henry Huxley, quickly styled 'Darwin's bulldog', who entered the lists on Darwin's behalf and became, at least for the younger generation, the hero of the struggle, the leader in the impartial search for scientific truth against the reactionary forces in biology, geology and theology.

Through his public lectures and his publications, both popular and academic, Huxley became a towering figure on the Victorian scene, defending Darwin against reactionary biologists, biology against the clergy, and State education against those who had faith in neither the State nor education, indeed entering into every dispute from negro slavery to the 'woman question'. To the general public he was the living embodiment of science militant, and certainly this mystique still clung about his person in 1884 when Wells entered the Normal School of Science. In 1901 Wells wrote of the admiration which, as a student, he had felt for Huxley:

> I do not know if the students of today will quite understand how we felt for our Dean – we read his speeches, we borrowed the books he wrote, we clubbed together out of our weekly guineas to buy the *Nineteenth Century* whenever he rattled Gladstone or pounded the Duke of Argyle. I believed then that he was the greatest man I was ever likely to meet, and I still believe that all the more firmly today. And when people ask, 'Were you at South Kensington in Huxley's time?' I answer with a vast amount of dishonest implication in my off-handed manner, 'Oh yes, *I was one of his men*.'[4]

Thirty-three years later, when writing his autobiography, he had not revised his opinion:

> That year I spent in Huxley's class was, beyond all question, the most educational year of my life. It left me under that urgency for coherence and consistency, that repugnance from haphazard

assumptions and arbitrary statements, which is the essential distinction of the educated from the uneducated mind. . . . For a year I went shabby and grew shabbier, I was underfed and not very well housed, and it did not matter to me in the least because of the vision of life that was growing in my mind.[5]

Thus Huxley's fascination for Wells was partly the result of his personality and reputation, which engendered in his students the excitement of being associated with a famous public figure, the sense of being at the centre of the intellectual world; but it was also, and in the long run more importantly, the result of his systematic and synthetic approach to knowledge, an approach which was the direct antithesis of the timid and muddled habits of Wells's family and class. Huxley believed passionately that a scientific education should accomplish two purposes – it should firmly inculcate the idea of causality and it should indicate the whole extent of the universe as known to science – its uniformity and diversity, its immensity and, equally, its limitations.

Wells described his biology course in retrospect as

a vivid, sustained attempt to see life clearly and to see it whole, to see into it, to see its interconnexions, to find out, so far as terms were available, what it is, where it came from, what it was doing, and where it was going.[6]

So vivid was the impact of Huxley, in whose class Wells was one of three to achieve a first-class pass, that he wished to continue with zoological research, but as there were no facilities available at that time for scholarship students, he was drafted into the physics class in his second year, and into geology in his third. Unfortunately, the professors of these subjects at the time proved incapable of fanning the flame of enthusiasm kindled by Huxley – partly because they were apparently less dynamic teachers, less compelling per- sonalities, and partly because, as Wells himself later declared, the science of physics, apart from its few fundamental laws of the conservation of energy and the indestructability of matter and force, was surrounded by a seemingly impenetrable fog, through which isolated experimental data loomed spasmodically, unconnected with any other known facts.

. . . in the whole world of physics at that time there was nobody with the grasp and power of exposition capable of translating the difficulties of material science into language understandable by the eager student or the unspecialised intelligent, educated man . . . my experience of it has remained that of an outsider trying to adjust his general ideas to what he can overhear. I have never been able to make that adjustment. I am still unable to realize what modern physics is up to. . . . My impression is that the Darwin and Huxley of physics have still to come.[7]

Thus the first-class student of biology failed his physics year, and, duly humiliated but subsequently no more inspired by his geology professor's pedestrian methods, proceeded to fail his third year also.

It is not surprising, then, that the chief formative influence on Wells's thought was that of Huxley. Even in his disappointing second year at South Kensington he had endeavoured in a halting way to apply the synthetic approach of biology to the basic questions of physics and thereby evolved his half-jesting, half-serious 'Universal Diagram', from which it should, theoretically, have been possible to derive a prediction of any phenomenon by mere deduction. This unsuccessful effort to devise a unified model of the science of physics later formed the basis of a paper, 'The Universe Rigid', which when submitted to the editor of the *Fortnightly Review* was, significantly, rejected as 'incomprehensible'.[8]

Evolutionary theory then seemed to Wells, and may still be regarded as, the nearest approach to a unifying factor in contemporary thought. Life, and even cosmology, could be seen as an unfolding of the same underlying process so that, although a missing factor might temporarily block one's understanding, all phenomena would ultimately be seen to obey universal laws. No other concept ever made an equivalent impact on Wells – rather the criteria of biology became his yardstick to measure the claims of all other disciplines – astronomy, physics, sociology, politics, even theology and art. Some idea of the extent of this influence may be gained by tracing in broad outline through Wells's work those principles which are also the basic assumptions of the scientific method, particularly of biology.

The first assumption, for Huxley as for all his contemporary scientists, was the necessity for an objective viewpoint, and it is clear that in virtually all the scientific romances and novels, with the partial exception of *Kipps*, *Tono-Bungay* and *Mr. Polly*, Wells's method of looking at the world was almost ruthlessly objective. This is one of the reasons why, although he was capable of expressing that depth of pathos which is the mark of great comedy, he was unable to write anything approaching tragedy; the latter presupposes an element of identification on the part of the audience with the protagonist while comedy depends, for its fullest effect, on the detachment or objectivity of the audience. Van Wyck Brooks has commented that Wells saw men chemically and anatomically, and the world astronomically, all of which terms presuppose an analytical gaze;[9] he might, with equal truth, have said that Wells saw life through a microscope or as stuffed remains. The biology course at South Kensington undoubtedly involved classes in microscopy (the atmosphere of these is vividly recaptured in *Love and Mr. Lewisham*, and in the short story, 'A Slip under the Microscope'), while the displays of stuffed animals in the adjacent Natural History Museum would certainly have furnished part of the visual aids in the study of evolution. Both these methods of looking at specimens involve the utmost alienation of the viewer from the object, which in the second instance is dead and in the first is either an organism on a scale remote from man or else a barely recognisable fragment. No other sections of biology are so far divorced from actual living organisms, and yet both seem to have had a marked influence on Wells's manner of looking at the world. Apart from those stories which deal directly with such studies – 'A Slip under the Microscope' and 'The Triumphs of a Taxidermist' – there is a significant number of stories in which one or more of the characters has the sensation of being watched like a specimen – 'In the Abyss', 'Under the Knife', 'The Crystal Egg', 'The Star', 'Pollock and the Porroh Man', 'Jimmy Goggles the God', *The First Men in the Moon* and *The War of the Worlds*. In three of these – 'In the Abyss', 'Jimmy Goggles the God' and *The First Men in the Moon* – there is even the simulated effect of looking, or being looked at, through a microscope on a larger scale; the circular glass windows of the diving sphere, of the diver's helmet and of Cavor's sphere, are emphasised as being the apertures through which strange forms are scrutinised, while the crystal egg in Mr Cave's shop and its facsimiles on Mars also suggest a lens in both shape and function. Again, in 'The Stolen Body', we are told that the disembodied Mr Bessel felt his observation of those around him to be 'like watching the affairs of a glass hive'.[10]

Wherever there is a sense of being observed, there is a corresponding sense of inferiority, the counterpart of the sensation felt by the

viewer through a microscope. When, in *Marriage*, Marjorie
Trafford sees the aurora for the first time, she experiences a deep
sense of insignificance and again Wells resorts to the microscope
image to describe her feelings:

> That night the whole world of man seemed small and shallow and
> insecure to her, beyond comparison; . . . one pricked the thin
> appearances of life with microscope or telescope and came to an
> equal strangeness. All the pride and hope of human life goes to
> and fro in a little shell of air between this ancient globe of rusty
> nickel-steel and the void of space; faint specks we are within a
> film; we quiver between the atom and the infinite.[11]

This sense of inferiority is particularly evident also in the dramatic
opening paragraphs of *The War of the Worlds* and in the final
paragraph of 'The Star' where the Martian astronomers, watching
for the changes on the earth as the star passes, perceive almost
nothing of those events which have loomed so catastrophically in
the experiences of men.

> 'Considering the mass and temperature of the missile that was
> flung through our solar system into the sun,' one wrote, 'it is
> astonishing what a little damage the earth, which it missed so
> narrowly, has sustained. All the familiar continental markings
> and the masses of the seas remain intact, and indeed the only
> difference seems to be a shrinkage of the white discoloration
> (supposed to be frozen water) round either pole.' Which only
> shows how small the vastest of human catastrophes may seem, at
> a distance of a few million miles.[12]

More subtle, but no less a part of this objective viewing of life, is
Wells's general approach to his characters. Rarely, even with
sympathetic characters, do we penetrate the wall erected by the
narrator's deprecatory humour: if a character is not absolutely the
butt of Wellsian wit, like Kipps, Edward Ponderevo, Mr Polly and
the other 'little men', he may frequently be distanced by an
indulgently avuncular tone which makes him appear significantly
smaller-than-life. Lewisham is introduced in this manner and never
wholly outgrows the initial diminishing effect:

> Mr. Lewisham is seen at his studies. . . . He was called 'Mr.' to

distinguish him from the bigger boys, whose duty it was to learn, and it was a matter of stringent regulation that he should be addressed as 'Sir'.[13]

The chief exceptions to this belittling process of characterisation are Wells's scientists, or those who, like Remington the politician, are seen as the progenitors of his ideal citizens of the future. That is to say, the chief exceptions are those who, in turn, regard the world scientifically and objectively and with a mind to impose order on its chaos. Even the scientists are not all exempt from gentle ridicule. Bensington, in *The Food of the Gods*, is introduced as being somewhat undersized in every sense:

> [He] was short and very, very bald, and he stooped slightly; he wore gold-rimmed spectacles and cloth boots that were abundantly cut open because of his numerous corns, and Professor Redwood was entirely ordinary in his appearance.[14]

Neither Bensington nor Redwood completely recovers from these humorous aspersions cast upon the social relevance of their early research; instead the suggestion of their being, in turn, specimens under Wells's searching gaze is strong.

The most striking manifestation, however, of Wells's objective viewpoint is his preoccupation with the future. His writings about it, far from being escapist in attitude, constitute the first literary experiment in deductive thinking about science. After the immediate success of his first essay on the future, *Anticipations*, he continued to analyse in increasing detail the implications of a future-based frame of reference. His lecture, 'The Discovery of the Future', delivered to the Royal Institution in January 1902, distinguishes and examines two fundamentally different ways of thinking:

> It will lead into my subject most conveniently to contrast and separate two divergent types of mind, types which are to be distinguished chiefly by their attitude towards time and more particularly by the relative importance they attach, and the relative amount of thought they give to the future of things.
> The first of these two types of mind, and it is, I think, the predominant type, . . . is that which seems scarcely to think of the future at all, which regards it as a sort of black non-existence

upon which the advancing present will presently write events.
The second type which is, I think, a more modern and much less
abundant type of mind, thinks constantly and by preference of
things to come, and of present things mainly in relation to the
results that must arise from them.[15]

Wells then proceeds to contrast our knowledge of the past, which is
essentially a personal memory of an individual past and only less
immediately and less reliably knowledge of impersonal or collective
events in the past, with our knowledge of the future, which must be
objective and general:

> The portion of the future that must remain darkest and least
> accessible is the individual future . . . the knowledge of the
> future we may hope to gain will be general and not individual.[16]

Now precisely because we may not know the future in any
personal and individual sense, we may experience an intellectual
hope for it, but not a deep emotion, not the emotion which can
mentally fondle the well-remembered experiences of the past or the
intimate sensations of the present. In this sense the phrase 'scientific
romance' is often a misleading term in the description of Wells's
work, for, traditionally, the romance, which seeks to elicit an
emotional involvement on the part of the reader with the events
described, has always, for the reasons indicated above, been set in
the past or, less often, in the present. On the other hand, in much of
Wells's work which is set in the future, we may experience
admiration, perhaps even some excitement for those

> . . . beings who are now latent in our thoughts and hidden in our
> loins, [who] shall stand upon this earth as one stands upon a
> footstool and shall laugh and reach out their hands amidst the
> stars.[17]

But it is a cold rather than a warm sentiment: the 'beings' (the word
itself is characteristically impersonal) seem closer to the stars than to
the present inhabitants of their footstool. This also suggests one
reason why the scientific romances, the future histories and the
utopias, have never been regarded as major works of literature or
even, by some critics, as literature at all. Their characters are too
deficient in human sympathy, precisely because they are credible

citizens of a future state and not of our past or present systems. The vistas of the dying world in *The Time Machine* or of the lunar dawn and the awakening of life in *The First Men in the Moon*, are magnificent in scope and descriptive power, but with the possible exception of the last Martian whose death-cries are heard on Primrose Hill, the characters of these stories fail to stir either love or hate. The only sensations we feel are vicarious ones on behalf of the protagonist – the disgust, for example, of the Time Traveller at the Morlocks – but even here the emotion experienced is at one or two removes and thus considerably attenuated.

A second fundamental scientific procedure and again a corner-stone of Huxley's system of education, is the desire to impose some order upon the universe, to collate the immense mass of data indiscriminately recorded by our senses and to evolve a unifying set of 'laws' which will both explain and predict the apparent confusion of phenomena. By the mid-nineteenth century, the Linnaean scheme of biological classification was already unable to cope with the abundance of observed species which seemed to defy the pigeon-holing mission of the classifiers. This was one explanation for the triumph of Darwinian theory over the static and cumbersome Linnaean system – it had provided a model which seemed capable of assimilating whatever variations Nature might produce in the future. A modern philosopher has said that

> the panorama presented by evolutionary biology is, though often terrible, magnificent; and to have brought the development of all living things within the scope of a single theory constitutes one of the achievements of the human mind.[18]

For Wells it was even more than this; by drawing together strands from all disciplines and relating them in one unifying theory, it seemed to him to symbolise order itself. The desire for order became a life-long craving in Wells, brought up in a world of confusion and incompetence.

Science had effectually rescued Wells himself from a drapery apprenticeship and shown him the possibilities of individual development. Small wonder if he believed it could perform the same miracle for the whole Victorian era. In his creed, discipline, research and planning are the sole means of saving the world from the insidious destroyer, waste, and hence the leaders of his utopias must display precisely these credentials if society is to be saved.

The principle of order, then, is Wells's remedy for virtually all social maladies but such an ideal might be thought to entail a cost in the sphere of personal life – the imposing of certain restrictions on individual freedom. But here another characteristic of Wells's utopias is important in moderating the regimentation which is usually regarded as inevitable in a highly-ordered society: that is, their non-static quality. The concept of an evolving utopia in which the ideal of perfection is itself changing is effectively a Wellsian innovation in the history of utopian thought, and one which has been largely overlooked by those later writers who have condemned Wells's utopias for the alleged exaction of conformity from all their members.[19] On the contrary, Wells regarded order as itself partaking of a kinetic quality, not a stasis: order means, for him, ordered change.

Like the other aspects of his thought discussed above, this non-static property of the utopias was also derived from Wells's implicit faith in the relevance of Darwinism to all facets of life. The Darwinian emphasis on the continual struggle for survival had made Wells keenly aware of the parallel existential struggle in sociology and politics.[20] In the history of evolution, failure to grow and adapt to change had repeatedly issued in the relative supersession of the static species, if not its total extinction, and Wells consciously applied the same moral to sociological development. Indeed he explicitly acknowledged Darwin's influence on the conception of his utopias, affirming that one can no longer imagine the kind of

> . . . Nowheres and Utopias men planned before Darwin quickened the thought of the world . . . [those were all] perfect and static states, a balance of happiness won for ever against the forces of unrest and disorder that inhere in things. . . . Change and development were dammed back by invincible dams for ever. The modern utopia must be a kinetic one, seen not as a permanent state, but as a hopeful stage, leading to a long ascent of stages.[21]

Wells's sociological theories are intended to parallel biological development. Thus his 'Open Conspiracy', for example, '. . . is the reaction of a rapidly progressing biological conception of the times. . . . It will [produce] . . . a survey of industry, business and finance biologically conceived and judged.[22]

A further important aspect of Wells's utopian novels and sociological writings is their internationalism, seen particularly in the emphasis on free discussion and the public accumulation of knowledge. Wells held firmly that universalism was the only possible creed for a sane, educated man and it seemed to him precisely because scientists most appreciated the necessity for a community of knowledge transcending political, social or religious frontiers that they had made such rapid, utilitarian progress in recent times. In *New Worlds for Old* (1908), Wells explicitly linked the socialist programme for governmental reform, which he at that time enthusiastically supported, with the communal, non-secret accumulation of knowledge which he saw as a fundamental characteristic of research:

> Knowledge is power: knowledge that is frankly and truly exchanged – that is the principal assumption of the *New Atlantis* which created the Royal Society and the organization of research . . . these two great processes of human thought [Science and Socialism] are further in sympathy in the demand they make upon men to become less egotistical and isolated. The main difference of modern scientific research from that of the middle ages, the secret of its immense successes, lies in its collective character, in the fact that every fruitful experiment is published, every new discovery of relationships explained. In a sense scientific research is a triumph over natural instinct, over that mean instinct that makes men secretive, that makes a man keep knowledge to himself and use it slyly to his own advantage.[23]

Again, in *Marriage*, Trafford, a crystallographer, speaks for Wells in contrasting the acquisitiveness of competitive private enterprise with the open exchange of data which has been the chief contributory factor in the emergence of science from mediaeval alchemy.[24] In his sociological writings Wells was to extend this principle to virtually every sphere of interest in an effort to lift men above their individual concerns and inspire them to think in terms of a wider frame of reference.

Although all these themes may be traced directly to Wells's science studies, the most striking evidence of Huxley's influence is to be seen in his concept of the dual nature of man. As a student of evolution, Wells was fully aware of the 'sub-human' elements in man; indeed Darwin's words at the conclusion of *The Descent of Man*,

'With all his noble qualities . . . with all these exalted powers, man still bears in his bodily frame the indelible stamp of his lowly origin,'[25] remained too controversial and too recent to admit of being forgotten in Wells's life-time. How little Wells was likely to forget man's 'lowly origin', *The Island of Dr. Moreau* shows only too clearly. But neither did he lose hope in the further evolution of man, for it was no inconsiderable triumph that the mind of man had advanced so far as to be capable of formulating an explanation of its own ancestry. *The Island of Dr. Moreau* displays both these aspects of man's nature – Moreau himself is the man endowed with creativity and understanding; the beast-men, with their recurrent regressions to a sub-human state, stand for those debased instincts which delay the progress of civilisation. The moral implications of this novel will be discussed at some length later but here it may be considered as a physical Jekyll and Hyde parable. Like Stevenson, Wells does not merely describe the duality of human nature; in both stories the 'beast' is victorious. But whereas Stevenson implies that this was the result of mere chance – because Dr Jekyll happened to drink the transforming potion first at a time when his sentiments were tending towards malevolence so that this side of his nature became exaggerated – Wells makes no such concessions. Reversion to the beast, in his novel, is the norm rather than the exception, as Prendick, like Gulliver, discovers on his return to so-called civilisation. *Dr. Moreau* is Wells's starkest and most sustained treatment of man's dual nature, but it is not the only example. The short story, 'The Reconciliation', describes a similar reversion to the beast of two apparently learned and cultivated gentlemen who deliberately and systematically attempt to batter each other to death over a five-year-old quarrel, while the closing chapters of *The Invisible Man* show not only the ruthlessness of the power-crazed Griffin, but also the savage emotions which come to the surface amongst the villagers once fear has stripped away the veneer of civilisation. Often these two elements of man's nature are dramatised as the intellectual and the sensual aspects, sometimes embodied in a pair of contrasting characters, the scientist and the sensualist, or the scientist and the irrational romantic – the narrator and the curate of *The War of the Worlds*, Cavor and Bedford in *The First Men in the Moon*, George and Edward Ponderevo in *Tono-Bungay*. In other instances they are dramatised as an internal, psychological conflict between two aspects of a single character – the ambitious, worldly facet and the gentle, escapist facet of Lionel

Wallace's personality in 'The Door in the Wall,' the political idealist at odds with the passionate lover in Remington and in the dream-protagonist of 'A Dream of Armageddon'. Or again, the conflict may be dramatised as a sociological confrontation between two groups or races – between Eloi and Morlocks, men and Martians, or men and Selenites.

At various stages of his career Wells's ideas about the possible outcome of these clashes alternated between hope and despair and frequently combined both to provide a warning and an incentive to action, but it is possible to find a basis in the biological climate of the time for each of these attitudes. Well's pessimism may have been partly innate, partly influenced by the prevailing *fin de siècle* atmosphere, as Bergonzi has claimed,[26] but the main source of it was the pessimism of Huxley, who was certainly not blind to the possibility of man's regression or extinction. Indeed, the impact of evolutionary thought on the humanitarian conscience has very frequently produced pessimism – in Huxley no less than in Tennyson, Arnold, Clough and Hardy. To what extent Huxley had imparted this attitude to his students at South Kensington one cannot be sure, and Wells himself makes no mention of it in his autobiography. As early as 1891, in 'Administrative Nihilism', Huxley had begun to emphasise the amorality and inevitable pain involved in the evolutionary process, but the clearest expression of his pessimism was his famous Romanes lecture, 'Evolution and Ethics'. Significantly, Wells's article 'On Extinction', which discusses the probable and disastrous outcome of man's perseverance along his current path, was published in the same year.

Basically, 'Evolution and Ethics' was an attempt to counter the facile optimism of those who blithely invoked evolutionary theory to justify *laissez-faire* socio-economic policies, and in it Huxley expressed a hitherto unsuspected depth of pessimism. The cosmic process, he declared, is a ferment of incessant struggle and change, inevitably entailing great suffering and death. But precisely because of his understanding of the evolutionary 'jungle', of 'nature red in tooth and claw' and of 'the ape and the tiger' aspects of man's nature,[27] Huxley also strove to see some alternative, some hope for the future of the race. This hope he formulated in his concept of an 'Ethical Process'. Though he believed this to have arisen through the natural mechanism of evolution, he saw as its main function the countering of the hitherto amoral evolutionary process and the substitution of willing cooperation for competitive struggle.

Cosmic evolution may teach us how the good and evil tendencies of man came about; but in itself it is incompetent to furnish any better reason why what we call good is preferable to what we call evil than what we had before. . . . The practice of that which is ethically best – what we call goodness or virtue – involves a course of conduct which, in all respects, is opposed to that which leads to success in the cosmic struggle for existence. . . . Its influence is directed not so much to survival of the fittest as to the fitting of as many as possible to survive. Let us understand once and for all, that the ethical progress of society depends not on imitating the cosmic process, still less on running away from it, but in combating it.[28]

Because man is only partially emancipated from nature, he still suffers pain, still struggles against the marks of his lowly origin, and Huxley did not blink from the spectacle of waste and suffering inherent in the natural process:

I deem it an essential condition of the realization of that hope [that evil may be abated] that we should cast aside the notion that escape from pain and sorrow is the proper object of life.[29]

In the Eloi of *The Time Machine* Wells created a literary symbol of precisely this warning. The Eloi desire above all else to escape from pain and effort, from seeing the unpleasant reality of their situation and seek only comfort and ease, the shallow happiness of an illusion. Their plight and their imminent evolutionary extinction are the natural and inevitable result of their childish hedonism.

Three years after 'Evolution and Ethics' Wells published *The Island of Dr. Moreau* in which the parallels are immediately obvious. Indeed there is almost nothing in Huxley's lecture which did not issue in a literary equivalent somewhere in Wells's work. Huxley had cited the extinction of the Tasmanian aborigines as a recent tragedy of evolution and the first chapter of *The War of the Worlds* draws an explicit parallel between the extermination of the Tasmanians and the conflict between men and Martians.

Huxley's emphasis on the 'cruel' amorality of Nature is restated at length in *Men Like Gods* where Urthred, spokesman for the superior race, answers Freddy Mush's sentimental and idealised speech about the 'balance of Nature', a favourite nineteenth-century delusion:

These Earthlings do not yet dare to see what our Mother Nature is. At the back of their minds is still the desire to abandon themselves to her. They do not see that except for our eyes and wills she is purposeless and blind. She is not awful. She is horrible. She takes no heed to our standards, nor to any standards of excellence. She made us by accident; all her children are bastards – undesired; she will cherish or expose them, pet or starve or torment without rhyme or reason. She does not heed, she does not care. She will lift us up to power and intelligence, or debase us to the mean feebleness of the rabbit or the slimy white filthiness of a thousand of her parasitic inventions. There must be good in her because she made all that is good in us – but also there is endless evil. Do not you Earthlings see the dirt of her, the cruelty, the insane indignity of much of her work? With man came Logos, the Word and the Will into our universe, to watch it and fear it, to learn it and cease to fear it, to know it and comprehend it and master it. . . .[30]

However, whereas Huxley's emphasis on ethics led him at times to mistrust even the intellect when it was divorced from a moral education, Wells came increasingly to place his hope for the future of mankind in intelligence and will as the means of overcoming the chance and cruelty of the evolutionary process. This purposive effort is certainly a moral one, but Wells (unlike Huxley) seems to have believed that it could be inspired by, and developed from, reason and intellect alone. The ideal life of his Samurai is assumed to be within the reach of anyone's 'better self', and thus evolutionary advance appears in his work to result from a better trained intellect and imagination which inevitably generate a more highly developed moral consciousness and will. Hence Wells's undisguised contempt for the 'natural man' who deliberately isolates himself from the social, and particularly the intellectual advances of utopia.

Nowhere in Wells's work, however, is his perception of the meaning and implications of evolution and of the dual nature of man so fully expressed as in the comparatively early novel, *The Island of Dr. Moreau*, which discusses, either directly or by implication, almost all the critical issues which have since been raised by neo-Darwinism. As such it merits a fuller discussion here since it illustrates both the facility with which Wells was able to examine and analyse the implications, many unrealised, of evolutionary theory and also the centrality of evolutionary assumptions in his thinking.

Throughout the second half of the nineteenth century evolutionary theories had been reflected with varying shades of accuracy in the English novel, but although these earlier treatments were, in general, better understood in their time than *Dr. Moreau*, they were universally more superficial and most are now fittingly forgotten.

Amongst the many and varied interpretations which reviewers attached to this story, several suspected an irreligious intent, and Wells later confirmed this when he referred to the novel as 'a theological grotesque',[31] but as very few of Wells's contemporaries realised the full extent to which Darwinism had overthrown the postulates of orthodox theology, it was natural that they should miss much of the point of the novel. The initial furore over the interpretation of Genesis was, in retrospect, seen to have been concerned with a minor issue, and gradually sank into relative oblivion when a tacit gentleman's agreement was reached by scientists and clerics alike not to poach on each other's territory. Deism, the belief that nature provides sufficient evidence for the existence of God, still flourished in the churches, even though most scientists believed that the universe was a closed, mechanistic system with no suggestion of a supernatural Engineer.

However, the major issues which Darwinian theory raised for liberal theology were not resolved by 'saving face' for the book of Genesis, by simply exchanging the notion of a single creative act in the past for one of continuous creation. There were at least three other aspects of the evolutionary process which struck deeply at both the Christian concept of a loving God, and the humanist belief in the essential goodness and nobility of man. These were, firstly, the stress on chance variations as the raw material for an arbitrary, non-directional evolutionary process; secondly the inevitable waste thereby involved, since those variations which proved less fitted for survival in the struggle for existence became extinct; and thirdly the consequent pain which must necessarily be suffered by the ill-adapted. A process involving any, much less all, of these aspects seemed irreconcilable with the character of a Christian God. Few of Darwin's contemporaries understood these difficulties fully and most who tried to grapple with them took refuge in the liberal Christianity which sought an amicable alliance with science by avoiding the more difficult areas of controversy. Wells, on the other hand, shows himself aware, in *Dr. Moreau*, of all these theological ramifications of Darwinism, although he is less concerned here with the implications for religious orthodoxy (which, at the time of writing the novel, he disavowed) than with the implications for scientific humanism.

The story in which he chose to examine these questions is, in itself, a remarkable strategem to which insufficient critical attention has been paid. Usually the thought of the evolutionary process fails to stir us intensely because our minds are incapable of coping with a span of twenty million centuries; the drama of successive triumphs and defeats is deadened for us by the weight of years and even the possibility of human extinction in some remote future time does not greatly appal us. Therefore, if he were to awaken his readers to the tense and imaginative involvement befitting a novel-reader, Wells had somehow to telescope the time scale to manageable proportions. Again, in the evolutionary drama, there are no human actors until the relatively brief few moments before the curtain falls on the present; yet the novel-reader's capacity for experiencing a sense of involvement in a non-human situation is limited. Moreover the 'director' of this drama is either supernatural or non-existent; in either case an audience which looks for a personality behind the scenes is unlikely to be deeply interested. All these difficulties Wells surmounted in his conception of Moreau who, while remaining an entirely credible if somewhat megalomaniac biologist, endeavours to effect a highly condensed form of evolution, to produce human beings, or their like, from their more remote ancestors without all the lengthy intermediate steps. Moreover, his own personal drama is inextricably linked with the whole process and therefore adds considerably to its interest.

This dramatic presentation necessarily involves a certain divergence from strict Darwinian theory, as Wells himself was doubtless aware, but the gain in literary potential is incomparably greater than the exactitude sacrificed in the process. The chief inconsistencies, moreover, are rather with neo-Darwinism than with Darwin's original formulation, for it must be remembered that Darwin himself was not entirely free from a vague, half-conscious hankering for a form of Lamarckism; he, like Wells at the time of writing *Dr. Moreau*, was ignorant of Mendel's work in genetics which could have helped him to explain the origin of the chance variations he had postulated but could not account for. Wells presents us with a Moreau who, while endeavouring to recreate an evolutionary situation, confuses cultural with genetic evolution. In fact, acquired cultural characteristics are transmitted by learning, both within and between generations, but acquired physical characteristics are not; yet Moreau expects that his grafting techniques will be as likely to succeed on a permanent basis as Montgomery's teaching of the Beast-People. In the event, they prove to be equally *im*permanent: regressions, both mental and physical, occur within one generation. It is possible that Wells may have stumbled upon the important distinction between somatic and cultural evolution during the writing of *Dr. Moreau*, for his article, 'Human Evolution, an Artificial Process', which clearly outlines the basic differences between the two processes, and which was probably the first published paper to do so, appeared in 1896, the year in which *Dr. Moreau* was completed.[32] However, within the context of the novel, the confusion between the two processes is virtually insignificant.

Moreau, who tries to force his beasts to evolve by non-genetic means, is fully aware of the three aspects of the process outlined above – chance, waste and pain; indeed he accepts them with no apparent signs of regret as obvious necessities. The element of chance in the novel is forced upon our attention repeatedly – the drawing of lots by the three castaways, that most arbitrary of all means of reaching a decision; the chance whim whereby Montgomery feels inclined to assist the dying Prendick – Montgomery himself stresses the extent to which this was mere chance when Prendick tries to thank him. Moreau certainly sees chance as the very basis of his 'design':

> I asked him why he had taken the human form as a model. . . .
> He confessed that he had chosen that form by chance. 'I might as well have worked to form sheep into llamas, and llamas into sheep.'[33]

This is perhaps the most brutal assertion of chance at the very centre of the evolutionary process for even the most materialistic and mechanistic scientists had tended to cherish a tacit regard for man as the crown of creation. Moreau's only concession is an almost arbitrary aesthetic one:

> 'I suppose that there is something in the human form that appeals to the artistic turn of mind more powerfully than any other

animal shape can. But I've not confined myself to man-making. . . .'[34]

Again, the result of one of Moreau's experiments 'got loose by accident – I never meant it to get away' – and killed a Kanaka.[35] When Prendick reflects on Moreau's experiment he is disgusted at the purposelessness of it all, just as Darwin's contemporaries found the idea of a cruel and purposeless Nature so abhorrent:

> It was the wantonness that stirred me. Had Moreau had any intelligent object, I could have sympathised at least a little with him. . . . But he was so irresponsible, so utterly careless. His curiosity, his mad aimless investigations, drove him on, and things were thrown out to live a year or so, to struggle, and blunder, and suffer; at least to die painfully. . . . I must confess I lost faith in the sanity of the world when I saw it suffering the painful disorder of this island.[36]

There could scarcely be a more concise account of the early reactions to Darwinian theory. The very boat in which Prendick eventually escapes, drifts 'on an aimless course'[37] towards the island, with no one to steer or direct it.

Even Darwin had had reservations about the centrality of chance in the evolutionary process; he wrote to fellow-biologist Asa Gray:

> I am inclined to look at everything as resulting from designed laws, with the details . . . left to the working out of what we may call chance. Not that this notion *at all* satisfies me. . . . The more I think, the more bewildered I become.[38]

But once chance is accepted, the implication of waste is inescapable. This was immediately seen to be one of the major evils of Darwin's scheme and a severe charge against a supposedly benevolent Creator. Cudworth's dilemma seemed oppressively relevant.[39] Moreau is no loving god; he personifies the insentient, mechanistic process which Tyndall and Huxley had so ruthlessly exposed.[40] This is stated quite explicitly by Prendick:

> A blind fate, a vast pitiless mechanism, seemed to cut and shape the fabric of existence, and I, Moreau (by his passion for research), Montgomery (by his passion for drink), the Beast-People with their instincts and mental reservations, were torn and

crushed, ruthlessly, inevitably, amid the infinite complexity of its incessant wheels.[41]

The six Kanakas he has originally brought to the island as servants are all presumed dead from 'accidental causes' and the early subjects of his experiments were failures:

> 'I began with a sheep, and killed it after a day and a half by a slip of the scalpel; I took another sheep . . . it looked quite human to me when I had finished with it, but when I went to it I was discontented with it, . . . then I took a gorilla. . . .'[42]

The almost arbitrary succession of beasts which passes through Moreau's hands re-enacts the idea of the evolutionary process as Nature's giant experiment, wherein much material must, of necessity, be lost for the sake of a few 'successes'. Moreau is as ruthlessly amoral as the Huxleyan view of nature; indeed his character is virtually a dramatisation of the dangers which Huxley had warned would result from an 'imitation' of the 'cosmic process', or from the attempt to derive a social ethic from it. Characteristically, Moreau endeavours to justify his relentless pursuit by just such an appeal to a 'natural' philosophy:

> 'I am a religious man, Prendick, as every sane man must be. It may be, I fancy, I have seen more of the ways of this world's Maker than you – for I have sought His laws, in my way, all my life. . . . To this day I have never troubled about the ethics of the matter. The study of Nature makes a man at least as remorseless as Nature.'[43]

Waste in any process involving living beings necessarily implies also pain, and pain is one of the most recurrent themes of the novel. It first assails Prendick through the agonised cries of the vivisected puma. To his raw and unaccustomed senses

> the emotional appeal of those yells grew upon me steadily, grew at last to such an exquisite expression of suffering that I could stand it in that confined room no longer. . . . It was as though all the pain in the world had found a voice.[44]

The contrast between Prendick's emotional reaction to the cries and

Moreau's unemotional acceptance of the necessity of pain epitomises the difference between the two men: the one cannot bear to know, or be forced to share in any sense the depths of suffering of living beings; the other extols suffering and inflicts it with a grim sense of inevitability. It might, of course, be argued that Moreau is at least the more honest of the two men, since Prendick admits:

> Had I known such pain was in the next room, and had it been dumb, I believe – I have thought since – I could have stood it well enough. It is when suffering finds a voice and sets our nerves quivering, that this pity comes troubling us.[45]

However, it is important to note that, though both men are biologists, they both differ recognisably from Huxley, Wells's ideal biologist, in their attitudes to pain. Huxley, like Moreau and unlike Prendick, did not close his eyes to the spectacle of waste and suffering involved in the evolutionary process; but Moreau does not merely accept the fact of suffering for himself and other creatures; he actively inflicts it – a course of action which Huxley had rigorously condemned. Moreau exploits the use of pain to the full: 'Each time I dip a living creature into the bath of pain, I say, This time I will burn out all the animal, this time I will make a rational creature of my own.'[46] This bath of pain through which the beasts must pass to be made whole, i.e. more human, is a highly significant symbol, for clearly it is intended to have overtones of the baptismal ceremony, a washing away of original sin and a passing from death into life, just as it is certainly intended to be reflected in Moreau's own name, a condensation of 'water of death'. This is sufficiently emphasised, if emphasis were needed, when Prendick hears Montgomery calling out the name as a disyllable – 'Mor – eau'.

Moreau is also associated with the deist idea of God and with several aspects of Judaeo-Christian orthodoxy. Apart from the oblique reference to the ceremony of baptism, the gatherings of the Beast-folk are, whatever the similarity to Kipling's *Jungle Book*, intended primarily as religious ceremonies involving a litany of prohibition, commandments delivered from on high, and a grovelling acknowledgment of Moreau's omnipotence and rights over them, as they sing hymns on the theme 'All Thine':

> His is the House of Pain,
> His is the Hand that Makes,

His is the Hand that Wounds,
His is the Hand that Heals.[47]

Moreau even follows the Genesis pattern of creation to the extent of
'creating' a serpent-devil: 'It was a limbless thing, with a horrible
face that writhed along the ground in a serpentine fashion.'[48] But
the most startling parallel with Christian orthodoxy is Moreau's
mock resurrection. Strangely enough, this episode, which one might
suppose would have been considered highly offensive, if not
blasphemous, seems to have passed unnoticed by critics; yet the
effect of this grotesque 'resurrection' cannot but be intended to
reflect upon the authenticity of Christian doctrine. The very
language used is highly reminiscent of the Gospel accounts of the
empty tomb:

> They seemed awe-stricken and puzzled. 'Where is he?' said
> Montgomery.
> 'Beyond,' and the grey creature pointed.
> 'Is there a Law now?' asked the Monkey Man. . . . 'Is he dead
> indeed?'
> 'Is there a Law?' repeated the man in white. . . . I suddenly
> stepped in front of him and lifted up my voice:
> 'Children of the Law,' I said, 'he is not dead! . . . He has
> changed his shape – he has changed his body,' I went on. 'For a
> time you will not see him. He is . . . there! – I pointed upward –
> where he can watch you. You cannot see him. But he can see you.
> Fear the Law'. . . .
> 'He is great, he is good,' said the Ape Man, peering fearfully
> upward.[49]

Moreau, then, represents a nightmarish hybrid, the logical and
inevitable outcome, as Wells saw it, of the desire to graft on to a
deistic belief in an omnipotent Creator, the postulates of Darwinian
theory including the assertion of a continuum of creation which
acknowledged no gap, no essential difference in kind, between man
and his forebears. Wells thus deliberately set out to destroy the hope
cherished by liberal theologians, that some valid, if tacit, compromise was possible between science and natural theology. But he was
not yet sufficiently interested in the fate of religion to launch out and
devise the outlines of a substitute faith, as he was to do later.
Bergonzi comments that not only must Moreau have offended

Wells's more traditionally-minded readers, who objected to the proposition that there was no essential difference between man and beast, 'but at the same time, the romanticising of Moreau, and his specific identification with the arbitrariness and indifference to suffering of what Huxley had called the 'cosmic process' would have offended scientifically-minded people'.[50] However, if 'scientifically-minded' readers were offended, this could only have been because they identified Moreau with their contemporary scientists, an identification which Wells was at pains to discourage by underlining the basic differences between his protagonist and that prototype of biologists, Huxley. Their fundamentally different attitudes to pain and suffering and their diametrically opposed ethical standpoints have already been discussed. Moreover, in Wells's allegory of an island cosmos, it would seem clear that Moreau is intended to represent not the biologist observing Nature – this is the role of Prendick who, if anyone, represents Huxley[51] – but rather the 'cosmic process' itself.

The scale of reality which Wells has succeeded in portraying in the handful of characters on his island (and we should not miss the irony that this island which disposes once for all of the romantic idea of the 'noble savage' is presumed in the Introduction to be Noble's Island) shows the extent of his mythopoeic capacities. Despite the apparent realism of the novel – and the recoil of his contemporaries from its vivid pictures of horror testifies to its atmosphere of authenticity and betokens a mind firmly grounded in facts[52] – Wells's success in creating the sense of a mythical dimension in the novel, resides in its very ambiguities. The images do not quite reinforce each other and the resultant blurred and composite picture seems to bespeak a complexity all the more striking because of the clarity of the surrounding detail. Thus, at one level, the Beast-People represent the dual nature of man – the bestial instincts which are his evolutionary inheritance, and the cultural acquirements uneasily and painfully superimposed upon them. But they also represent the nineteenth-century confusion as to man's origins. Just as in pre-Darwinian belief man was regarded as a fallen angel, so Prendick at first assumes that Moreau's grotesques are degenerate and muti-lated human beings, until Moreau shows him that they have in fact been developed from lower forms.

Even more significant is the reaction that Prendick, like Gulliver, experiences towards his compatriots after returning to England:

I could not persuade myself that the men and women I met were not also another, still passably human, Beast People, animals half-wrought into the outward image of human souls, and that they would presently begin to revert to show first this bestial mark and then that.[53]

Similarly Moreau himself has an ambiguous role in the novel. He seems to be both fully human in that he errs and proceeds by trial and error, and also a parody of the Old Testament Jehovah, in that he is both Creator and Law-Giver. Moreover he is both an individual scientist and an allegory of the evolutionary process. In the coalescence of these suggestions lie the fascination and the subtlety of Wells's modern myth.

Apart from these specific biological concepts which are central issues in Wells's thought, it remains to consider his attitude to the general principles of the scientific method since these are frequently considered alien to the literary mind.

The basis of the experimental method, and necessarily therefore one of the cornerstones of scientific theory, is a rejection of fixed and determined 'laws', of unquestionable authorities and infallible doctrines. In one of his earliest writings, 'The Chronic Argonauts' (1888), Wells was already stressing this. Dr Nebogipfel explains to the bewildered minister:

'Opinions of all sorts. . . . – Scientific Theories, Laws, Articles of Belief, or, to come to elements, Logical Premises, Ideas, or whatever you like to call them – all are, from the infinite nature of things, so many diagrammatic caricatures of the ineffable – caricatures altogether to be avoided save where they are necessary in the shaping of results – as chalk outlines are necessary to the painter and plans and sections to the engineer.'[54]

This firm belief in the uniqueness of every entity was, in Wells's case, derived from Darwinism. It is arguable that, by dissolving the Linnaean distinctions between categories, and showing that species were located along a continuum, Darwin had demonstrated the inadequacy of categories and labels and thus, by implication, affirmed the uniqueness of every entity. In 'The Rediscovery of the Unique' Wells made this connection explicitly:

The work of Darwin and Wallace was the clear assertion of the uniqueness of living things; and the physicists and chemists are now trying the next step forward in a hesitating way.[55]

Clearly, Wells mistrusted labels under which, on the basis of similarity, similar entities were grouped and thereafter tacitly considered to be identical. He then proceeded to argue that this mistrust was a necessary basis of the scientific method which repudiated tradition and authority in any guise. Indeed the anti-authoritarian aspect of science made an immediate and lasting appeal to Wells's intrinsically rebellious nature, and it continued to play an important role not merely in his thinking about the philosophy of science, but in his political and sociological thought also. Unlike orthodoxy in other fields, scientific method makes no claim to infallibility and refuses to rest content with the results it has obtained in the past. The same continued questioning of current hypotheses is one of the most striking characteristics of Wells's scientific romances in which current scientific assumptions are no more exempt from rigorous reconsideration than are political or religious ones, for he saw that those who accepted the 'authority' of science as absolute were in fact farthest from understanding the true scientific method.

Whether consciously or unconsciously on his part, Wells's awareness of the limitations of scientific 'truths' led to an interesting feature of his utopias. In science, the greater the number of trained men, the stronger the likelihood of its advance; in authoritarian systems, on the other hand, the greater the numbers of educated and enquiring minds, the stronger the likelihood of the system's breakdown, for with the growth of intellectual independence, dissension under a restrictive system becomes almost inevitable. Hence, in a totalitarian state, complete authority is always vested in a relatively small number of people. In common with most scientists, Wells mistrusted the power of those in authority, realising the ease with which their judgment might be corrupted through their office; yet he also recognised the need for dedicated and strong men in the struggle to institute order and efficiency in society. It is thus significant that in nearly all his plans for a utopia, he depends for leadership chiefly on the scientists of the society. They, because of their training, are considered sufficiently impartial and morally reliable to remain uncorrupted by the mantle of authority; again, because their major interests lie elsewhere they will be glad to lay down their interim power when the masses have been sufficiently educated for self-government; and, perhaps most importantly they, because of the strongly anti-authoritarian bias of their training, will continue to examine, question and test the fundamental assumptions and beliefs of their society, and educate others to do likewise. Thus Wells's utopias, unlike almost all that have followed them, pursue the actual policies of scientific method, not some authoritarian travesty of these, stressing the equal responsibility of all citizens, and working towards the elimination of any separate governing class.

Having now examined the extent to which the assumptions and methods of science, and in particular fundamental, biological concepts, came to form the central issues and themes of Wells's thought and work, it is necessary to consider next whether his manner of thinking, as distinct from the topics with which he dealt, was scientific also, or whether he merely attempted to disguise an essentially non-scientific mode of reasoning by the glib use of overtly scientific material couched in a judicious selection of technological terms.

2 Scientific Method and Wells's Credentials

While no reader can fail to have been struck by the emphasis on science in Wells's work, there has been no universal agreement amongst critics as to whether Wells's thought was consistent with, or influenced by, scientific method. The most interesting point to emerge from a survey of the critical estimates is that while those scientists who are familiar with Wells's work have for the most part applauded his treatment of scientific interests, even, in a few cases, regarding it as germinal to their own ideas, literary critics, after the first wave of somewhat indiscriminate enthusiasm, have tended to denigrate Wells's scientific ability and to dismiss his work as, at best, interesting fantasy. Such a strange division of opinion would be worth examining in its own right, but it is especially interesting here for the light it throws on the popular misconceptions of science which Wells was concerned to erase.

In examining first the estimate of the scientists, Wells's technical qualifications are relevant as a basis for appraisal.

Although he left South Kensington without the coveted B.Sc. degree, Wells seems to have had little trouble in remedying this deficiency in subsequent years. In 1889, while teaching at Henley House School, he passed the Intermediate Science Examination with honours in zoology, and gained the diploma of Licentiate of the College of Preceptors. The following year, while coaching at Briggs's Tutorial College, he was finally awarded the B.Sc. degree from London University, with honours in zoology and geology. During this period too, Wells, frustrated by the textbooks currently available to his students, published a *Textbook of Biology* remarkable for its clarity and readable style.

After the attainment of these formal qualifications, there was a lapse of fifty-one years before Wells submitted to London University a thesis 'On the Quality of Illusion in the Continuity of the Individual Life in the Higher Metazoa, with particular reference to

39

Homo Sapiens', and was awarded his doctorate, but during the
interim the esteem in which his scientific reputation was held by his
contemporaries may be partially gauged from the fact that, as early
as 1902, he was invited to lecture to the Royal Institution, an
honour usually reserved for eminent specialists. The text of his
lecture was printed in full in *Nature* (6 February 1902), and in the
Smithsonian report for the same year, both publications of the
highest repute in the scientific world. Later, following the publication of his book, *Natural Science and the Classical System in Education*,
he was elected to write the 1916–1918 report of the League for the
Promotion of Science in Education. He was also invited to
contribute to the 1925 edition of the *Encyclopaedia Britannica* a sixty-
page section entitled 'A Forecast of World Affairs'.

These were no mean distinctions to be conferred on someone who
was not a professional scientist. Moreover, apart from these formal
honours, there exists considerable evidence of the regard in which
Wells was held by contemporary scientists. When he wrote to
Arnold Bennett, 'Ray Lankester will tell you I've never jarred on
the exacting sensibilities of a critical scientific mind,'[1] he was not
overstating the case. Ray Lankester, formerly a fellow-student at
South Kensington, was at this time Director of the Natural History
Department and Keeper of Zoology at the British Museum, and
soon to be knighted for his outstanding work in zoology. He
remained a firm friend of Wells, whose work he clearly admired
since he was not only a consultant for the *Outline of History*, but also
edited Wells's *Natural Science and the Classical System in Education*, and
reviewed *Anticipations* for *Nature* in the following enthusiastic terms:

Mr Wells has a thorough knowledge of and considerable training
in, the great branches of science – physics, chemistry, astronomy,
geology and biology. This course of study operated, in the case of
Mr Wells, upon a mind naturally gifted with an extraordinarily
vivid imagination . . . the really wonderful range of knowledge . . . the scientific accuracy of the abundant details, the
absolute restraint of the weird histories recounted, within the
limits of what scientific criticism must admit as possible – nay,
even probable, given the one initial miracle of anyone having and
recording experience of such things – lend a special charm to Mr
Wells's writings wanting in those of all other masters of this kind
of literary craft from Swift to Jules Verne.[2]

In January of the same year, an anonymous review of *The First Men in the Moon* had appeared in *Nature*,[3] making similar, almost eulogistic claims, and Arnold Bennett recorded that:

Those who prefix 'pseudo' to the scientific part of Mr Wells's novels are not the men of science. One may pleasantly observe the experts of *Nature*, a scientific organ of unrivalled authority, discussing the gravitational phenomena of *The First Men in the Moon*, with the aid of diagrams, and admitting that Mr Wells has the law on his side.[4]

Later, the physicist Ludwig Silberstein, in his *Theory of Relativity*, quoted with approbation the words of Wells's Time Traveller:

There is no difference between Time and Space except that our consciousness moves along it. It is interesting to remark that even the forms used by Minkowski to express these ideas as 'three-dimensional geometry becoming a chapter of four-dimensional physics', are anticipated in Mr Wells's fantastic novel. Here is another sample illustrative of what is now called a 'World tube': 'For instance, here is a portrait (or say a statute) of a man at eight years old, another at fifteen, another at seventeen, another at twenty-three, and so on. All these are evidently sections, as it were, Three-Dimensional representations of his Four-Dimensional being which is a fixed and unalterable thing.' Thus Mr Wells seems to perceive clearly the absoluteness, as it were, of the world tube and the relativity of its various sections.[5]

One of the most remarkable of Wells's 'prophecies', that of atomic warfare in *The World Set Free*, was fully appreciated by both contemporary scientists and later physicists. Although Wells was originally inspired by Soddy's *Interpretation of Radium*, physicists had, in 1913 when the novel was written, no proposals for splitting the atom; yet 1933, the year in which the scientists of the novel first allegedly succeeded in constructing fission bombs to be used in the 1956 holocaust, was actually the year in which the Joliot-Curies first produced radioactive phosphorus by bombarding aluminium with beta particles, the first step in tapping atomic energy. Again, in the novel, Wells's scientists discover a substance, carolinium, which has the same properties and uses as plutonium, an element isolated only much later and which, with uranium, is now the most important atomic fuel. The concept of using atomic degeneration to provide nuclear power, the possible uses of this power, and the details of the process as described in this novel elicited probably the most interesting tribute of all to Wells's scientific ability, for the distinguished physicist Leo Szilard acknowledged a practical debt to Wells, as though to a fellow-scientist:

> In 1932, while I was still in Berlin, I read a book by H. G. Wells. It was called *The World Set Free*. This book was written in 1913, one year before the World War, and in it H. G. Wells describes the discovery of artificial radioactivity and puts it in the year 1933, the year in which it actually occurred. He then proceeds to describe the liberation of atomic energy on a large scale for industrial purposes, the development of atomic bombs, and a world war. . . . He places this war in the year 1956, and in this war the major cities of the world are all destroyed by atomic bombs. . . . This book made a very great impression on me, but I didn't regard it as anything *but* fiction. It didn't start me thinking whether or not such things could in fact happen. I had not been working in nuclear physics up to that time. . . .[6]

Later, however, Szilard realised how a chain nuclear reaction could be set up, and hastily applied for a patent to cover his invention because, he writes, 'knowing what this would mean – and I knew it because I had read H. G. Wells, – I did not want this patent to become public'.[7]

In 1936 Wells was again invited to lecture to the Royal Institution, this time on his ideas for the setting up of a world encyclopaedia which should be the work of the best minds of each generation in every country. The following year, he developed this concept further in an analytic lecture to the British Association for the Advancement of Science, 'The Informative Content of Education'.

More recently, Julian Huxley, himself a distinguished biologist, has described Wells as

> a rare combination of scientist and humanist. . . . If his agility of mind and the insatiable range of his interest stood in the way of that focussing of his energy on a particular problem, which is needed for successful scientific research, yet he certainly was one of the chief agents in bringing the free curiosity and the

experimental spirit of modern science, to bear upon political and social thought and action.[8]

In the light of such testimony from scientists, the adverse criticism of the non-scientists who have doubted the validity of much of Wells's work is the more difficult to understand; yet they have become, if anything, more numerous over the years. The diversity of opinion is, in many cases, the result of a fundamental misunderstanding by non-scientists about the scientific method and the claims which science actually makes, and it is therefore necessary to resolve this anomaly first. The issue is further clouded by the fact that, in philosophical terms, the progress of science involves both nominalism and realism, two positions generally considered to be opposites. Wells's own statement of these two doctrines as they relate to science remains one of the clearest and justifies quotation:

The essence of this vast dispute between Nominalism and Realism which was already beginning in the Greek discussion between the One and the Many . . . may be stated in a few paragraphs. Indeed one may get very near the heart of the matter in a sentence. We have already said that there are three ways of thinking about words; one may think they are truer or less true than fact, or that they are *accurate* and fit the fact exactly. For the Realist the word was truer than the experience; for the Nominalist the experience was truer than the word. . . . The Realist believed that all individuals are imperfect specimens of the perfect 'type'; the Nominalist ignored the perfect type. . . . The practical defeat of Realism over the larger areas of human interest was obviously a necessary preliminary to the release of experimental science. You could not get men to look at reality until verbal Realism was abandoned. It was so much easier to deduce your beliefs from first principles than to go out to make observations, and, according to the Realists, it was a sounder process. The protest of Roger Bacon was the outcry of a Nominalist in a Realist Age. . . . It was Roger Bacon who was the first to ascribe to experiment its proper importance in the pursuit and discipline of knowledge . . . he was almost the first human being to stress the supreme importance of verificatory experiment in the search for knowledge.[9]

And he went on to characterise scientific method as the endeavour to

> 'Observe, try, record, speculate logically, try out your specu-
> lation, confirm or correct, *communicate to other investigators, hear their
> communications, compare, discuss logically,* establish, and so onward.'
> This, for all practical purposes, is the method of sci-
> ence. . . . Distrust every term, every name you use. Logic is very
> serviceable as an aid to judgment, but not as a final judge. All
> the terms you use *fit loosely on fact.* That is the key persuasion
> behind the experimental method.[10]

Now this programme presupposes a Nominalist scepticism, and a
consequent determination to test all theories against repeated
experimentation, but it also assumes that phenomena can be
rationally understood and that, at least at a statistical level, order
and predictability will eventually become evident when sufficient
data has been obtained. Thus the scientific method in its entirety
involves both Nominalism (in its experimentation) and Realism (in
its theorising), both aspects being equally necessary for the overall
progress of scientific investigation. Nevertheless one group of
Wellsian critics asserts that Wells was committed, by his Nominalist
position, to an essentially anti-scientific view of the universe. Thus,
Anthony West links Wells's position with the extreme materialist
view of Hobbes that there is 'Nothing in the World Universal but
Names, for·the things named are, every one of them, Individual and
Singular.'[11]
     West claims that Wells was therefore committed to the mechanis-
tic viewpoint:

> according to which the whole world is nothing but a mere heap of
> dust, fortuitously agitated; and the universe a similar abnegation.
> It is impossible to believe in progress if you believe in a universe in
> which mind figures as a local accident, and which, by its nature,
> cannot support any permanent moral order or indeed, any
> permanent thing. That Wells was deeply committed to this view
> is evident from his first novel, *The Time Machine.*[12]

But Wells dealt quite explicitly with this objection to Nominalism.
After emphasising the uniqueness of every entity and the need for

repeated experimentation to check each generalisation posited, he
continues:

> This pragmatical view of nature leaves a working belief in
> causality intact. We can still believe that exactly the same cause
> would produce exactly the same effect. We are sustained in this
> belief almost invincibly by the invariable experience that the
> more similar the cause the more similar the effect. Our minds
> seem to have been built up from the beginning of time upon such
> experiences. Nevertheless we can recognize that there is a quiver
> of idiosyncrasy in every sequence and that nature never repeats
> herself. There never has been, it seems, exactly the same cause
> and exactly the same effect.
>   Because the universe continues to be unique and original down
> to the minutest particle of the smallest atom, that is no reason for
> supposing it is not nevertheless after the pattern of the rational
> process it has built up in the human mind . . . the direct,
> adequate, dynamic causation of every event, however minute,
> remains the only possible working hypothesis for the scientific
> worker.[13]

The other basic misunderstanding arises from the false reverence
with which many laymen regard science. They tend to believe that
scientific theories are established facts and fail to realise that in
science theories are not proved, they are merely waiting to be
disproved. Theories constitute a proposed explanation of the
observed phenomena, but one contradictory fact, if established,
may topple or modify even the most long-standing theories and
'laws'; thus Einstein's work modified Newton's and awaits further
modification. The scientist, then, sits lightly on his theories; there
are no infallible laws save that which says no laws are infallible.
  In an early essay, 'The Rediscovery of the Unique', Wells
expressed just this necessity for scepticism about scientific laws:

> Those scientific writers who have talked so glibly of the reign of
> inflexible law have been under a serious misconception. It [the
> rediscovery of the unique] restores special providences and
> unverified assertions to the stock of credible things, and liberty to
> the human imagination. . . . Science is a match that man has just
> got alight. He thought he was in a room – in moments of
> devotion, a temple – and that his light would be reflected from

and display walls encrusted with wonderful secrets and pillars carved with philosophical systems, wrought into harmony. It is a curious sensation now that the preliminary splutter is over, and the flame burns up clear, to see his hands lit, and just a glimpse of himself, the patch he stands on visible, and around him in place of all that human comfort and beauty he anticipated – darkness still.[14]

Yet Bergonzi has seen in this appraisal a 'scepticism about the beneficent possibilities of science',[15] and uses it as evidence for the view that Wells was fundamentally a pessimist about science and progress, and that any writings to the contrary were the result of self-delusion. Such a view involves a total misreading of the article. When Wells speaks of 'those scientific writers who have talked so glibly of the reign of inflexible law', he is clearly not intending to imply that all scientists do so, for in the same article he cites the work of Darwin and Wallace as a 'clear assertion of the uniqueness of living things'. Moreover, although Wells was certainly not blind to the limitations of scientific theory and experimental procedures, he was nevertheless sure that they were the best equipment we at present have in the search for truth: it is the 'physicists and chemists who are now trying the next step forward in a hesitating way'. Indeed, the point of the parable is not the feebleness of the glow produced by science, but rather the fact that it illuminates the darkness at all, since, in the terms of the metaphor, nothing else has previously done so. Science shows us at least where we are and hence the point from which we must proceed in our exploration of the universe. Even though the more we learn the more we realise the extent of our ignorance, this realisation is itself a salutary one.

Wells is merely affirming here, as he almost invariably does, the genuinely scientific view that a theory is never an end in itself, but only a tool, an effort to coordinate and explain the phenomena which we observe and that it can never be more than a model of reality. The model approximates most closely to the reality in sections of atomic physics; it is least accurate in biological systems; but in no case can it ever be equivalent to the reality itself.

Science never professes to present more than a working diagram of fact. She does not *explain*. *She states the relations and associations of facts as simply as possible.*
Her justification for her diagrams lies in her increasing power

to change matter. The test of her theories is that they work. She has always been true and continually she becomes truer. But she never expects to reach Ultimate Truth. At their truest her theories are not, and never pretend to be, more than diagrams to fit, not even all possible facts, but simply the known facts.[16]

Wells's recognition of the limitations of science then, is certainly no reason for considering his mode of thinking anti-scientific; rather it suggests the contrary position, for flexibility and a willingness to modify, to change or even to demolish a previously held theory or diagram, is one of the most essential characteristics of the scientific method.

But to vindicate Wells from the charge of an anti-scientific philosophy does not necessarily mean that he was successful in his attempts to express scientific thought, or that his own thought was scientifically accurate. Jules Verne was amongst the first to assert that Wells's stories did 'not repose on very scientific bases . . . Wells is a true representative of the English imagination', and many later English critics have pronounced him deficient as a scientific thinker.[17]

More recently, Bergonzi, developing Anthony West's thesis that Wells's thinking was basically not scientific but imaginative, claims that pseudo-scientific elements, grafted on to an essentially romantic education, were never quite at home in his mind. He writes:

I refer to them as 'romances' rather than 'scientific romances' since, apart from anything else, the adjective is not always appropriate. There are no 'scientific' elements for instance, in a novel such as *The Wonderful Visit*, or in stories like 'The Country of the Blind' and 'The Door in the Wall'.[18]

This assessment appears to have arisen from an implied definition, unjustifiably narrow, of 'scientific' as meaning actual, or scientifically possible, for Bergonzi goes on to cite *The Invisible Man* as an example of a non-scientific, because fundamentally impossible, situation. However, all four of these examples are in fact related to scientific concepts in ways less superficial than the mere use of technological jargon, and it is worth discussing them briefly both in an effort to resolve the anomaly between the disparate assessments of Wells's work, and because they typify some of the common misconceptions held by non-scientists about science.

Certainly *The Wonderful Visit*, which has the form of a fairy tale
with a bias towards social satire, is one of the least scientific of the
romances, and clearly the Angel is not intended to be regarded as a
member of some new species. Nevertheless, even within such an
unlikely framework, Wells has inserted a small satirical vignette of a
scientist in Dr Crump, the village physician, who, so to speak,
cannot see the wood of reality for his preconceived theoretical trees.
More important than the particular figure of Crump, however, is
the fact that the basis and moral of the story is quite definitely a
scientific one in that it calls for a fresh investigation of phenomena,
without any labels, preconceptions or formulae. The vicar confesses
to the Angel, 'I had taken it as a matter of course until you came into
my life.'[19] This taking things 'as a matter of course' is the antithesis
of the scientific attitude and Wells almost never does it. The impulse
underlying the scientific romances, and stated explicitly in *The
Wonderful Visit*, is the refusal to take things at their traditionally
accepted value; beneath the varied shades of wit, humour, pathos
and beauty of the story, is the firm nominalist intention to question
everything and to discover the reasons for its existence.

When we turn to 'The Country of the Blind', which contains an
expanded form of the moral hinted at in Dr Crump – the intolerance of men towards whatever they do not understand (one is,
of course, reminded of the further proverb implicit in the story,
'there are none so blind as they that won't see') – we find again an
'unscientific' setting, for the story is cast in almost mythical terms.
But the way in which the theme is worked out is evidence of a
biologically-trained mind behind it. Wells's ultra-montane race is
blind for micro-biological reasons, and he has shown in some detail
how cultural evolution, through acquired adaptive characteristics,
enables men to overcome a disability which might otherwise have
led to their extinction. This is seen much more clearly if the story is
read in conjunction with Wells's article, 'Human Evolution, an
Artificial Process', in which he compares the different contributions
of two kinds of evolution, genetic and cultural:

> Natural Selection is selection by death. . . . The evolutionary
> process now operating in the social body is one essentially
> different from that which has differentiated species in the past
> and raised man to his ascendancy among the animals. It is a
> process new in this world's history . . . a different sort of
> evolution altogether, an evolution of suggestions and ideas.[20]

In order to appreciate fully the originality of 'The Country of Blind', it is necessary to understand how new this concept of cultural evolution was in 1904. Wells realised that only by this means could survival be ensured in an ecological situation which would normally decimate a population, if not render it extinct within a single generation; but few, if any, of his contemporaries understood the significance of the idea. They tended either to embrace whole-heartedly Lamarck's theory of the inheritance of acquired charac-teristics, or else to reject completely any evidence which seemed to support it. Thus the story is, amongst other things, a biological parable, however little it has been recognised as such.

'The Door in the Wall' also partakes very largely of the aura of fairy tale, even of myth, albeit one that is psychologically valid. It concerns the politician Lionel Wallace, who once, as a child of a joyless, inhibiting home, discovered a door to a visionary garden of happiness. This door presented itself to him as simultaneously attractive and illicit, and it has reappeared temptingly at critical moments throughout his distinguished public career. Hitherto he has remained true to the latter, passing by 'the door that goes into peace, into delight, into a beauty beyond dreaming, a kindness no man on earth can know.'[21] Wallace is subsequently found dead in an excavation, having one night apparently mistaken the workmen's door in the hoarding for the door in the wall of his garden. The story poses a question to which Wells returned repeatedly in his writing – the contrast between the aesthetic and the practical, scientific inclinations of man and the difficulty of choosing between them.

> I am more than half convinced that he had, in truth, an abnormal gift, and a sense, something – I know not what – that in the guise of wall and door offered him an outlet, a secret and peculiar passage of escape into another and altogether more beautiful world. At any rate, you will say, it betrayed him in the end. But did it betray him? There you touch the inmost mystery of these dreamers, these men of vision and the imagination. We see our world fair and common, the hoarding and the pit. By our daylight standard he walked out of security into darkness, danger and death.
> But did he see like that?[22]

This theme recurs in several guises in Wells's work, being part of a wider contrast between tangible and imaginative elements of experience, or between science and aesthetics, a conflict which was all too pertinent to Wells's own experience. Wells has often been seen as being caught on an intellectual battle-ground between his scientific training in rational thought and his native gift of a vivid imagination. He himself was apparently aware of this conflict intermittently during his science course at South Kensington, when poetry seduced his attention from geology practical work,[23] and he portrayed a similar struggle in several student characters – in Lewisham and in William Hill of 'A Slip Under the Microscope' – and at greater length in George Ponderevo's dalliance with art. Thus even in a manifest fairy story, 'The Door in the Wall', Wells is preoccupied with a question, partly psychological, partly sociological, raised by his own experiences as a science student. It is certainly conceivable that this divided intellectual allegiance still beset Wells in the literary field – how far was his imagination justified in leaping beyond the limits of the scientifically acceptable postulates of his day? Or alternatively, how far did a desire to put forward a point of view as scientifically as possible emasculate his potential literary gifts?

However, the most surprising of Bergonzi's examples of an 'unscientific story' is *The Invisible Man*. Certainly, in a letter to Arnold Bennett, Wells admitted that the process described in the novel as producing invisibility in living tissues was not scientifically possible, and himself pointed out to Bennett another yet more awkward difficulty in the scientific rationale of the story:

> There is another difficulty . . . which really makes the whole story impossible. I believe it to be insurmountable. Any alteration in the refractive index of the eye lens would make vision impossible. Without such alteration the eyes would be visible as glassy globules. And for vision it is also necessary that there should be visual purple behind the retina and an opaque cornea and iris.[24]

But he goes on to indicate why, although well aware of these biological shortcomings of his story, he nevertheless persevered with it: 'On those lines [i.e. taking account of the above] you would get a very effective short story but nothing more.'[25] Indeed these objections scarcely affect the story at all as a scientific romance. The whole atmosphere of the story is matter-of-fact, as though Wells has accepted the challenge to take one of the most magic of fairy-tale situations, the cloak of invisibility, and treat it scientifically. This he does with manifest success. Instead of the standard *coup d'oeil* transformation, we have a careful analysis in optical terms of what invisibility would entail, reinforced by scientific parallels and analogies together with a suggestion, albeit impossible in practice, as to how such a process might be effected, the whole passage being treated in a deliberately prosaic manner:

> The essential phase was to place the transparent object whose refractive index was to be lowered, between two radiating centres of a sort of ethereal vibration of which I will tell you more fully later. No, not these Röntgen vibrations – I don't know that these others of mine have been described. Yet they are obvious enough. I needed two little dynamos, and these I worked with a cheap gas engine. . . .[26]

But, striking as this technique of simulating authenticity is, it is not the most important aspect of the story. Wells is far more concerned with the psychological effect on a scientist, Griffin, of this power placed so suddenly within his grasp. As such, the relevance of the story to science and scientists was already considerable in Wells's own day and even more pertinent today.

At the end of his study of the scientific romances, Bergonzi sums up his thesis that Wells's attitudes and interests are basically aesthetic and literary rather than scientific:

> The picture that will have emerged from them [the preceding chapters] of the young Wells as a symbolic and mythopoeic writer whose work has closer affinities to poetry than to the conventional realistic fiction of his time, will no doubt seem strange and even incredible to those who are more familiar with his later career. . . . It is true of course that Wells had received a scientific education and that his later attitudes were severely positivistic. Yet, as we have seen, he had been absorbing fictional romance from childhood, long before he embarked on his studies at South Kensington.[27]

Wells himself was certainly aware of these rival claims. In his autobiography he recalls the conflict between them during the years 1897–1910 (that is, the period during which the short stories and the major novels were written); but he himself believed firmly that his scientific training outweighed the aesthetic strain in his personality:

> So far . . . I have tried to show the pull of two main groups of
> divergent personalities, and two main sets of tendency upon my
> character, during those still plastic days at Sandgate, and to
> indicate something of the quality of my response. . . . The
> scientific pull was the earlier and the stronger. I moved more and
> more away from conscious artistry and its exaltations and
> chagrins; I was strengthened against self-dramatization and
> confirmed in my disposition to social purposiveness.[28]

How then are the opposing critical estimates of Wells's scientific
reasoning to be resolved? The objections raised by most of the
literary critics result from their failure to understand fully the
nature of the scientific method and in particular of twentieth-
century physics, and hence to appreciate how completely Wells
relied on such reasoning, not only in the scientific romances, but
throughout all his work.

Until the twentieth century, the prevailing mechanistic view of
the universe obliged scientists to cultivate detachment and rigorous
objectivity, but with Heisenberg's enunciation of the Uncertainty
Principle (1927) this concept of science became untenable.
Mechanism was shown to be an inadequate way of explaining the
world of atoms and electrons.[29] Ironically the physicist Sir James
Jeans, in describing the new approach to physics, virtually
paraphrased Wordsworth's dictum, 'we murder to dissect':

> Every observation destroys the bit of the universe observed, and
> so supplies knowledge only of a bit of the universe which has
> already become past history . . .

and he goes on to elaborate:

> The old science which pictured nature as a crowd of blindly
> wandering atoms, claimed that it was depicting a completely
> objective universe, entirely outside of, and detached from, the
> mind which perceived it. Modern science makes no such claim,
> frankly admitting that its subject of study is primarily our
> observation of nature and not nature itself. The new picture of
> nature must then inevitably involve mind as well as matter – the
> mind which perceives and the matter which is perceived – and so

must be more mental in character than the fallacious one which preceded it.[30]

This *volte-face* is of course relevant chiefly to the field of submolecular physics but there is a wider sense in which popular opinion ascribes to science a certainty which is possible only in the deductive procedures of pure mathematics and formal logic, procedures which are not concerned with natural phenomena at all but only with the logical connections between statements. On the contrary empirical (or natural) science involves a very large element of induction, an educated guess, which leaps beyond the observed facts and suggests a further hypothesis or a new synthesis of previously-known facts. A genuinely scientific hypothesis has implications, it makes predictions which can be tested by comparing them with the observed facts, but it cannot claim certainty. (If it does it is not an induction at all but a disguised deduction in which the conclusions are, by definition, already implicit in the premises.) Any hypothesis achieves scientific respectability only after rigorous experimentation has failed to disqualify it, and even then it still has a provisional quality, as evidenced by the very word 'theory'. The so-called 'laws' of science were the formulations of a less scientific age, and nearly all have since been qualified in some degree.

Now it is precisely for their inductive procedure that Wells's scientific romances have sustained the most criticism. Typically he puts forward some novel postulate and then proceeds to demonstrate with great precision the consequences and implications, so that, if we are once led to accept his initial supposition, we can scarcely dispute the conclusion. Once we grant the possibility of a substance such as cavorite, we can scarcely fault the description of the flight to the moon; once grant the possibility of an atmosphere on the moon and there is no clear point where we can logically take exception to the evolving story of the Selenites and their civilisation; so too with 'Boom-food' in *The Food of the Gods* and time-travel in *The Time Machine*. Thus, in the best scientific tradition, Wells postulates a condition and then proceeds to deduce the consequences. If he at times waived current theories concerning the nature of the physical universe, it was not usually in order to usher in a fantastic world where physical laws were inoperable, but rather in order to test and question common assumptions by considering the possible alternatives.

This comparative freedom from the trammels of conventional

preconceptions enabled Wells at times to consider apparent impossibilities which were later developed and shown to be feasible. A more closed mind, such as Verne's, made fewer blunders, but it also necessarily forfeited the possibility of more fundamental insights.

The most fascinating example of an hypothesis which Wells developed perhaps at first only incidentally, is that of time as the fourth dimension. Although the explanations of time-travel given within *The Time Machine* are, technically, only preliminaries to the main sociological point of the story, they show Wells's careful examination of what such a concept would entail. Indeed, for scientific readers they must assume an extraordinary stature in so far as Wells's discussion of the fourth dimension not only predates any other, but proceeds with meticulous clarity and accuracy.

It is clear that the concept of time-travelling, rather than the sociological fable, was the nucleus of *The Time Machine*, for its precursor was a serial, 'The Chronic Argonauts', which Wells wrote for *The Science Schools Journal* in 1888. The grandiose title is symptomatic of the poor writing of this early draft, 'loaded', as Wells later realised, 'with irrelevant, sham significance',[31] and with unnecessary and distracting incidents. Nevertheless, these stylistic imperfections should not lead us to forget that the idea of time-travelling had already taken shape in Wells's mind by this earlier date of 1888 when the concept of a fourth dimension was still only dimly imagined by scientists. He records that:

> In the universe in which my brain was living in 1879 there was no nonsense about time being space or anything of that sort. There were three dimensions . . . and I never heard of a fourth dimension until 1884 or thereabout. Then I thought it was a witticism.[32]

The only literary precursors of the idea of a fourth dimension were Charles Hinton's *Scientific Romances*[33] and Oscar Wilde's casual allusion in his short story 'The Canterville Ghost', and in both of these, the proposed fourth dimension is a spatial one.[34] How, then, did Wells conceive of the idea of *time* as a dimension analogous to the Euclidean spatial dimensions, in particular the idea of differential movement along such a dimension and, in the light of later physics, how successfully did he grapple with its implications?

The celebrated Michelson-Morley experiment in 1887 struck the

first definitive blow to the concept that light-propagation necessitated an ether through which energy, in the form of waves, travelled
and it later became the starting-point for Einstein's work. However,
by the close of the nineteenth century there was still no recognition
by physicists of the basic relations between the systems of electro-
magnetic and mechanical observations which necessitated cor-
rections to the latter. Those who preferred to preserve the integrity
of the whole corpus of Newtonian physics against the results of a
single experiment failed to see the implication of the 'negative'
result of the Michelson-Morley experiment: namely that the
velocity of light is not affected by the motion of the earth, and hence
that there is no *absolute* frame of reference for the earth's
motion.

Undoubtedly this experiment must have caused at least some
physicists to question the traditional concepts of velocity and hence
of time, but it is understandable that none of their inconclusive
speculations would be published. Reputable journals of physics are
restricted to publishing experimental results, or, at most, closely-
knit mathematical formulations, not wild guesses. It is therefore not
unlikely that Wells's only source material for the ideas underlying
The Time Machine should have been, as he himself claimed, a paper
read at the South Kensington Debating Society. Bergonzi has
concluded that this paper was, in all probability, that read on 14
January 1887, by a fellow-student of Wells, E. A. Hamilton-Gordon
who, in his address, 'The Fourth Dimension', discussed the
probabilities of multidimensional Euclidean geometry and suggested, apparently at random, time, life and heaven as three possible
candidates for the fourth dimension.

Characteristically Wells chose the least obscure of these suggestions to develop, notwithstanding the current popularity of
Hinton's *Scientific Romances* which elaborated the idea of a fourth
dimension of *space*. Thus, quite without benefit of scientific
precursors, Wells launched into an imaginative exploration of what
movement in time would mean. It was another seventeen years
before the publication of Einstein's Theory of Special Relativity,
where the concept of a time dimension was first treated in a scientific
paper.[35] Here Einstein showed that a clock, attached to any moving
system, runs at a different rate from a stationary clock, slowing
down as its velocity increases, not by virtue of any mechanical
changes in the clock (for an observer travelling with the clock would
not notice the changes); only an observer stationary relative to the

moving system would find that the moving clock had slowed down with respect to his stationary clock.

Einstein's example of the clocks is particularly relevant to *The Time Machine*, and it is interesting to examine in some detail how successfully Wells's descriptions of the Time Traveller's experiences compare with what we might now predict from the Theory of Special Relativity.

The first page of *The Time Machine* opens with a clear statement of the concept of a fourth dimension by analogy with the three spatial dimensions, and then proceeds to clarify the basic assumptions involved in the idea of time as a dimension. Characteristically, Wells did not attempt to derive such a concept mathematically, but merely from common experience, and he then traced its implications. It is significant, however, that the Time Traveller states categorically (Wells's italics): ' "*There is no difference between Time and any of the three dimensions of Space except that our consciousness moves along it.*" '[36] As if to emphasise the essential similarity between time and the three spatial dimensions, the Time-Traveller has constructed his machine not merely to travel in time, but to 'travel indifferently in any direction of Space and Time as the driver determines'. One of the guests, the Psychologist, raises what seems to common-sense experience an obvious point, namely that the model time machine, having disappeared, must have gone into the past, if it has indeed travelled in time, because, ' "I presume that it has not moved in space, and if it travelled into the future, it would still be here all this time, since it must have travelled through this time" '.[37] This is virtually the same objection which the critic Pitkin raises but Wells explicitly dealt with it several times.[38] When it is first raised by the Psychologist, the Time Traveller replies;

'It's presentation below the threshold, you know, diluted presentation.' 'Of course,' said the psychologist, and reassured us. 'That's a simple point of psychology. I should have thought of it. . . . We cannot see it, nor can we appreciate this machine, any more than we can the spoke of a wheel spinning, or a bullet flying through the air. If it is travelling through time fifty or a hundred times faster than we are, if it gets through a minute while we get through a second, the impression it creates will of course be only one-fiftieth or one-hundredth of what it would make if it were not travelling in time. That's plain enough.'[39]

Similarly, when the Time Traveller departs into the future, his housekeeper Mrs Watchets, who enters the laboratory just after he has started the machine, does not see him, for he has already attained such a speed in time that she, walking at 'normal' speed, appears to rocket across the room according to his frame of reference.

Later, the Time Traveller elaborates on the risk which he runs in coming to a stop in any future time:

'The peculiar risk lay in the possibility of my finding some substance in the space which I or the machine occupied. So long as I travelled at a high velocity through time, this scarcely mattered. I was, so to speak, attenuated – was slipping like a vapour through the interstices of intervening substances! But to come to a stop involved the jamming of myself, molecule by molecule, into whatever lay in my way; it meant bringing my atoms into such intimate contact with those of the obstacle that a profound chemical reaction – possibly a far-reaching explosion – would result and blow myself and my apparatus out of all possible dimensions.'

Hence, when he does stop, 'there was the sound of a clap of thunder in my ears . . . but presently I remarked that that confusion in my ears was gone'.[40] And again, when the Time Traveller departs on his machine for his second and last expedition, there is a corresponding implosion, as molecules of the surrounding medium rush to fill the vacuum suddenly formed. The narrator relates that he heard

a click and a thud. A gust of air whirled around me as I opened the door, and from within came the sound of broken glass falling on the floor. . . . A pane of the skylight had, apparently, just been blown in.[41]

Wells is also careful to draw our attention to the fact that the time machine has travelled under its own power only in one dimension. It reappears in the laboratory against the north-west wall although it had started from the south-east corner, the amount of displacement being the exact distance which the Morlocks had carried it from its position on the lawn to the pedestal of the White Sphinx. All these points in the story are entirely consistent with Einstein's Theory.

A further point, with which Pitkin takes issue, is the idea of traversing a 'great deal of time' in a 'little time', for, he reasons:

> To do this, time itself must have a time-velocity which the time machine can exceed. And this a pure contradiction: for velocity is a ratio within the time continuum.[42]

Pitkin seems here not to understand the concept of velocity. Velocity is defined as the distance moved along *any* axis per unit time. Once the concept of time as a dimension is understood, there is no difficulty in substituting an increment of time for an increment of length, whereupon the velocity along the time axis becomes the movement in time with respect to the basic unit of time. This is precisely the concept used by Wells when the Time Traveller speeds up or slows down his machine. Pitkin's objection to the detail that when the Time Traveller returns from the future he is no older and wears the same clothes merely shows that even in 1914, nine years after the publication of Einstein's work, Pitkin has not understood the implications of Relativity Theory. Consistently with Special Relativity Theory, the Time Traveller, while on the machine, exists in one frame of reference with it and, within that frame, time for him appears to pass 'normally'. Likewise, time for those outside this frame also appears to pass 'normally'. It is only in the interaction of the time machine frame with any other frame of reference that velocity along the time-axis occurs. Therefore there is no reason why the Time Traveller should age, since, as far as he is concerned, and as far as his 'biological clock' is concerned, the only time he has experienced is the period of 'normal' time spent in the seat of the time machine together with the time spent in the course of his three halts – a total of some eleven days in all. His clothes are dusty and torn and his shoes lost only because of his experiences during the time he was *not* in the time machine.

More serious than any of Pitkin's charges was that made by Israel Zangwill in the year of publication of *The Time Machine*. His primary objection springs from his belief in a strict chronological determinism which, from the point of view of physics, creates paradoxes as yet unresolvable when held in juxtaposition with the idea of time-travelling, although this latter concept is, in itself, mathematically valid. Zangwill makes the point that the Time Traveller is agitated at the thought that he might have to remain in the year 802,701,

. . . into which he has recklessly travelled; nor does it ever occur to him that in the aforesaid year he will have to repeat these painful experiences of his, else his vision of the future will have falsified itself – though how the long-dispersed dust is to be vivified again does not appear.[43]

Zangwill assumes that this objection, which is partially valid in itself, has invalidated the whole concept of motion in time, and concludes that 'There is no getting into the Future, except by waiting'.[44] In fact, both arguments, for and against time-travel, are theoretically valid, creating a paradox which has so far remained unresolved. Wells's 'error' lies in avoiding the implications, both physical and logical, of the Time Traveller's sudden appearances and disappearances in time, but clearly this 'error' had to be made if there were to be a story at all. His achievement, which far outweighs this, lies not only in his literary power but also in his analysis of the mathematical concept of a fourth dimension of time and his highly original deduction in considerable detail of the side effects upon a body moving differentially along the time axis. On the other hand, those critics who claim to have refuted Wells's reasoning have, in general, not understood the concept of a fourth dimension.

Ironically, in those cases where there has been a partial vindication of Wells's postulates, but where details differ from those of current scientific knowledge, critics have tended to shift their ground of attack. Now Wells is frequently criticised for being 'wrong' rather than for postulating the impossible. But to be wrong is not to be unscientific – rather the contrary in one vital sense, for it is characteristic of a scientifically presented hypothesis that it should make predictions definite enough to admit of being proved wrong if they *are* wrong; on the other hand there are scarcely any circumstances under which an unscientific theory could be disproved, since it does not make sufficiently precise predictions.

The great faith which Wells habitually placed in scientific method as the only effective means of organising society, of preventing waste and of facilitating progress, is further evident in his own sociological outlines, many of which read like brief scientific treatises. *The Open Conspiracy* and *First and Last Things* are set out as a coherent piece of that same scientific reasoning which they exhort others to use. In their format and style they are closest to Wells's early article 'The Things that Live on Mars', itself a conscious and highly successful attempt to derive a hypothetical picture of the surface and inhabitants of Mars from the few scattered facts then known from observation. Two of Wells's earliest essays, 'Zoological Retrogression' and 'On Extinction', already demonstrate this procedure which was to form the basis of much of his most successful writing – broad generalisation on a subject, followed by careful reference to facts which have been marshalled in support of the postulate and made palatable by imaginative presentation. In conclusion there is a prediction, derived from the foregoing. This is the closest literary equivalent of the procedure customarily employed in the presentation of a scientific paper.

Nevertheless there are areas in which Wells's scientific approach faltered. When making use of a scientific background for his stories, he did endeavour to construct this as accurately as possible, but there were times when this background research proved inadequate. Ironically, Burke detects a weakness in the Wellsian armour at a point where it might have been thought least vulnerable – biology. He claims that Wells seems not to have been aware, when writing his *Short History of the World*, of the later developments in biology:

> Not a word about Neo-Darwinism. Neither Weissmann, nor Mendel, nor de Vries, nor Bateson on discontinous variation and heredity, appears to have attracted his attention. The blood test method due to Professor H. F. Nuttall of Cambridge, affording as it does evidence of man's relationship to the apes, is passed over as though it were unknown. And the more recent work of Keith and others on hormones . . . appears to have completely escaped his attention. In truth, Mr Wells writes as if he were almost a contemporary of Huxley, Tyndall or Father Gerrard; of the science of the nineteenth century and the first few years of the twentieth.[45]

Again, the publication of *Dr. Moreau* elicited, apart from the wrath of literary critics on ethical grounds, a stern note in *Natural Science* pointing out the scientific inaccuracy involved in the description of Moreau's transplantation techniques:

> From the scientific side, however, Mr Wells seems to us to have allowed his imagination too free a run in his new story . . . Mr Barfurth sums up recent work on transplantation and transfusion conclusively against the success of operations conducted upon

animals of different species. Transplantations from one species to another almost invariably have proved unsuccessful.[46]

A celebrated spokesman for medical research, P. Chalmers Mitchell, also raised doubts about the validity of the central idea of the romance.[47] Wells had stated in a note appended to the novel that:

> There can be no denying, whatever amount of scientific credibility attaches to the details of this story, that the manufacture of monsters – even of quasi-human monsters – is within the possibilities of vivisection.

Mitchell replied:

> The most recent discussion of grafting and transfusion experiments is to be found in the treatise by Oscar Hertwig, the translation of which Mr. Heinemann announces. Later investigators have failed to repeat the grafting experiments of Hunter.[48]

Since these criticisms, we have of course seen an enormous development in transplant techniques, with results more practical if less exotic than Moreau's, and this might be seen as a partial vindication of Wells, but the question remains whether this, like some of his other 'prophecies', was not a lucky guess rather than prediction based on scientific data. Wells was certainly of the opinion that tissue-transplants, even between animals of different species, had already been proved possible. In an article published before *Dr. Moreau* he affirmed that:

> The medical man will at once recall Hunter's cock's spur flourishing on the bull's neck. . . . It is a possible thing to transplant tissues from one part of an animal to another, or from one animal to another, to alter its chemical reactions and methods of growth, to modify the articulation of its limbs, and indeed to change its most intimate structure.[49]

But *Dr. Moreau* went further in its scope than current research warranted, just as in the early articles Wells could not resist

speculating about the future of surgery in terms which at times seem
wantonly calculated to alienate scientists:

> If we concede the justifications of vivisection, we may imagine as
> possible in the future, operators armed with antiseptic
> surgery . . . taking living creatures and moulding them into the
> most amazing forms; it may be even reviving the monsters of
> mythology, realizing the fantasies of the taxidermist, his mer-
> maids and whatnot in flesh and blood.[50]

Behind the highly-coloured and emotive journalism of these early
articles and the blood-stained horrors of Moreau's laboratory,
however, there is a serious moral question which Wells at once
perceived, even from the preliminary transplant experiments of his
day – and one which the perfecting of such surgery has only served
to emphasise more strongly – namely, the question of the sanctity of
identity. What in fact constitutes personal identity, when the
possibilities of transplantation, not only within a species but even
between species, become theoretically limitless? The title of Wells's
early article, 'The Limits of Individual Plasticity', implies a
question which has not yet been answered. The related problem,
more topical today, that of the sanctity of the donor and his rights –
what constitutes a voluntary donation of vital organs? Must such a
donation be always voluntary? – Wells apparently did not foresee,
but his moral comment as a whole remains no less valid and may
perhaps be seen as partial justification for his use of exaggeration to
force his point upon his readers' attention.

Wells was not basically interested in the slow detailed accumulation of evidence or in the painstaking accuracy of experimental
method, but rather in broad theories. He did not go on to test his
hypotheses experimentally for his limited training in research, his
personal inclinations and his literary intentions were all against it;
and to this extent his scientific thinking was seriously flawed. Wells
himself was not unaware of this. In his autobiography, while
speaking of his 'relative readiness to grasp form and relation . . . a
brain good for outlines', he admits:

> It scarcely needs criticism to bring home to me that much of my
> work has been slovenly, haggard and irritated, most of it hurried
> and inadequately revised. . . . I am tormented by a desire for
> achievement that overruns my capacity and by a practical

incapacity to bring about for myself the conditions under which fine achievement is possible.[51]

Despite these defects, which are undeniable, it must also be remembered that with the obvious exceptions of his *Honours Physiography*, his *Textbook of Biology* and later *The Science of Life*, Wells's primary aim was never simply an explication of scientific data. His early years as a teacher had aroused his critical interest in the processes of education and with maturity he showed an increasing commitment to the task of educating a public hitherto largely ignorant of scientific principles and equally devoid of scientific reasoning. Having suffered, as he believed, from the uninspired teaching of two professors at South Kensington, Wells held strongly to the view that the facts could and should be made interesting to the general public, especially since the increase in the reading public as a result of the 1870 Education Act gave an unprecedented educational opportunity to his generation of writers and educators. He therefore castigated those scientists who, in lectures and articles, talked down to their audience and substituted witticisms for facts:

> It is a far more difficult thing than is usually imagined, but it is an imperative one, that scientific exponents who wish to be taken seriously should not only be precise and explicit, but also absolutely serious in their style. If it were not a point of discretion, it would still be a point of honour. . . . Very few books and scientific papers appear to be constructed at all. The author simply wanders about his subject. . . . This is not simply bad art; it is the trick of boredom. A scientific paper for popular reading may and should have an orderly progression in development. Intelligent common people come to scientific books neither for humour, subtlety of style, nor for vulgar words of the 'millions and millions and millions' type, but for problems to exercise their minds upon. The taste for good, inductive reading is very widely diffused; there is a keen pleasure in seeing a previously unexpected generalisation skilfully developed.[52]

Wells's failure to pursue a life of concentrated scientific research was undoubtedly the reason for his failure to be elected a Fellow of the Royal Society, perhaps the recognition which he most desired. This disappointment may have contributed to his sometimes scathing attitude towards that body for its refusal to recognise what he considered the wider applications of science, in particular the social sciences and theories of education:

> It is not always the professors, experts and researchers in a field of human interest, who are the best and most trustworthy teachers of that subject to the common man. This is a point excessively ignored by men of science. They do not realise their specialised limitations. They think that writing and teaching come by nature. They do not understand that science is something far greater than the community of scientific men. It is a culture and not a club. The Royal Society resists the admission that there is any science of public education or social psychology whatever.[53]

In *Tono-Bungay*, Edward Ponderevo, whose early life closely follows Wells's own, does attain to a Fellowship of the Royal Society but as a free-lance scientist, often dilettante, he remains critical of the traditional scientific training in research. Reviewing his achievements, he asks (with Wells):

> Could I have done as much if I had had a turn for obeying those rather mediocre professors at the College who proposed to train my mind? If I had been trained in research – that ridiculous contradiction in terms – should I have done more than produce additions to the existing store of little papers with blunted conclusions, of which there are already too many? . . . Suppose I had stamped down on the head of my wandering curiosity, locked my imagination, in a box just when it wanted to grow out to things, worked by so-and-so's excellent method and so-and-so's indications, where should I be now?[54]

But if Wells criticised the Royal Society for its stress on detailed research at the expense of fostering a more flexible educational system, the alternative which he envisaged was, in his view, not less but more valuable for the future of science since it involved training the next generation of scientists. The kind of mind which makes scientific predictions from existing theories and data is characteristically one which thinks in a future frame of reference; its preoccupations tend to be general and statistical rather than individual or personal. It was this kind of thinking which Wells believed education should encourage – hence the need for scientists to be involved in reforming the educational system to promote such an awareness. Not only the utopian novels but most of Wells's sociological writings also urge this revolution from a past- to a future-oriented mode of thinking. In *The Science of Life* he writes about the influence which science has had in changing the emphasis of education from a tradition-centred approach to a forward-looking attitude:

> In education the human young learnt the wisdom of its forefathers. Education was an entirely conservative force, it functioned to preserve the traditional state of affairs. So it is still over large parts of the world. . . . But in quite a little space of years, the conception of education in many progressive minds has undergone the most revolutionary developments. The introduction of scientific work has infected even the most dogmatic centres with a sense of intellectual incompleteness. Even the most traditional education glances now, ever and again, almost unwittingly towards the future.[55]

Judged by this criterion of a non-personal and forward-looking attitude, which, if it seems on occasions too all-inclusive a definition, is still no less appropriate than the too-narrow alternative adopted by many of his critics, Wells's thinking was indeed scientific. His preoccupation was increasingly with society as a whole and less with the few remarkable individuals within it. Similarly, his synthetic approach to data caused him to stress the relationship of any one fact to the existing body of facts, even to subjects previously considered somewhat disparate – science and social morality, science and economics, science and politics. This integration of science into the wider discussion of society remains, in many ways, Wells's most important contribution to both science and literature. Our increasing awareness today of society's collective responsibility for the results and ramifications of scientific research has tended to obscure the fact that Wells was a pioneer of this way of thinking, that he coined such phrases as 'social biology' and 'human ecology' which are now part of our common vocabulary. Throughout his career, he came to treat science less as an end in itself, and increasingly in relation to sociological development, particularly in relation to the moral issues raised at the social level. This change in perspective is already apparent between the wholly theoretical 'Chronic Argonauts' and *The Time Machine*, in which the sociological questions raised by the society of AD 802, 701 have almost overshadowed the author's fascination with the physics underlying the concept of time-travel. Wells had already begun to take his prophetic and educational role very seriously in 1901, when he wrote to R. A. Gregory, 'I am going to write, talk and preach revolution for the next five years'.[56]

Part II
Science in Society

3 Science and Technology

The pursuit of science involves an advancement in the understanding of the way in which the world functions, but it does not necessarily make a society immediately richer or stronger, or give it any greater power over nature. Technology, on the other hand, does not significantly add to one's understanding of the laws of nature, but it does increase the possibility of control over one's surroundings. Today it is often assumed that these are, if not identical, then necessarily interacting processes, scientific discovery leading to technological innovation which, in turn, suggests further experimentation. This is true in modern Western society, but the correlation is by no means inevitable. It is possible to have both technological societies devoid of science (as in the so-called hydraulic societies of Peru and Ceylon) and others, such as those of ancient Greece and India which, while developing abstract scientific theory to a considerable degree, have regarded engineering and applied or experimental science of any kind as a pursuit unworthy of the educated mind. In fact the combination of both procedures in a fruitful partnership is peculiar to modern industrial societies. However, precisely because of this close integration of the two elements, the basic and important distinction between them is only infrequently realised.

From the time of Blake, whose hatred of the dark Satanic mills was matched only by his scorn of Newton's somnolent single vision, the attitudes expressed in nineteenth-century English literature showed an overwhelming confusion of science with technology and a painful ambivalence towards both. Most writers welcomed, at least tacitly, the materialistic comforts made possible by technology, but cried out against the physical ugliness and moral corruption it occasioned.[1] On the other hand, many hated the deterministic rationalism which formed the basis of theoretical science but were forced to admire the unprecedented success of theories such as Darwinism in explaining natural phenomena.

Wells was certainly the first writer to be fully aware of the basic distinction between science and technology, and to assert the moral responsibility of scientists for such technology as resulted from their researches – an issue which remains highly controversial to this day.

Wells's attitudes were not, however, always homogeneous. There is a marked development from the earlier writings which still reflect the common nineteenth-century resistance to, and fear of, the machine, to the later sociological novels which welcome scientific advances not merely as inevitable but as almost wholly beneficial and liberating. These scientifically advanced societies are shown as making possible a more creative and enriching life for both the individual and his community.

It is noteworthy that even in the earlier romances, where the resistance to technology is maximal, the actual principles of theoretical science are, for the most part, exempt from castigation. The criticism is levelled at technology or at those who attempt to prostitute scientific knowledge for other 'non-scientific' motives, for self-aggrandisement, power or financial gain. Pure science, and those who pursue it faithfully, are in general applauded. However, in these early works the 'noble' scientists are almost invariably depicted as being powerless to curb the evil machinations of the 'false' scientists or to control the amoral progress of technology. This comparative impotence of scientists is not only reflected in their failure to dominate the technological scene but is also implied in the recurrent theme of their inability to account for the unexpectedness of nature. Events, unpredicted and often inexplicable, even in retrospect, continue to baffle scientific theory, a point which is emphasised by the personal discomfiture, physical, intellectual, or sometimes both, of scientists in the face of surprising occurrences. 'Aepyornis Island', 'The Remarkable Case of Davidson's Eyes', 'The Plattner Story', 'In the Abyss', 'The Sea Raiders', 'In the Avu Observatory', 'The Crystal Egg' and 'The Stolen Body', all stress the inadequacy of scientists in the face of the apparent eccentricity of Nature. The able, dedicated and virtuous scientists are far outnumbered in this period of Wells's writing by the helpless and demented ones. There is thus in effect a repeated warning against the expectation that technological progress divorced from the principles and philosophy of an essentially benevolent science, can effect any permanent good for society.

In the earliest fictional example, *The Time Machine*, the Time Traveller, in so far as he is characterised within the story, is essentially a sympathetic figure – the dedicated scientist steadfastly seeking knowledge at whatever personal risk, and despite the ridicule and lack of understanding of his friends. Moreover, he is not merely a cloistered, theoretical scientist, isolating himself in obscure research; his instinctive moral reactions of justice, benevolence and pity lead him to become involved in the affairs of the Eloi and to strive for the welfare of their community. Yet, in the same sequence, there is a description, rendered all the more vivid by its mythic overtones, of the evil and degrading effects of a technology devoid of morality, and overall this latter picture far outweighs the small human touches of the Time Traveller's concern and Weena's pathetic gratitude. Indeed the Morlocks and their underworld are painted in colours that recall the tradition of Dante and Milton rather than the late nineteenth-century novel; their subterranean factories, their predatory, nocturnal raids, their distorted forms and the dark outlines of their machines are all reminiscent of the classical trappings of an infernal hell and its denizens. Nevertheless, it should be noted that, even at this stage of his writing, when the bias against technology is greatest, Wells does not, on that account, necessarily revere the earlier pre-industrial tradition as the Pre-Raphaelites had done in their reaction against mechanisation. The Eloi, with their gentle, childlike pastimes, their free-flowing dress, their dancing and harmless play, their diet of fruit and their wilful isolation from unpleasant social situations, represent all too obviously the pastoral heaven of the Pre-Raphaelites. The Time Travellor at first responds to the Eloi in the Romantic manner, being enchanted, if perplexed, by their way of life, until it is forced upon his understanding that this Arcadian leisure is inextricably bound to, and indeed dependent upon, the brutalising mechanical labour of the machine-tenders. His disenchantment, however, leaves him with no positive view to uphold. If he can no longer respect the fatuous Eloi, neither can he endorse the brutality of the Morlocks. His predicament is, in fact, that of Wells himself, who, while renouncing the impractical dreams of Ruskin and Morris, nevertheless saw only too clearly the potential danger of a society in which a sense of the inevitability of technological advance has subtly infected the public consciousness with an amoral, machine-derived ethic.

In 'The Lord of the Dynamos' (1894), one of his almost perfect short stories, Wells attempted a less mythical but still allegorical rendering of a similar theme. The stark simplicity and brevity of the story underlines the issues more clearly than the novels of the same period, and it is therefore worth looking at in some detail.

The shed housing the dynamos which supply the electric railway at Camberwell is a model for the technological society, its chief and most obvious attribute being power, and to it come representatives of three modern attitudes towards the machine. Holroyd, the 'practical electrician', has substituted his machine for traditional gods and ethics, and thus its 'morality', the principle of power, dictates his: 'He doubted the existence of the Deity but accepted Carnot's cycle and he had read Shakespeare and found him weak in chemistry.'[2] Holroyd reveres the dynamo partly because it is more powerful than he, and partly because it lends support to his innate desire to exercise physical power over his subordinates. 'Holroyd liked a nigger help because he would stand kicking – a habit with Holroyd . . . to James Holroyd bullying was a labour of love.'[3] He thus embodies the *laissez-faire* policies and social exploitation of the nineteenth-century captains of industry who also worshipped technological power. It is not accidental that he is described as delivering 'a theological lecture on the text of his big machine': ' "Kill a hundred men. Twelve per cent on the ordinary shares, and that's something like a Gord." '[4] This half-jocular outburst reveals only too accurately the technology-worshipper's personal ideals – power to kill and power to make money. When Azuma-zi, provoked beyond endurance by Holroyd's bullying, flings him to his death on the live terminals, he merely performs the literal extension of what Holroyd has already become symbolically – a part of the machine.

If Holroyd reveres the machine for its power, Azuma-zi, the primitive, suddenly confronted by this glittering representation of technology, also deifies it, though in his mind its power is associated with the 'natural' sense impressions – noise, rhythm, colour, vibrations – rather than the materialistic considerations which weigh so heavily with Holroyd. His voluntary death fused to the dynamo is again an extension of his sense of mystic communion with his Lord.

The third character, the scientific manager, represents the 'true scientist', the expert. He does not deify the machine; he simply uses it. He alone combines an objective rationalistic viewpoint with a humane morality. On the one hand his approach is all efficiency – after Holroyd's death 'the expert was chiefly anxious to get the machine at work again, for seven or eight trains had stopped'; yet later, realising why and how Holroyd has died, he feels pity concomitantly with his sense of duty – ' "Poor Holroyd! I see it now." Then almost mechanically he went towards the switch. . . .'[5]

It is interesting that several critics have noted in 'The Lord of the Dynamos' a close resemblance to Kipling's style – 'A tale worthy of Kipling when he is very near his best',[6] commented *The Critic*, while Raknem remarks that Kipling and Wells 'stand apart from other short story writers in their adoration of machinery'.[7] If Wells's style in this story is close to Kipling's (and there are suggestions of a similarity in the descriptions of Azuma-zi and in the ascribing of human qualities to the dynamo by Azuma-zi) then this is more likely to be an additional level of irony than an indication of parallel views on the part of the two authors. It should be clear that, so far from conforming to Kipling's values, Wells is in fact satirising the attitude of which Kipling was the leading spokesman – that of imputing human characteristics to machinery. Both Holroyd and Azuma-zi in their diverse ways do this and thereby perish. For Wells, on the other hand, the machine or any scientific apparatus, was not an end in itself but only a useful servant. The 'hero' of the story, therefore, is certainly not the dynamo, much less its various devotees, but the scientific manager who, neither worshipping nor hating the machine, understands its value and purpose, and controls it.

This view of the machine was to be elaborated and clarified throughout Wells's later work, but never revoked. During the years between 'The Lord of the Dynamos' (1894) and *A Modern Utopia* (1905), it lay in abeyance, and there appeared a vague inconclusiveness about Wells's treatment of the subject in the interval but this was because he was still endeavouring to determine how a scientific élite, fully in control of technology yet retaining the morality of pre-industrial man, might arise in the community. Until he could satisfactorily envisage the means whereby such a social revolution might be effected, Wells was unwilling to depict this result, however desirable it might seem to him. Hence, in this decade, the pictures of an uncontrolled technology recur with the increasingly strong suggestion that technological advance is inevitable and with the repeated warning that unless it were controlled it would surely destroy all the humane qualities of society, for there could be no return to a pre-machine age.

In *The War of the Worlds* (1898) the Martians' fighting machines which invade the earth demonstrate, more obviously than the dynamo, the potential for cruelty and exploitation in the purely rationalistic mind, but it is nevertheless stressed that the Martians are not 'evil', only amoral and highly efficient. Their fighting machines are simply their means of trapping or over-running a more vulnerable species – a practice which Wells compares to the British colonisation of Tasmania. *The War of the Worlds* provides no answer. Despite the final optimistic hope for a new world from the ruins, there is no effective counter-impression to that of confused, self-centred men fleeing in confusion before the advance of an efficient, amoral, technological power.

In *The Sleeper Awakes*, the story of the twentieth-century Graham who, falling into an unnaturally deep sleep, awakens in the twenty-first century, there is still no viable alternative to sheer power. Ostrog represents the amoral scientist manipulating the machinery of his world as a totalitarian technocrat, but here the opponents, Ostrog and Graham, are more evenly matched than the men and Martians, and Wells does not shrink from portraying the dichotomy as actually being present within Western society. On the one hand, there is Graham, the 'natural man', awakening to find that technology has advanced beyond what he could have imagined possible, thereby rendering him ignorant, redundant and powerless before its all-encompassing mechanical progress.[8] On the other hand, there is his opponent Ostrog, the 'organisational man', alert to the opportunities, technologically competent and hence powerful, a Nietzschean Superman and presumably an evolutionary advance on nineteenth-century man, produced by the natural selection of the machine-age.[9] Yet, in his self-justifying speech to Graham, Ostrog unwittingly indicates that the machine is the cause as well as the symbol of his authoritarian technocracy, for he pleads expediency – no other approach, he maintains, is possible. Thus, while seeming to control the mechanisation of his world, he is in fact controlled by it, even in his nature and personality.

Clearly there was much about Ostrog that Wells admired, for he continued to portray his qualities of efficient leadership in his Utopian heroes. But Ostrog, despite his power which finally overcomes Graham,[10] is ultimately condemned on moral grounds, for he fails to unite with his technological acumen the humane qualities of Graham. Several critics have suggested that Wells did not permit Graham to defeat Ostrog because his intrinsic sympathies lay with the latter, but this argument is weakened when we look at Ostrog's opponent, Graham. He is shown as being at pains to overcome his ignorance of technology and social organisation, so that he does embody the best of both approaches – the organisational and the humane. Like Helen Wotton, the intelligent girl who first denounces Ostrog's regime to him, Graham remains an implacable critic of the system and is, himself, a Christ-like figure, associated with suggestions of both resurrection and parousia.

Thus it seems far more likely that the major reason for Wells's insistence on Graham's ultimate defeat was that at this stage he was still not clear in his own mind how humane justice and egalitarian- ism could triumph over ruthless power and dehumanising in- efficiency in a technological society.[11] Bergonzi[12] and Parrinder[13] have suggested that Wells, at least subconsciously and perhaps even consciously, approved not only of Ostrog but also of what he stands for: that he welcomed the huge bee-hive cities described in *The Sleeper* (where London has a population of three hundred million) and in 'A Story of the Days to Come', and approved of the mass eating-houses with their much-processed food of esoteric origin. However, a comparison with *Anticipations* and the later utopian writings must suggest the contrary view. In these later works Wells clearly disapproves of over-population and its local manifestation, huge cities. In *A Modern Utopia* and *Men Like Gods* he favours rigid birth-control to obtain an optimum population and describes at some length the importance of individual houses with surrounding gardens for the well-being of the inhabitants. Indeed *A Modern Utopia* pictures the idealised form of those innovations which in *The Sleeper* and 'A Story of the Days to Come' occur only in a perverted and degraded form and indicates that the earlier accounts are to be read as satire.

The First Men in the Moon (1901) elaborates a more subtle but no less dangerous emotional cost of scientific rationalism. Cavor, the scientist who discovers how to travel to the moon, is not portrayed as overtly evil – he would never actively or deliberately harm anyone – yet he represents the amoral scientist who feels no responsibility for the results of his invention, cavorite, a substance allegedly immune to gravity. He is thus a potential agent of destruction. Relatively early in the novel he is explicitly compared to a machine:

> When he said it was 'the most important' research the world had ever seen, he simply meant it squared up so many theories, settled so much that was in doubt; he had troubled no more about the application of the stuff he was going to turn out than if he had been a machine that makes guns.[14]

In Cavor's view individuals are decidedly inferior to machines and his emotional poverty suggests that he is approaching the state of the passionless Grand Lunar who rules the Selenites, inhabitants of the moon. Cavor reports on the Selenites' conditioning of their offspring and the consequent orderliness of their society with profound admiration: 'Each is a perfect unit in a world machine'.[15] Thus in one sense the otherwise comic Cavor epitomises the insidious evils of the scientist who acknowledges no responsibility for his inventions.

Anticipations, which appeared in the same year, marks a turning-point in Wells's thought, for although its ostensible method is one of extrapolation from existing trends (and it is this illusion which accounts for much of its plausibility), Wells introduces a new factor – namely a proposal of the possible means whereby a scientific élite which understood the dangers of technology but was capable of mastering them, might attain to a position of benevolent control over society. The means he envisages here are crude by his later standards – there is resort to overt warfare – but they nevertheless indicate his hope that such an outcome might be feasible.

Thus in 'The Land Ironclads' (1903), a short story concerned with the clash between English disorganisation and non-English scientific expertise, those who act with scientific understanding but without sacrificing their humane qualities are permitted to be victorious against the reactionary non-scientific forces. These successful 'young engineers' are among the first fictional examples of Wells's fully endorsed scientific men; they are in fact a recognisable development from the soldiers of *Anticipations*. Rational and efficient, they exploit all the possibilities of the machine as the Martians and Ostrog had done, yet now Wells is ready to admire them, even to prefer them to the sentimental, patriotic image of the well-meaning if muddled English soldier. His own change of allegiance is dramatised within the story by the wavering of the war-correspondent, 'one of those inconsistent people who always want the beaten side to win'.[16] For Wells, however, the preference is not 'inconsistent' but based on a rational decision. When order and efficiency are embodied not in alien forms like those of the Martians and Selenites, or in obviously immoral figures like Griffin or *The Invisible Man* and Ostrog of *The Sleeper Awakes*, but in intelligent, moral individuals, Wells's admiration is unbounded.

In 'The Land Ironclads', as in *Anticipations*, technological progress is shown as being inevitable and Wells's contemporaries are therefore counselled to accept it out of necessity whether they like it or not, but two years later in *The Food of the Gods* it is not merely inevitable, but wholly desirable. This changed attitude on Wells's part seems to spring from the fact that he had now evolved what he considered an infallible plan for controlling technology and preventing it from falling into unscrupulous hands. It is especially interesting that in this attempt to describe his new ruling class of the future, Wells pictures its members as children and youths rather than as a parent generation of fully-fledged scientists. Sussman has objected to this on the grounds that Wells is postulating a change in human nature as a result of the Boom food, whereas the giant rats produced under the action of the same chemical suffer no such personality change for the better.[17] This interpretation, however, misses an important part of the moral of the story. The good nature of the giant children is intended to be seen not as something extraordinary or alien to the race, but rather as an intensification of the intrinsic goodwill of all human beings. The difference lies merely in the fact that because these particular children are either outcasts from society (and hence left largely to their own devices) or educated in an enlightened manner, their natural instincts have not been corrupted or distorted by the prejudices of the adult world. The giant children thus embody the best characteristics of both worlds – inherent good nature which develops into a sense of social and moral responsibility, together with an education which stresses the scientific virtues of efficiency and rationalism.

Having evolved to his own satisfaction, at least in broad outline, the concept of a scientific élite comprising individuals who were also morally upright and virtually incapable of a selfish use of power, Wells proceeded to elaborate in a series of propagandist novels a detailed picture of the society which such an élite would institute. In *A Modern Utopia*, the paradigm of the Utopian novels which followed it, the Samurai or ruling class are also the prototypes of Wells's noble scientists. They create a firmly oligarchic society, technologically efficient but still permitting its citizens scope for creative freedom. The 'natural' man whom the visitors to Utopia encounter and who inveighs against all mechanisation and progress, is clearly intended as a parody of Morris and Ruskin, but the parallel is scarcely justified, for the social evils decried by the Pre-Raphaelites no longer exist in the humanised technocracy of Utopia.

Thus Wells's proposed solution to the blot on the landscape

occasioned by nineteenth-century industrialism was not to return to a pre-industrial state – for indeed such a return on a sustained basis is impossible outside literature – but to remake the technological state. Even ugliness, to the Pre-Raphaelites the cardinal sin of technology, has allegedly been overcome in Utopia – machinery too is aesthetically pleasing.

> There is nothing in machinery, there is nothing in embankments and railways, and iron bridges and engineering devices, to oblige them to be ugly. Ugliness is the measure of imperfection; a thing of human making is, for the most part, ugly in proportion to the poverty of its constructive thought, to the failure of its producer fully to grasp the purpose of its being. . . . This is the misfortune of the machine and not its fault.[18]

But even in the later utopian novels, all set in highly sophisticated technological states, there is still a concomitant warning against any expectation that technology, divorced from the disinterested attitudes of science, can achieve any permanent good. In *The World Set Free* (1914) Wells wrote scathingly, and, in the event, prophetically, of such a divided state, where the desire for profits from technology is in conflict with pure research: 'What chiefly impressed the journalists of 1933 was the production of gold from bismuth and the realisation, albeit upon unprofitable lines, of the alchemist's dreams.'[19] For this society is basically an unhealthy one:

> Beneath that brightness was a glittering darkness, a deepening dismay. If there was a vast development of production, there was also a huge destruction of values. . . . There was an enormous increase in violent crime throughout the world. The thing had come upon an unprepared humanity; it seemed as though human society was to be smashed by its own magnificent gains.[20]

The War of the Worlds, *The War in the Air* and *The World Set Free* all warn of the levels of violence to which warfare must inevitably escalate if the resources of technology are turned simply to the task of producing the most efficient weapons possible, without heed to the morality of their use. *The War in the Air* makes explicit the connection between scientific industrialism and the catastrophic war to which it leads in the hands of those not morally equipped to deal with it:

[New York] was the first of the great cities of the Scientific Age to suffer by the enormous powers and grotesque limitations of aerial warfare. . . . Given the circumstances the thing had to be done. . . . The catastrophe was the logical outcome of the situation created by the application of science to warfare. It was unavoidable that great cities should be destroyed. . . . It was the dissolution of an age; it was the collapse of the civilisation that had trusted to machinery, and the instruments of its destruction were machines.[21]

There is a more subtle but no less insidious example of the perversion of scientific knowledge for destructive purposes when the mind in control has no guiding principles in *Tono-Bungay*. At the conclusion of the novel, George Ponderevo, the coldly rational scientist who has observed, without any attempt at moral intervention, the vast 'spectacle of forces running to waste', rounds off his career by using his scientific training and skill to build 'destroyers'. Mark Schorer believes that Wells did not intend this final image of the destroyer as ironic:

> As far as one can tell, Wells intends no irony, although he may here have come upon the major irony in modern history. The novel ends in a kind of meditative rhapsody which denies every value that the book has been aiming towards. For, of all kinds of social waste which Wells has been describing, this is the most inclusive, the final waste.[22]

But Wells is surely conscious of the irony. George's comment, 'And now I build destroyers!' is emphasised as an exclamation and stands as the culmination of a paragraph enumerating the manifold forms of waste which have been described in the novel. Moreover the destroyer is named, significantly, 'X_2', that is, a double unknown, representing the double-edged and unknown quantity of science which has potential for either good or evil in the community.

Whether the immense power of science *would* in fact be used for good or evil remained an open question in Wells's mind to the end of his life, for, perhaps more clearly than anyone else of his period, he saw that the danger of confusing science with technology was that technology came to be revered as science. The fictional holocaust of *The World Set Free* proved to be uncomfortably close to the reality of the decades which followed its publication. Nevertheless, even in

The World Set Free, Wells was still confident that there was an answer. Late in the novel, after the holocaust, Karenin reflects upon the changed attitude to science, contrasting the appreciation of its true value by the citizens of the new World Republic, with the estimate of it held in the nineteenth century by those who confused it with technology:

> It is wonderful how our fathers bore themselves towards science. They hated it. They feared it. They permitted a few scientific men to exist and work – a pitiful handful. . . . 'Don't find out anything about us,' they said to them; 'don't inflict vision upon us, spare our little ways of life from the fearful shaft of understanding. But do tricks for us, little limited tricks. Give us cheap lighting. And cure us of certain disagreeable things, cure us of cancer, cure us of consumption, cure our colds and relieve us after repletion. . . .' We have changed all that, Gardener. Science is no longer our servant. We know it for something greater than our little individual selves. It is the awakening mind of the race.[23]

This is the apotheosis of science in Wells's work. It is now recognised as being on a different plane from technology, from knowledge. It has become a spiritual power, Truth. Not least amongst the ironies of *Tono-Bungay* is the fact that even George, the designer of destroyers, realises something of this.

> Through the confusion something drives, something that is at once human achievement and the most inhuman of all existing things. . . . How can I express the values of a thing at once so essential and so immaterial? It is something that calls upon such men as I with an irresistible appeal. . . . Sometimes I call this reality Science, sometimes I call it Truth.[24]

Thus Wells's attitude to Science passed through four distinct stages: from a vote of no-confidence, through a grudging acceptance of its inevitable importance in society, to a wholehearted approval of a utopia governed on scientific principles, and finally to an almost mystic reverence for science as the purest and most selfless of human endeavours. He came at last to believe that in science lay the only hope for the survival of the human race which was otherwise doomed to destruction by its selfish individualistic strivings and vast, amoral technology. Thus like Samuel Butler, and later Aldous Huxley, who also began with a mechanistic interpretation of the universe and a rigorous belief in scientific method, Wells eventually adopted a vitalist position. Science, for him, came to be identified with a power which he called the 'Mind of the Race' and which, like Butler's 'race memory', was essentially mystical, related to technology only in so far as the latter was a tool useful in promoting the development of the species. From being at the mercy of a diabolical technology, as in the early works, Science has attained in the last writings a high-priestly role, the *sine qua non* of utopia, and the only hope of salvation for *Homo sapiens*.

4 Science and Government – the Wellsian Utopia

The development of Wells's attitude towards the machine and technology, from the traditional view that it was a dangerous and perhaps evil power but nevertheless inevitable, to the view that it could be entirely beneficial if controlled and directed towards the welfare of society, was dependent on the further question whether, given the immense potential of modern technology for destruction, it could be controlled in time to save mankind from self-inflicted disaster, perhaps even the total annihilation of the human race.

A parallel succession of attitudes is observable in Wells's views about government, for he was intensely aware of the 'incompatibility of the great world order foreshadowed by scientific and industrial progress with the existing political and social structures'.[1] While the various proposals which he made in the realm of sociology and government appear at first glance disparate, even at times incompatible, they may nevertheless all be seen as emanating from the desire for order and efficiency with which he had been imbued as a science student. His ideas about the best means of implementing these principles in the realm of government varied with the fluctuations of the world political situation, with his own moods and with his developing understanding of people, but his allegiance to the ideals themselves rarely wavered, however optimistic or pessimistic he might feel about the general human response to them.

It is pertinent here to ask briefly why Wells, without benefit of any political training or experience, should have considered himself equipped to deal at length with such questions. He himself apparently felt that in this sphere non-involvement and inexperience were themselves credentials – an attitude which he would certainly have condemned in almost any other field:

> The fact that I regarded myself as a complete outsider in public affairs . . . probably helped importantly in the liberation of my

mind to these realizations, and supplied the disinterested vigour with which I worked them out. I could attack electoral and parliamentary methods, the prestige of the universities, and the ruling class, the monarchy and patriotism, because I had not the slightest hope or intention of ever using any of these established systems for my own advancement or protection. For a scientific treatment of the theory of government, my political handicap was a release.[2]

Although the major part of Wells's political thought is contained in the utopian novels, and in the more didactic works of the same period, it is important to realise that these form part of a continuing development of thought, which began as early as *The Time Machine* with its description of a bifurcate society ruled by ruthless technocrats. Here already is the germ of an idea which was to be developed more fully in the major scientific romances, and in the novels of the period 1896 to 1901 – the idea of a natural aristocracy of talent and intellect which rules by right of its innate superiority. In *The Time Machine*, which may be seen sociologically as an extension of Disraeli's contention that England had become a country of two distinct nations, Wells is still ambiguous in his attitudes towards a 'superior' race. The Morlocks are certainly intended to be regarded with disgust, but the ineffectual Eloi are scarcely to be whole-heartedly approved. They are pitied in a rather superficial way, but never fully endorsed.

By the time of writing *Dr. Moreau* and *The Invisible Man*, however, Wells seems already to have associated the idea of a ruling class with the related question of the rights of scientists and technologists to assume command, in the name of order, over their less intelligent and less efficient fellows: should a scientist's intellect and scientific capability entitle him to perform his research at the expense of consequent pain to animals or to other members of society? Prendick who, if anyone in the novel, represents Wells's views, never entirely supports Moreau's experiments, but neither does he altogether condemn them – chiefly because he sees no possibility of a stable system based on the primitive instincts of the Beast People.[3] Certainly Moreau foreshadows the ruthless ruler of the modern scientific state in much of the later science fiction, a ruler devoid of ethical considerations, but armed with all the knowledge of biological and psychological conditioning necessary to give him complete control over his ignorant subjects.

Griffin, the invisible man, has, like Moreau, gained knowledge and lost all sense of ethical and human sympathy. Hillegas has pointed out 'how perfect a symbol of a science without humanity is an invisible man without scruples'.[4] Yet, despite his ultimate downfall, and Wells's censure of him on moral grounds, it is clear that this figure of a brilliant scientist who considers that his gifts endow him with the right to govern – ruthlessly if necessary – held a certain qualified fascination for the young Wells, contemptuous of the disorganised multitude. Our final condemnation is intended to fall not merely on Griffin and his proposed reign of terror, but also on the sadistic reprisals of the undisciplined mob.

The same ambiguity recurs in *The War of the Worlds*, where, it is implied, the blindly ignorant and egotistical crowds fully deserve their defeat by the efficient and orderly Martians. Indeed, the only incident approaching pathos in the novel is the defeat of the Martians by a cause beyond their control. In this novel Wells is unable to identify fully with either group of participants. As far as is intellectually possible he supports the cause of the Martians, while emotionally his sympathies must still lie with the helpless men whom he despises. It is this ambiguity of allegiance which underlies the peculiarly disturbing effect of the novel.

There are several other examples of ambiguity in his work at this time besides that of *The Sleeper Awakes*, which has already been discussed. The conditioned Selenites in *The First Men in the Moon*, each perfectly adapted to his own niche in the social hierarchy and kept under sedation if he becomes temporarily redundant, are intended to shock, and Cavor's admiration for this way of life is partly a judgment on his own character; but his interview with the Grand Lunar, like Gulliver's with the King of Brobdignag, functions also as satire directed against the smug inefficiency of contemporary English society where *laissez-faire* policies ensured that workers were 'free' to starve, to be unemployed, to be untrained for any useful work.

Compared with these authoritarian predecessors, the New Republicans of *Anticipations* appear at first to represent a morality closer to the democratic ideal approved, at least in theory, by Wells's contemporaries, in that they serve a purpose not their own – described rather vaguely as 'the purpose that presents [God] without presumption, and without fear'.[5] Moreover, the 'cause' of the New Republic is described as emerging for the most part without the need for violence or revolution.[6] However, a closer examination reveals that they are almost as ruthlessly intent as their predecessors on purging society of misfits and socially unattractive personalities, and here the similarity of their programme to Ostrog's can scarcely be ignored,

> It has become apparent that whole masses of human population are, as a whole, inferior in their claim upon the future, to other masses, that they cannot be given opportunities, or trusted with powers as the superior people are trusted, that their characteristic weaknesses are contagious and detrimental in the civilising fabric, and that their range of incapacity tempts and demoralizes the strong. To give them equality is to sink to their level.[7]

Even in retrospect Wells continued to approve of his new Republicans and considered his chapter on government, 'The Greater Synthesis', the most interesting part of *Anticipations*. Apparently, far from regretting his uncompromising autocracy, he later criticised what seemed to him the benign nineteenth-century liberalism of the book with its pious hopefulness that the New Republic would emerge of its own accord without any need for force, and appears to have forgotten that he had made full provision for the use of violence should it prove necessary for the overthrow of democracy.[8]

Characteristically, the New Republican spearhead is the body of scientists who will constitute a guild of social engineers from the middle classes. They are the forerunners, the first draft, as it were, of the later Samurai, who appear less ruthless only because, owing to an improved education system, their society is apparently prepared to accept without question their superiority and their right to govern.

By the time of writing *A Modern Utopia*, Wells had mellowed considerably in the extent to which he was prepared to advocate force in the reform of society, for he now believed that a revolution was less likely to succeed than a gradual evolution in education and social awareness, such as that outlined in *Mankind in the Making*. Although he despised what he considered the timidity of the Fabians, their values appear to have tempered his zeal for precipitating a class war. Henceforth, the new society is to be ushered in by peaceful means – education, discussion, and the gradual diffusion of a spirit of goodwill – although Wells still has little faith in the concept of democracy. The organisation of the

Samurai is seen as a 'quite deliberate invention' urged by the enthusiasm of genuine altruists bent on saving the world from democratic chaos.[9] Thus the Samurai still embody Wells's autocratic contempt for the ordinary man, the dull, the stupid, and the average. It must therefore be asked whether rule by such an élite would not lead to ruthless discrimination against, and even extermination of, the ungifted citizen. *First and Last Things* contains a further anti-democratic discussion[10] and such outbursts show no sign of abating in the novels of his middle and later years. Remington, from the time of his unfortunate schoolboy encounter with a gang of lower-class youths who rob him of his penknife, retains a deep dislike and mistrust of the working class.[11]

In 1902, in a letter to Arnold Bennett, Wells cited *The Invisible Man*, *The First Men in the Moon*, *Anticipations*, Chapter 9, 'The Discovery of the Future' and *Love and Mr. Lewisham* as the emerging thread of 'a new system of ideas'[12] and in retrospect it becomes clear that after 1900 Wells had turned his attention from the ideal ruling figure and from questions of the relation between a talented individual and his inferiors, to the broader concept of the ideal society – what constitutes a utopian society, and how may it best be instigated? Thereafter government and governors feature in his work only in relation to the ordering of the whole society. Wells had found no solution to the problem posed by Moreau, Griffin and Ostrog, but after *Anticipations* he apparently ceased to toy with it, for his talented individuals no longer attempt to seize power for themselves and to function alone; rather, they have formed a group, eventually an entire social class, which toils responsibly and untiringly for the public good. Wells believed, with Comte, that spiritual reform must precede political reconstruction, and hence the Samurai represent our 'best selves'. Their moral awareness is highly developed and they can apparently be trusted not to resort to the crude discriminatory methods of nineteenth- and twentieth-century autocrats. Moreover, by virtue of the proposed eugenics programme and an enlightened education system, it is assumed that after some few generations no inferior individuals will have survived; instead, the Samurai class will include virtually all members of the world state, as it does in *Men Like Gods*. This is Wells's final, and perhaps ultimately the only answer to the otherwise insuperable problems posed by the two-class systems of *The Time Machine* and *The Sleeper*.

After *The Sleeper*, the 'Overman' philosophy carries sinister connotations in Wells's work even when described in humorous terms. In *Kipps*, young Walshingham, who has been reading Nietzsche, comes to believe that in all probability he is the 'Non-Moral Overman' referred to[13] and this identification with an essentially amoral figure is shown as subsequently tainting his legal ethics until he ends by embezzling from his clients. Chester Coote has already described him, earlier in the novel, as: ' "Gifted. And yet, you know – utterly sceptical. Practically altogether a Sceptic . . . full of this dreadful Modern Spirit – Cynical! All this Overman stuff. Nietzsche and all that . . ." '[14] And Kipps himself, with full authorial approval, pronounces upon Walshingham's overbearing demeanour:

'He's getting too big for 'is britches . . . 'e's seemed to think I've got no right to spend my own money. . . .'
'Overman indeed!' he added. 'Overmantel! . . . 'E tries that on with me – I'll tell 'im something 'e won't like.'[15]

Again, in *The War in the Air*, Bert Smallways, on returning from his experiences in the war, is forced to fight the formidable Bill Gore for the love of his faithful Edna. Bill is described in antipathetic terms which include, as final condemnation, the fact that:

There had been a strain of advanced philosophy about the local nobleman, and his mind ran to 'improving the race' and producing the Overman, which in practice took the form of himself especially, and his little band in moderation, marrying with some frequency.[16]

Throughout the later work also there are spasmodic outbursts against the Caesars and Napoleons who have sought glory and power as individuals, regardless of the suffering caused to their fellows.[17]

In considering the development of Wells's utopian ideals for society as a whole it seems most useful here to trace first their progressive emergence through both the novels and the more doctrinaire works, *Anticipations*, *New Worlds for Old*, and *The Open Conspiracy*, with which he interspersed them, before examining in detail the characteristics of his more mature conception of utopia.

Anticipations (1901) was the first of Wells's prophetic tracts, endeavouring to predict the future by the scientific procedure of induction from current and potential sociological trends. Wells professed to present a vivid and rational picture of the future as though it were based on universally accepted data and as though the full text, with detailed citation of proofs were readily available and had been thoughtfully abridged only to spare the non-specialist reader. The work is in fact an almost wholly imaginative effort, but Wells's guesses were for the most part accepted by his contemporaries as virtual facts, and his broad generalisations as natural laws. The government which he envisages in his future world state is characteristically a technocracy, socialist in economy and politically authoritarian, ruled by an élite of 'functional men', mostly scientists, who would seize power during a crisis and retain it through their efficiency and general ability. This first book outlining a future state is the least didactic of Wells's sociological works. It does not argue for any principles or even, overtly, press for any reforms; it simply outlines a picture of the future, with the assurance of presenting the inevitable.

Soon after the publication of *Anticipations*, Wells became a member of the Fabian Society and the tone of his writing changed markedly. Thereafter his sociological-prophetic books and pamphlets became as propagandist as they were prolific, and correspondingly poorer in literary merit.

The first fictional work of the series, *A Modern Utopia* (1905), makes only a token gesture towards a story, by far the greater part of the book being a description of the way of life to be observed in this utopia of the year 2100, and an explanation of the form of government behind it. Utopia is governed by a ruling class, the Samurai, a rank to which anyone may aspire at any time, whatever his birth, provided only that he is prepared to follow the 'Rule', a code of behaviour embracing physical, intellectual and moral aspects of life. Wells lays considerable stress on the parallels between his utopian system and the world-wide House of Salomon envisaged in Bacon's *New Atlantis*,[18] so that in this fundamental respect it is alleged to be firmly based on scientific principles. Wells never explicitly states that the Samurai are to be identified with scientifically trained men, as the New Republicans had been in *Anticipations*, but clearly their mode of thinking is patterned on scientific procedures.

In *Men Like Gods*, where the utopia is represented as being three thousand years ahead of the 'Last Age of Confusion' (the latter, presumably, equivalent to nineteenth-century England), all formal government has become redundant.

> Utopia has no parliament, no politics, no private wealth, no business competition, no policeman, no prisoners, no lunatics, no defectives, no cripples, and it has none of those things because it has schools and teachers who are all that schools and teachers can be. . . . There is no rule nor government needed by adult Utopians because all the rule and government they need they have had in childhood and youth. Said Lion, '*Our education is our government*.'[19]

This education for government apparently involves a knowledge and understanding of the Five Principles of Liberty 'without which civilisation is impossible': the Principle of Privacy, the Principle of Free Movement, the Principle of Unlimited Knowledge, the Principle that Lying is the Blackest Crime, and Free Discussion and Criticism.[20] The last four of these are in effect the principles most conducive to research, and it is therefore not surprising that science has flourished so prolifically in this utopia.

Written much later and subtitled 'Blueprints for a World Revolution', *The Open Conspiracy* was an avowed attempt to justify the ideas proposed in *A Modern Utopia* and *Men Like Gods* by outlining how such a change in society might be effected, that is, how a conversion from self-seeking to altruism might be induced amongst a significant proportion of the population. Typically the people to whom Wells looks as leaders in exemplifying and popularising his programme for reform are the scientists and other specialists who, in the Wellsian canon, are presumed to be, merely by reason of their training, men of good will.

In *New Worlds for Old* Wells explicitly identified his programme with the socialist platform, and both with the principles of scientific research, indicating that the aims of all three are closely parallel if not identical:

> The fundamental idea upon which Socialism rests is the same fundamental idea as that upon which all real scientific work is carried on. It is the denial that chance impulse and individual will and happening constitute the only possible methods by which things may be done in the world. It is an assertion that things are, in their nature, orderly; that things may be computed,

may be calculated upon and foreseen. In the spirit of this belief, Science aims at a systematic knowledge of material things . . . the Socialist has just that same faith in the order, the knowableness of things, and the power of men in co-operation to overcome chance. . . .

Just as Science aims at a common, organized body of knowledge, to which all its servants contribute, and in which they share, so Socialism insists upon its ideal of an organized social order which every man serves and by which every man benefits.[21]

The World Set Free contains not only a description of the world holocaust which, it is claimed, would inevitably result from the current trends of individual egotism and its national correlative, jingoism, but also an outline of the new world state which is to replace the previous system of mutually antagonistic regimes. Once the conflict has exhausted itself, the leaders of the nations convene at Brissago to draft a new pattern of world government. There the axiomatic truth of the principles of science, as being, by definition and necessity, acceptable to all nations, is explicitly affirmed. These principles alone are seen as a viable starting-point for discussion, and the only infallible guide in framing a constitution. King Egbert discusses with the American President during the peace talks, the proposed government of the nascent world state:

'Science,' the King cried presently, 'is the new king of the world.'

'Our view,' said the President, 'is that sovereignty resides with the people.'

'No,' said the King, 'the sovereign is a being more subtle than [the masses]. And less arithmetical. Neither my family nor your emancipated people. It is something that floats about us and through us. It is that common impersonal will and sense of necessity of which Science is the best understood and most typical aspect. It is the mind of the race.'[22]

This is virtually the climax in the evolution of Wells's utopian thought; it is the ideal which he believed must inform any government attempting to provide maximum scope for the expression of individual initiative commensurate with the growth and development of the whole society. After *A Modern Utopia* he did not significantly alter his ideals but only refined them and speculated on various methods for setting up a world state. It is thus possible to consider the Wellsian utopia as a relatively homogeneous concept and to examine here its underlying assumptions and characteristics, before discussing the various criticisms which have been levelled against it.

Wells's first assumption, derived directly from Huxley, was that the cosmic process of evolution was basically amoral, and could not be expected in itself either to produce a more moral species than *Homo sapiens*, or to provide the principles for an ethically conscious society.[23] Thus, there being no inherent virtue in nature, man must strive to direct and control his own evolution, including the evolution of society, and not merely accept or blindly follow the Darwinian process. The Primitivists before Wells, and many writers since, have held the contrary view – namely that to tamper with Nature, to go against natural processes, can produce only harm. This view assumes that there is already an optimal natural balance which any interference will destroy. The two views are debated in *Men Like Gods* between the English politician Rupert Catskill and the utopian, Urthred, authorial approval clearly resting with the latter.

The second assumption, also strongly criticised by later anti-utopians, is the belief that science and technology are in themselves fundamentally good and wholly beneficial to mankind if properly controlled and understood. In Wells's view the virtues of technology were twofold: firstly the power it offered for effecting a change in evolution, a possibility which would be unthinkable without modern scientific knowledge and technological efficiency, and secondly the opportunity provided thereby for increased leisure and cultivation of the individual personality in a society where manual labour had been rendered obsolete by machinery. *A Modern Utopia* contains Wells's manifesto on this subject, an expansion of Bacon's similar statement in *New Atlantis*:

> The plain message physical science has for the world at large is this, that, were our political and social and moral devices only as well contrived to their ends as a linotype machine, an antiseptic operating plant or an electric tramcar, there need now at the present moment be no appreciable toil in the world and only the smallest fraction of the pain, the fear and the anxiety that now make human life so doubtful in its value. There is more than enough for everyone alive. Science stands, a too-competent

servant, behind her wrangling under-bred masters, holding out resources, devices and remedies they are too stupid to use. And on its material side, a modern utopia must needs present these gifts as taken, and show a world that is really abolishing the needs of labour, abolishing the last base reason for anyone's servitude or inferiority.[24]

Of the utopian characteristics which Wells advocated, perhaps the most important contribution to the history of utopian thought was his stress on internationalism. This is virtually a necessary consequence of the second assumption outlined above, for where technology has inevitably shrunk distances by improved communications and transport, no non-military utopia could hope to survive in isolation from neighbours who were not similarly motivated. Enclosure being thus rendered impossible, the only alternative was to envisage utopia as a world-state from the outset. In *The War in the Air*, Wells analyses explicitly the way in which the growth of science has rendered both isolationist and aggressive policies untenable:

The essential fact of the politics of the age in which Bert Smallways lived – the age that blundered at last into the catastrophe of the War in the Air – was a very simple one if only people had had the intelligence to be simple about it. The development of Science had altered the scale of human affairs. By means of rapid mechanical traction, it had brought men nearer together, so much nearer socially, economically, physically, that the old separations into nations and kingdoms were no longer possible. A newer, wider synthesis was not only needed, but imperatively demanded. . . .[25]

Thus Wells frequently describes his utopias as being instituted after the holocaust of war has shown the inadequacy of the previous separatist system. *The War of the Worlds, The World Set Free* and *The Shape of Things to Come* all follow this pattern. The benefits of a world-state in the efficient organisation and development of society are obviously enormous – the saving in money, time, men and resources formerly devoted to defence systems and warfare; the automatic sharing of all scientific and cultural advances made by any one group to enrich the whole species; the stimulating effect of being free to travel to any part of the globe without fear of restriction or hostility; the added efficiency of specialised research, when workers are no longer competing against each other and thereby duplicating their efforts, but exploring varied aspects of the same problem. These are but some of the manifest advantages of a world-state; yet earlier utopian literature had concentrated almost exclusively on personal relations, on questions of duty between individuals, and between individuals and God, or had in their widest scope been extended to include national values. Wells was perhaps the first writer to consider in depth a world-centred morality which looked beyond both individualism and patriotism to a community of mankind.

Another unique feature of Wells's utopias was their essentially kinetic quality. Perfection was, for Wells, no static concept, but, like the evolutionary panorama, continually changing and developing. In *A Modern Utopia* this conceptual debt to Darwin was explicitly acknowledged[26] and Wells would certainly have been familiar with Huxley's stress on ceaseless change as the primary characteristic of nature:

The more we learn of the nature of things, the more evident is it that what we call rest is only unperceived activity; that seeming peace is silent but strenuous battle. . . . Thus the most obvious attribute of the cosmos is its impermanence. It assumes the aspect not so much of a permanent entity as of changeful process, in which naught endures save the flow of energy and the rational order which pervades it.[27]

Thus, in Wells's utopian thought, achievements are regarded as merely vantage points for envisaging the next goal.

From this dynamic view of a cosmos in which no final goal can be envisaged, Wells derived his utopians' awareness of the adventure and excitement of life, a spirit which is baffling, even depressing, to an outsider. Barnstaple, on his first encounter with it, muses:

Knowledge swept forward here. . . . Life marched here; it was terrifying to think with what strides. Terrifying – because at the back of Mr. Barnstaple's mind, as at the back of so many intelligent minds in our world still, had been the persuasion that presently everything would be known and the scientific process come to an end. And then we should be happy for ever after.

He was not really acclimatised to progress. He had always

thought of Utopia as a tranquillity with everything settled for good.[28]

A further characteristic of *A Modern Utopia* which has been too frequently overlooked by critics is the stress on individuality and non-uniformity. In *A Modern Utopia* the individuals have far greater freedom than has ever been seen in past or present societies. Wells repeatedly affirmed the value of individuality, not only as a passport to intellectual and moral growth, but as an end in itself, and he continued to maintain that such freedom would be fostered, rather than subdued, by a cooperative and well-organised state.[29]

A Modern Utopia is explicit on this question of the rights and freedom of the individual in many respects not previously considered, for example the freedom to travel,[30] and Wells repeatedly affirms the value of individuality, not only for the personal satisfaction and fulfilment of the individual himself but for the enrichment of the society of which he is a part.

> So long as we ignore difference, so long as we ignore individuality, and that I hold has been the common sin of all Utopias hitherto, we can make absolute statements, prescribe communisms or individualisms and all sorts of theoretical arrangements. But in the world of reality, . . . which is nothing more nor less than the world of individuality, there are no absolute rights and wrongs, there are no qualitative questions at all, but only quantitative adjustments.[31]

For similar reasons, Wells preserves the family unit which many previous utopians, concerned to eliminate competitive allegiances which might stand in the way of the individual's duty to the state, had proscribed.[32] Wells saw the family as the nursery of individuality, and hence of initiative. Indeed, one of the scandals of the world of *The Sleeper* is the system of Child Education Refineries, where

> the wet nurses [are] a vista of mechanical figures with arms, shoulders and breasts of astonishingly realistic modelling, articulation and texture, but mere brass tripods below, and having in place of features, a flat disc bearing advertisements likely to be of interest to the mothers.[33]

Characteristically, Wells's stress on individualism in the utopias is, for him, scientifically founded. The relation between the individual and the utopian world-state is virtually that between the individual and the biological species:

> As against the individual, the state represents the species; in the case of the Utopian world-state, it absolutely represents the species. The individual emerges from the species, makes his experiment and either fails, dies and comes to an end, or succeeds and impresses himself in offspring, in consequences and results, intellectual, material and moral, upon the world.[34]

An essential part of Wells's utopian scheme was the role of the Samurai, the 'voluntary nobility' of *A Modern Utopia* and of several later didactic works. All political power is in their hands, for they are the sole administrators, lawyers, practising doctors and public officials, and also the only voters. Yet, if these privileges seem somewhat extreme, it must be remembered that no one is excluded from the Samurai class except by his own choice in refusing to follow the 'Rule'. Both the New Republicans and the Samurai are closely modelled on Wells's emerging conception of the 'new scientist' who supposedly combines knowledge and efficiency with a high moral code and sense of social responsibility. However, since, with the exception of Bacon, earlier utopian writers had conceived of their ideal states as being ruled by military power, hereditary dynasties, or philosopher-kings, and since at the time of Wells's writing there was little to suggest the emergence of a technocracy, it is worth considering why he should, at this stage, have stressed so firmly and repeatedly the necessity for a scientific élite – or at least an élite which embodied the characteristics he ascribed to scientists – to rescue the world from its governmental and sociological confusion.

By both training and instinct, scientists strive to impose order upon the universe and to work and think efficiently; thus it might reasonably be assumed that they would introduce an orderly and efficient administration – not as an end in itself, but as the *sine qua non* of more important and more creative activities in the community. The integral relation of this desire for order to the details of Wells's sociological thought will be considered in Chapter 5, but there are several other important factors contributing to his faith in scientists. We have seen that no governmental or sociological reform seemed to Wells even potentially viable unless it were a world-wide one, and since scientists were the only major group in the community with a firm tradition of non-nationalistic thinking he believed that only their internationalism could circumvent the secret treaties and intrigues which bedevilled politics and hampered world peace. Ironically, since Wells began to urge upon the whole community the traditional freedom of scientists to surmount political barriers, the scientists themselves have become progressively less free. Einstein's proposal in 1940 that he, Nils Bohr, Lord Cherwell and Peter Kapitsa should jointly publish the details of the atomic bomb to the world to prevent its becoming the monopoly of any one power, was never seriously considered by the governments concerned, and the extent to which scientists were made the virtual prisoners of their governments during the Second World War has been revealed only too clearly.[35] More recently, Rose and Rose, in their sociological survey of science report that:

> Research linked closely with industry, or, more significantly, with defence, and supported by 'tied money' with restraints on freedom to publish – and on those selected to carry out the research – exemplify these trends. The existence of large areas of 'secret research' in many U.S. universities financed by the U.S. Department of Defence exemplifies this. In Britain in 1967, there were 786 research contracts, worth some £1·4 million, placed in the universities by the Ministry of Defence and of Technology with restrictions on publishing buried in the small print.[36]

These objections in no way undermine Wells's belief that universalism is an essential part of the scientific tradition; they merely show the power of governments to threaten such a tradition, thereby restricting the progress of science. Yet from their statistical considerations the above authors conclude that:

> To argue that science is, by its very nature universalistic, increasingly falls into the fallacy of confusing an *is* with an *ought*. What remains true is that the explicit credo of many – perhaps most – of the outstanding basic scientists has such a universalism about it. There are two consequences of such a universalism. One is an *élitist* belief that scientists, *qua* scientists, are capable of rescuing the world from the worst abuses of its nationalist divisions. This belief has long historical antecedents, stretching

back to the days of the scientific religion founded by Saint-Simon in the early nineteenth century and runs through H. G. Wells's *Open Conspiracy* of intellectualists and scientists who would manage the world in its own best interests. . . . A contemporary descendant of this type of internationalism is the scientists' Pugwash Association.[37]

The reasons advanced as evidence for the limitations of Wells's view reside less in the character of the scientists themselves than in the power of governments which hold the purse-strings of research finance. Clearly, Wells was not unaware of this political danger for his utopias describe a simple – perhaps too simple – expedient whereby the potential 'taming' of scientists and the tailoring of their ideals to governmental policy might be averted – namely the identification of the government with the scientists, rather than of the scientists with their governments.

A further reason for Wells's faith in the integrity of scientists and in their mission to govern the world seems to have been derived from a not irrational supposition that those whose primary commitments and interests lie elsewhere than in the political arena are perhaps the only ones fit to be entrusted with political power. Like Plato's philosopher-kings, they will doubtless be unwilling rulers, but they will therefore be the more ready to relinquish the mantle of power after their term of office.

It is important to stress here that Wells's scientists are considered best fitted to govern not primarily because of any intrinsic moral superiority, but chiefly because they are the custodians of the principles of science and might therefore be expected to see more clearly their social implications. Wells was never beguiled, as some of the early utopians had been, into imagining that men of the future state would be automatically kind, gentle and good. In *A Modern Utopia*, he explicitly disclaims the idea of 'dolls in the likeness of angels – imaginary laws to fit incredible people'[38] – and concedes that perhaps only the environment may be changed, not man's essential nature, but even that is a considerable advance, for it involves

. . . a free hand with all the apparatus of existence that man has, so to speak, made for himself, with houses, roads, clothing, canals, machinery, with laws, boundaries, conventions and traditions, with schools, with literature, and religious organizations, with creeds and customs, with everything, in fact, that it lies within man's power to alter.[39]

Clearly, then, a major part of Wells's sociological writing is concerned with ethical questions raised within the scientific community, questions of leadership, of the use of power to enforce what seems good for the majority, of the system of priorities to be observed if the will of the individual should conflict with that of the state. He was thereby attempting to force upon scientists a sense of moral responsibility for the by-products of their research, and upon laymen the question whether they were ready to receive and cope with the new knowledge becoming available.

Nevertheless, despite approbation from at least two authoritative critics – Connes, who maintained that the utopias were Wells's greatest imaginative achievement,[40] and the sociologist Lewis Mumford who describes Wells's work as 'the quintessential Utopia'[41] – Wells's utopian works have elicited a considerable volume of adverse criticism from the time of their first publication. The criticism, which is basically of four distinct kinds, has been directed against the feasibility of the proposed government and social reform, the literary appropriateness of Wells's didactic method, the originality of his proposals, and the morality of his utopian schemes.

The first of these criticisms was occasioned by *Anticipations* and concerned chiefly the role of the scientist élite. Beatrice Webb read the book in December 1901, and the subsequent entry in her diary shows that she levelled this criticism almost immediately.

The most remarkable book of the year: a powerful imagination furnished with the data and methods of physical science, working on social problems. The weak part of Wells's outfit is his lack of any detailed knowledge of social organizations – and this, I think, vitiates his capacity for foreseeing the future machinery of government and the relation of classes.[42]

Later, having come to know Wells himself better, she declared that he had

. . . an immense respect for science and its methods. But he is totally ignorant of the manual worker on the one hand, and of the big administrator and aristocrat on the other; . . . he does not appreciate the need for a wide experience of men and affairs in administration. A world run by the physical scientist straight from his laboratory is his ideal: he does not see that specialized faculty and knowledge are needed for administration exactly as they are needed for the manipulation of machinery or forces. . . . He has no great faith in government by the 'man in the street' and, I think, has hardly realised the function of the representative as a 'foolometer' for the expert.[43]

Beatrice Webb's complaint that Wells 'does not see that specialised faculty and knowledge are needed for administration' indicates her failure to grasp the point of his emphasis on a scientific élite. Professional administrators were precisely the men whom Wells most mistrusted because their training was in diplomacy, in secrecy, in 'giving nothing away', in delaying tactics, indeed, in all the political subterfuges which Wells abhorred, believing, as he did, that the chief requisites for practical and peaceful government were openness and efficiency.

Nevertheless the criticisms of his system continued rather than abated after the publication of *A Modern Utopia*. Shaw had parodied Wells's 'functional men' in the figure of 'Enry Straker, the Cockney engineer of *Man and Superman* (1903) and later spoke vehemently against the whole concept of an élite at the First Public Conference on Mr Wells's 'Samurai'.[44] Shaw's attack was two-pronged – charging firstly that

the discipline described by Mr. Wells falls ridiculously short of the discipline I have put upon myself . . . the error is the outcome of supposing that character and morals are simple things; but they are outrageously difficult things.

and secondly that the very existence of an élite was the essence of Toryism and therefore suspect, if not disastrous:

The present state of our civilisation has been brought about precisely as the result of a Samurai idea. Why, every Tory would cordially agree with Mr. Wells; only he would say that in the English gentleman we have already got our Samurai. He is sent to Oxford where he undergoes most of Mr. Wells's discipline, including the cold bath and daily shave. He is duly turned out with a degree certifying his proficiency as a gentleman. . . . This is just the very thing that every superior mind does his very best to avoid.[45]

Crozier, a sociologist whose criticism of Wells's work seems to have been motivated, at least in part, by his resentment at Wells's cavalier disregard of current sociological theory, was nevertheless essentially correct when he charged that 'This Utopia of Mr. Wells is a purely personal imagination of its author, founded like any other millennial dream on what he personally would like to see realised.'[46] This claim was later repeated by Belgion, who maintained that all Wells's plans for reform sprang from an emotional desire to change whatever he, personally, did not find agreeable in society.[47] This does not, of course, necessarily invalidate them.

More frequent were the criticisms from those who realised that all Wells's sociological reforms did in fact, whatever his claims to the contrary, presuppose a change in human nature, and doubted whether this were possible. Conrad, who admired and sympathised with Wells on many counts, wrote to him: 'The difference between us, Wells, is fundamental. You don't care for humanity, but think they are to be improved. I love humanity, but know they are not.'[48] Again G. K. Chesterton, in his allegedly complimentary chapter on Wells in *Heretics*, also criticises the feasibility of Wells's utopia:

> The weakness of all Utopias is this, that they take the greatest difficulty of man and assume it to be overcome, and then give an elaborate account of the overcoming of smaller ones. They first assume that no man will want more than his share, and then are very ingenious in explaining whether his share will be delivered by motor car or balloon.[49]

Anthony West makes a similar but more thorough-going attack in his *Encounter* article, maintaining that the idea of a change in human nature is the *sine qua non* of all Wells's utopias and that in the end Wells conceded such a change to be impossible. West claims that *Men Like Gods* is the point of concession, for here the utopians are special creations designed, like the giant children of *The Food of the Gods*, to evade the truth about human nature. Therefore their universe is outside the earth's spatial scheme altogether and unlike *A Modern Utopia*, the novel is thus not even a debate between man-as-he-might-be and man-as-he-is but an essentially sterile confrontation between reality and an unattainable ideal.

Now in theory neither Chesterton's nor West's criticism is justified, for Wells himself explicitly denied that his utopians were beyond normal human limitations, maintaining, on the contrary, that:

> We are to restrict ourselves first to the limitations of human possibilities as we know them . . . and then to all the inhumanity, all the insubordinations of nature. We are to shape our state in a world of uncertain seasons, men and women with like passions, like uncertainties of mood and desire to our own.[50]

Moreover, in both *A Modern Utopia* and *Men Like Gods* it is stressed that utopian societies have developed from a precedent resembling Wells's contemporary world – an 'Age of Confusion' – which has been gradually overcome by a reformed education system and a humane programme of negative eugenics. Wells may not have succeeded in convincing his readers that such deep-seated and thorough-going reforms were possible, but this arises chiefly from a failure to make vivid his impressions of the intervening reform period, rather than from a failure to recognise the difficulties involved in instituting such reform. In fact Wells himself later admitted that in *A Modern Utopia* 'I presented not so much my expectations for mankind as my desire',[51] and in the later novels his ideas oscillated between optimism and pessimism. The picture of man in *The Croquet Player* (1937) is darker than any Wells had hitherto drawn. Norbert, the psychiatrist, asserts that man is still as he was 100000 years ago, and that any apparent progress is a delusion.[52] A similarly pessimistic outlook underlies *The Brothers* (1938), where the irrational elements of life become predominant; yet the enlightened forces striving to introduce 'The New Society' are pictured as successful in *The Holy Terror*, published the following year. However, since Wells's hopes for the inception of utopia depended so strongly on the formation of the élitist ruling class – whether scientists or Samurai – the most serious criticism may well be his own admission in the allegory, *All Aboard for Ararat* (1940):

> Our élite is our necessity and our menace. The primary danger, I take it, is that the élite will become a self-conscious, self-protective organisation within the State. It will taste the joys of authority and aristocracy, and instead of quickening and keeping alive the general sense of freedom, it will adopt the far easier line of

humbugging the common man, and fighting down any competing system of humbug . . . such has been the fate of *all* élites in
the past.[53]

Moreover, a closer examination of the central argument implicit
in the genesis of the new society as described in *A Modern Utopia*
shows that it is in fact circular in its essentials, for it fails to explain
convincingly how such a utopia is to be instigated without the use of
force, at least in the first stages of reform, and concentrates instead
on the details of its functioning and development once its principles
have been accepted by a significant majority of the population. The
Samurai, and indeed all the orders with the exception of the Base,
are willing to support the system, presumably because it provides
them with all the essentials of life as well as the stimulus and
opportunity for further development. Yet these benefits are possible
only because of the efficient social system which prevails and which
is shown as being conceivable only under Samurai rule. The
methods of procedure outlined in *The Open Conspiracy* are clearly
intended to suggest a way whereby the general populace might
become converted to utopian principles but Wells himself was more
often sceptical of such pious liberal hopes. To this extent the
objections of Chesterton and West do hold in practice, although in
theory Wells apparently believed that he had dealt with them.

A further variation of this criticism has been advanced by Orwell,
who disputes the possibility of combining technological progress
with the development of those qualities of personality and physique
which are generally admired and which Wells had also professed to
admire:

> All mechanical progress is towards greater and greater efficiency;
> ultimately therefore towards a world in which nothing ever goes
> wrong. But in a world in which nothing ever goes wrong many of
> the qualities which Mr. Wells regards as godlike would be no
> more valuable than the animal faculty of moving the
> ears. . . . The tendency of mechanical progress is to make your
> environment safe and soft; and yet you are striving to keep
> yourself brave and hard. You are, at the same moment furiously
> pressing forward and desperately holding back. . . . So, in the
> last analysis the champion of progress is also the champion of an
> anachronism. . . . The truth is that many of the qualities that we
> admire in human beings can only function in opposition to some

kind of disaster, pain or difficulty; but the tendency of mechanical progress is to eliminate disaster, pain and difficulty.[54]

Whether or not Wells was successful in countering Orwell's criticisms must remain a matter for subjective assessment, but certainly he attempted to forestall them. The Samurai 'Rule' insisted upon physical fitness and enforced this rigorously by stipulating that every member of the Samurai class should spend annually a period of seven consecutive days alone in a wild and physically testing situation for private meditation and for physical and moral strengthening.[55] There is apparently ample scope for the expression of those qualities which Orwell is concerned to uphold – bravery, generosity and physical strength – in the utopia of *Men Like Gods* since the physique of the utopians is demonstrably superior to that of the Earthling visitors, and mechanical progress seems to complement rather than render redundant feats of physical strength and bravery.

Wells's hopes of eliciting a spirit of 'goodwill' in men, and of directing their energies towards the community rather than for their individual profit, came to rest in education and in the institution of the socialist state. He wrote later in retrospect that he had returned from America in 1906

> . . . to begin a confused, tedious, ill-conceived and ineffectual campaign to turn the little Fabian Society, wizened already though not old, into the beginning of an order akin to those Samurai in *A Modern Utopia*, which should embody for mankind a sense of the State. . . . We would attack the coming generation at the high school, technical college and university stage, and our organisation would quicken into a constructive social stratum.[56]

For three vigorous years, 1906–8, this liaison with the Fabian Society markedly coloured Wells's sociological thinking, and led to the spate of propagandist literature which alienated many of his literary critics to such an extent that some have doubted whether the sociological novels could be regarded as literature.[57] When Wells first promulgated his prophecies of a new world-state and its Samurai élite, his ideas were still so novel and his imagination so fertile and vivid that he scarcely needed to write well in order to attract readers. Later, when his books became repetitive he still did not realise, despite remonstrances from Bennett and James, that it was then necessary to concentrate more carefully on style and expression. The vivid descriptions strung together with poorly integrated propagandist speeches, such as Urthred's in *Men Like Gods*, continued and gradually their impact not only as literature but as popular sociology decreased. Shanks commented that:

> Most of his novels since about 1906 have been clearly didactic, propagandist and controversial in nature. They are written 'about' contemporary topics: the characters are invented to discuss and illustrate contemporary problems. . . . Mr. Wells never plays quite fair with his characters here; no artist who turns to propaganda can ever do so.[58]

The third charge, lack of originality, or, in its extreme form, plagiarism, was less common, for Wells had never claimed complete originality for his utopian ideas and had repeatedly throughout *A Modern Utopia* acknowledged his indebtedness to earlier writers.[59] The idea of a world-state, which Wells regarded as a basic feature of his utopia was not, in essence, original. It was first mooted by Adam Müller (1816) and then by Carlyle (1832), Emerson (1856) and J. A. Froude (1870). The idea had also recurred in Lord Erskine's *Armanta* and in Havelock Ellis's *The Nineteenth Century: A Dialogue in Utopia* (1900), which condemns militaristic nationalism, imperialism and any exploitation of subject races, and sees a world-state as the only viable alternative. It was probably this latter source which influenced Wells most directly, although, despite his friendship with Havelock Ellis, he does not record having read this particular work.

Crozier disputed whether Wells's utopia was, as he claimed, kinetic and evolving.

> As for his Utopia being one with a principle of evolution in it and not rigid and fixed like those of his predecessors – had he embodied his ideas in an abstract discourse they would have been seen to be as immovable and fixed as the statues of the gods around the walls of a pantheon, but by draping his figures, after the manner of the novelist, in the appropriate costume, he would lead us to believe . . . that his Utopia is really alive and moving with all the possibilities of evolution and progress in it.[60]

Crozier cites no other basis for this criticism which, as it stands, is exaggerated. In one sense it was impossible for Wells, or indeed anyone, to predict in detail the lines along which a society would evolve, any more than it is possible to predict precisely the probable evolutionary development of any single organism. One can only, as Wells did, speculate upon various general possibilities. Wells's Martians, Selenites, Sea Raiders and giant ants are mere guesses – educated guesses but guesses nevertheless, not scientifically respectable predictions. Yet natural selection operating upon a society, and especially on a world-society, is far more diverse and subtle than the elements of selection which individual species undergo, so that any detailed picture of that evolution in progress is, *ipso facto*, impossible. It should however be possible to describe an environment which would offer maximum possibilities for the individual variations upon which selection might act and this Wells did with considerable success. His peculiarly futuristic outlook on life allowed him to participate in, and to describe vividly, the dynamic character and movement of modern life, and the forward-looking attitude of his utopians is a dramatic extension of this.

These three prongs of critical attack have appeared infrequently and are, on the whole, of minor importance. The more sustained attack on the utopias has been the moral one, first voiced in detail by Chesterton who claimed that Wells's utopia was too mechanised, too scientific and materialistic, and made no allowance for any spiritual qualities of man, for the emotional and religious life.[61] Apart from his stress on rationalism as opposed to emotional guides to action, the moral feature which most distressed Wells's contemporaries was his attitude to eugenics. He had first broached the topic in *Anticipations* where he stressed the importance of Malthusian doctrine for any practical utopia, and derided any reform movement which chose to ignore the issue:

Probably no more shattering book than the *Essay on Population* has ever been, or ever will be written. . . . It has become apparent that whole masses of human population are, as a whole, inferior in their claim upon the future to other masses, . . . To give them equality is to sink to their level, to protect and cherish them is to be swamped in their fecundity. The confident and optimistic Radicalism of the earlier nineteenth century and the humanitarian philanthropic type of Liberalism, have bogged themselves beyond hope in these realizations. The Socialist has shirked them as he has shirked the older crux of Malthus.[62]

By 1903 Wells's views were less extremist: *Mankind in the Making* rejected the whole idea of positive eugenics. But Wells was never to repudiate the necessity for negative eugenics. It is present, though not unduly stressed, in *A Modern Utopia* and *Men Like Gods*, and Wells's last word on the subject, in *The Science of Life* (1931), is the claim that, although perhaps not practical in our present age, eugenics must nevertheless eventually become so. Clearly he regrets only the delay in implementing a eugenics programme:

> At present eugenics is merely the word for what still remains an impracticable idea. But it is clear that what men can do with wheat and maize may be done with every living species in the world – including his own. It is not ultimately necessary that a multitude of dull and timid people should be born. That is how things have to be today, but it is an unnecessary state of affairs. . . . Once the eugenic phase is reached, humanity may increase very rapidly in skill, mental power, will and general vigour.[63]

Wells's continued support for a eugenics programme, in some form at least, undoubtedly arose from his desire for order and for control over nature, for the elimination of inefficiency from every sphere of individual life and from society as a whole. Hence his continued and characteristic intolerance of the average, dull, inefficient citizen whose pattern of living was based on uncontrolled instincts, egotistic social conventions and fossilised codes of behaviour rather than on rationalism, social-minded aspirations, and initiative. In Wells's view these obstacles to progress had somehow to be overcome. The eugenic method was the most ruthless and probably the quickest; education was another, slower but perhaps no less sure in the long run. He never ceased to stress the importance of both methods in the struggle to eliminate the 'natural man' for whom his scorn, with the two notable exceptions of Kipps and Mr Polly, was unlimited. The hero of Romanticism and Rousseauism, 'unimproved man', represented by the anachronistic individual whom the travellers first encounter in *A Modern Utopia*, is described as 'a most consummate ass' and subsequently as an 'incredibly egotistical dissentient . . . with a manifest incapacity for comprehensive co-operation'.[64] Wells believed firmly with Huxley that man must become the antithesis of 'natural man', the arbiter of evolution and not its passive product. In such a scheme, the 'acceptance' of nature, or indeed of the *status quo* in anything, appeared both cowardly and ridiculous.

This contempt for the popular concept of the 'natural man' is expressed uncompromisingly in *The World Set Free*, when Karenin remarks:

> There is no natural life of man. . . . It was the habit of many writers in the early twentieth century to speak of competition and the narrow private life of trade and saving and suspicious isolation as though such things were in some exceptional way proper to the human constitution, as though openness of mind and a preference for achievement over possession were abnormal and rather insubstantial qualities. How wrong that was, the history of the decades immediately following the establishment of the world republic witnesses.[65]

Huxley had delivered a similar, detailed warning to those who attempted to derive a 'gladiatorial' social ethic from evolutionary studies:

> There is another fallacy which appears to me to pervade the so-called 'ethics of evolution'. It is the notion that because, on the whole, animals and plants have advanced in perfection of organisation by means of the struggle for existence, and the consequent survival of the fittest, therefore men in society, men as ethical beings must look to the same process to help them towards perfection. I suspect that this fallacy has arisen out of the unfortunate ambiguity of the phrase 'survival of the fittest'. 'Fittest' has a connotation of 'best'; and about 'best' there hangs a moral flavour. In cosmic nature, however, what is 'fittest' depends upon the conditions. . . . Men in society are undoubtedly subject to the cosmic process. . . . But the influence of the cosmic process on the evolution of society is the greater the more rudimentary its civilisation. Social progress means a checking of the cosmic process at every step, and the substitution for it of another, which may be called the ethical process, the end of which is not the survival of those who happen to be the fittest, in respect of the whole of the conditions which obtain, but of those who are ethically the best.[66]

However, despite this stress on the importance of the moral factor in

the evolution of society, Wells's readers continued to be alienated by
any suggestion of a need for selection – moral or otherwise – in a
utopian society. His emphasis on the need for efficiency elicited the
frequent charge of arrogance. A critic writing in *T.P.'s Weekly*
claimed that to Wells '. . . other people were 'silly' – his favourite
epithet. A whole class he would sum up with the aid of that pet word
of his.'[67] Indeed the very names by which he designates the inferior
classes of his utopia, the Dull and the Base, betray this characteristic
impatience and intolerance. Dullness in the Wellsian canon is a
crime quite as heinous and infectious as moral turpitude. It is
interesting that in *The Star Begotten*, the intelligent and highly
developed future race is described as having a 'hard, clear mind'.
Wells instantly qualifies this, to avert the unsympathetic reaction
which such a phrase might evoke from his readers, and characteristically his defence involves an appeal to intelligence as a self-
evident virtue: 'A hard clear mind does not mean what we call a
hard individual. What we call a hard man is a stupid man, who
specialises in inflexibility to escape perplexity.'[68] Edward Shanks
attempted to explain this characteristic impatience of Wells as a
result of his birth and education:

> One of the most remarkable things about him . . . is that the past
> has no native roots in his mind; and it might be said that the
> future has taken its place. It is natural for a man so constituted to
> be impatient. He can foresee in an hour more than can happen in
> a century; and he demands that the procession shall be
> accelerated.[69]

It is indicative of this native impatience that, whatever his hopes
for the future development of *Homo sapiens*, Wells never, at any time
of his writing, showed any faith in the average man and least of all in
the crowd which, he believed, was by nature reactionary.
Democracy he had explicitly denigrated in *Anticipations* for the same
reasons:

> I know of no case for the elective Democratic government of
> modern States that cannot be knocked to pieces in five minutes. It
> is manifest that upon countless important public issues there is no
> Collective will, and nothing in the mind of the average man
> except blank indifference . . . the case against all prolusions of
> ostensible Democracy is indeed so strong that it is impossible to

consider the present wide establishment of Democratic institutions as being the outcome of any process of intellectual conviction.[70]

And he apparently saw no reason to reverse this judgment. In *Men Like Gods*, the authorial Barnstaple reflects upon a unique feature of the new utopia into which he has come:

> There is no Crowd. The Old World, the world to which I belong was, and in my universe alas still is, the world of the Crowd, the world of that detestable crawling mass of unfeatured, infected human beings.[71]

In one of Wells's last attempts to picture a utopian society, *The Star Begotten*, a sudden accretion of cosmic rays produces an increased mutation rate in human genes, and ultimately a race of beings who are wiser, and more developed morally than ourselves. It is emphasised that these beings, who are highly individualised, resist utterly any shadow of a crowd mentality or mass prejudices. Thus only in the intermediate stages does Wells see the need for the strict regulation of the crowd, for in the future and more perfect society the crowd has dispersed, it has become individuals again, each unique and free to express his personality, accomplishments and will. It is ironical that later writers and critics should have derived from Wells's work the opinion that he aimed to subdue all individualism and to crush initiative, and that he was the predecessor, albeit unwittingly, of *Brave New World* and the later twentieth-century anti-utopias. Wells himself explicitly dealt with this objection in so far as it was raised by *Brave New World*, the whole conception of which he vigorously repudiated. In both *Guide to the New World* and *The Fate of Homo Sapiens* he criticised the utter lack of imagination of those who assume that a utopia must, by definition, be regimented and boring:

> Many unimaginative people who can still think only in terms of getting a living, believe that this release of energy [from the business of wage-earning] means only an increase in that terrible, boring vacuity of time called Leisure. . . . One finds this sort of thing in Aldous Huxley. . . . His mind is evidently enormously obsessed by thoughts of sex and bodily vigour, and in his *Brave New World* he makes sexual and athletic elaboration the chief

employment of human leisure. To that he thinks our reason leads us.

But healthy, educated children – and men and women with a lively interest in life, do not succumb to these fundamental urgencies. They will be untroubled by either morbid excesses or morbid abstinence or jealousies. In this world of realized possibilities, the concept of life after the Aldous Huxley pattern, is, to say the last [sic] of it, improbable.[72]

Yet, although Wells continued to believe in the possibilities of utopias, if only man or his improved descendants could muster sufficient will and expertise to reform society, he did come to abrogate his earlier conception of a scientific élite which would instigate the sociological changes and preside over the new world state until education had rendered government redundant. After 1936 he proceeded to discard the idea of a scientific élite – not directly for any of the reasons advanced above, but because he no longer believed that the scientists could fulfil the particular function assigned to them in his utopian system – namely the instigation of an orderly and efficient society. This is further support for the contention that it was not the scientists themselves whom Wells believed important, but rather the principles which he had supposed them to embody. When he came to believe them incapable of performing their role adequately, he did not scruple to demote them to a different and less prominent role. Character-istically, his objections are couched in terms of efficiency:

We have to face the fact that from the point of view of general living, men of science, artists, philosophers, specialized in-telligences of any sort, do not constitute an élite that can be mobilized for collective action. They are an extraordinarily miscellaneous assembly, and their most remarkable common quality is the quality of concentration in comparative retirement – each along his own lines. They have none of the solidarity . . . that lawyers, doctors or any of the really socially-organized professions, for instance, display. A professor-ridden world might prove as unsatisfactory under the stress of modern life and fluctuating conditions as a theologian-ridden world.[73]

Instead, the scientists, the technicians and artists, the specialists in all fields, are to be employed in the compilation of a vast, and continually updated world encyclopaedia which will embody the collective wisdom of the world's best brains on every conceivable issue, and thus furnish a vast and immediate reference, not only for the more efficient working of other research specialists, but for the consultation of governments which will thereby act with increased understanding and wisdom.

Thus despite Wells's changing views on government and the optimum organisation of society, the principles underlying his ideas at any one time did not vary. They were consistently the two closely interrelated principles which had impressed him most strongly during his years as a science student. Whether they were embodied in a ruthless technocracy, such as that of Ostrog, or in a benevolent and numerically increasing élite, the Samurai, which should eventually embrace the whole population, whether they were to be implemented through the socialist programme or by the setting up of a world-encyclopaedia from which all governments might derive information, the basis of each suggestion was Wells's overriding desire for order and efficiency. He would certainly not have considered his later views any less scientific merely because they were no longer dependent on a scientific élite for their implementation. It was the principle which was all-important. Scientists had been seen as a possible tool in effecting a desirable end, but if there were a better tool, or a more efficient method of deploying these scientists, then this alternative would be adopted without regret.

5 Waste and Disorder or Order and Uniformity?

We have seen in Chapter 1 that the study of science, and in particular of evolution, instilled in Wells a desire for order amounting almost to an obsession. His family background of a disordered and incompetently run home, an unprofitable, ill-managed shop and an apparently ineffectual mother, came to symbolise for him all that disorder and concomitant waste which undermined the social structure at every level.[1] The Bromstead described in *The New Machiavelli* is a vivid picture of the impression which his own native Bromley had seared upon his mind: 'Chaotic indiscipline, ill-adjusted effort, spasmodic aims, these give the quality of all my Bromstead memories'.[2] There is a similar picture of the Leadford home in *The Days of the Comet* and almost exactly the same atmosphere is described in Wells's autobiographical account of his childhood.[3] This impatience with semi-accurate, muddled thinking even finds expression in several of the scientific romances, frequently in humorous situations such as that described in 'The Truth about Pyecraft', concerning the strange experiences of a corpulent man who carelessly expresses a desire to 'lose weight' when he really wishes to 'lose mass'. Unfortunately for him his wish is granted, and he finds himself as bulky as ever, but almost weightless, floating helplessly about the ceiling until supplied with lead weights in his pockets to bring him down to earth.

Even the easier circumstances of Wells's later life failed to erase this scar, for waste, the natural and inevitable result of disorder, became a perennial theme in his work – waste and inefficiency in domestic arrangements, the waste of natural resources, the wasted potential of men and women unable to make their full contribution to society (Beatrice, Trafford, Remington and Isabel) or those who, like Griffin, pervert their talents to ill effect; waste in personal relationships and in international relations, culminating in the immense waste of every kind involved in a world war.

Spasmodic outbursts against one or several of these aspects of waste occur in most of the early works, while *Tono-Bungay* surveys virtually the whole spectrum of waste in society, tracing the causal relations between its various manifestations. One of the most striking features of this novel is the related imagery of disease and decay which predominates throughout. At the end George reflects: 'Again and again in this book I have written of England as a feudal scheme overtaken by fatty degeneration and stupendous accidents of hypertrophy'.[4] In *Tono-Bungay* the sense of decay pervades every sphere of life. Socio-economic decay is apparent in the very success of Tono-Bungay, Uncle Ponderevo's patent medicine which purports to be a panacea for all conceivable ailments; it is equally apparent in the final failure of the enterprise, for the evaporation of the Ponderevo fortune is not the result of a sudden, nationwide enlightenment as to the real nature of the spurious product: it is brought about by angry speculators whose expectations of dishonest profits have been frustrated. The decadence of the Bladesover estate, and, by explicit analogy, of the whole English class system, is stressed repeatedly. Even George, who observes and diagnoses all these instances of illness, does not remain uncontaminated; appropriately he suffers from a similar 'fatty degeneration'. When he throws in his lot with his uncle and the Tono-Bungay enterprise begins to produce rich profits, George grows flabby and dull:

With the coming of plenty, I ate abundantly and foolishly, drank freely and followed my impulses more and more carelessly. I felt no reason why I should do anything else. Never at any point did I use myself to the edge of my capacity . . . I became an inordinate smoker; it gave me moods of profound depression, but I treated these usually by the homeopathic method – by lighting another cigar. I didn't realise at all how loose my moral and nervous fibre had become.[5]

His life story presents one example of waste after another, in both the social and the individual sphere. Even the temporary gratification of George's passion for Beatrice is seen as futile and without future:

For nearly a fortnight we two met and made love together. Once more this mighty passion, that our aimless civilisation has fettered and maimed and sterilized and debased, gripped me and filled me with passionate delights and solemn joys – that were all, you know, futile and purposeless.[6]

The whole 'quap'-seeking episode, which several critics have found so irrelevant and discursive, is a further elaborate allegory of the social disintegration of England, permitting the introduction of symbolic comments which could not have been made in the main sequence of events without destroying the illusion that George, the semi-flippant social observer, is the narrator. George is serious only about science, and thus, in the midst of a scientific discourse on radio-activity he can legitimately digress and compare it with social decay, while all the time the comparison is equally effective for the reader in the converse direction:

Those are just little molecular centres of disintegration, of that mysterious decay and rotting of those elements, elements once regarded as the most stable things in Nature. But there is something – the only word that comes near it is *Cancerous* – and that is not very near, about the whole of quap, something that creeps and lives as a disease lives, by destroying. . . . It is in the matter exactly what the decay of our old culture is in society, a loss of traditions and distinctions and assured reactions.[7]

So many aspects of waste and confusion are represented and discussed in *Tono-Bungay* that George is eventually moved to a more explicit outburst:

As I turn over the big pile of manuscript before me certain things become clear to me, and particularly the immense inconsequence of my experiences. It is, I see now that I have it all before me, a story of activity and urgency and sterility. I have called it *Tono-Bungay* but I had far better have called it *Waste*. I have told of childless Marion, of my childless aunt, of Beatrice wasted and wasteful and futile. What hope is there for a people whose women become fruitless? I think of all the energy I have given to vain things, I think of my industrious scheming with my uncle, of Crest Hill's vast cessation, of his resonant strenuous career. . . . It is all one spectacle of forces running to waste, of people who use and do not replace, the story of a country hectic with a wasting, aimless fever of trade and money-making.[8]

The cancer image of waste and decay in society recurs in 'A Story of
the Days to Come', and in *In the Days of the Comet* where Denton
rages against civilisation as a 'vast lunatic growth', while in *The New
Machiavelli* the disorder of society is described in another image, that
of a careless, unplanned experiment, the mark of an incompetent
scientist:

> The Victorian epoch was not the dawn of a new era; it was a hasty
> trial experiment, a gigantic experiment of the most slovenly kind.
> I suppose it was necessary; . . . I suppose that before men will
> discipline themselves to learn and plan, they must first see in a
> hundred convincing forms the folly and muddle that come from
> headlong, aimless and haphazard methods.[9]

Later in the novel Remington discourses with some heat on the
subject of 'muddle' to his fellow students at Cambridge, setting forth
what is to be one of the major themes:

> 'Muddle,' said I, 'is the enemy.' That remains my belief to this
> day. Clearness and order, light and foresight, these things I know
> for Good. It was muddle had just given us all the still freshly
> painful disasters and humiliations of the war, muddle that gives
> us the visibly sprawling disorder of our cities and the industrial
> countryside, muddle that gives us the waste of life, the limitations,
> wretchedness and unemployment of the poor.[10]

In *The New Machiavelli*, this theme of waste has various ramifications in personal as well as social relationships, its central example
being the alleged waste of Remington's potential as a political
leader, rejected by a society which cannot reconcile his personal and
moral life with the image to which it requires that a statesman
conform. Ironically, Remington himself, before he is attracted to
Isabel, acknowledges the waste of individual energy involved in an
earlier illicit relationship:

> The interim was full of the quality of work delayed, of time and
> energy wasted. . . . These furtive scuffles, this sneaking into
> shabby houses of assignation, was what we had made of the
> suggestion of pagan beauty. . . . We had laid hands upon the
> wonder and glory of bodily love and wasted them. . . . It was the
> sense of waste, of finely beautiful possibilities getting entangled

and marred for ever that oppressed me. I had missed, I had lost.[11]

In *The Passionate Friends*, Stephen Stratton and Lady Mary Justin discover a similar limitation in their relationship, together with a consequent draining of their intellectual and spiritual potential through the channels of an illicit physical passion:

> . . . from the day that passion carried us and we became, in the narrower sense of the word, lovers, all the wider interests we had in common, our political intentions, our impersonal schemes, began to pass out of our intercourse. Our situation closed upon us like a trap and hid the sky. Something more intense had our attention by the feet and we used our wings no more.[12]

Marriage too is concerned largely with aspects of waste in personal relationships and in society. Marjorie confesses to having squandered Trafford's money and, through her demands on his time and resources, ruined his career as a research chemist. Here, as in *Tono-Bungay*, waste is seen as the great crime of society, because it is fundamentally a crime against nature. Again, childlessness – that of Aunt and Uncle Plessington, of Daffy and Magnet – is symbolic of a barren social order, characterised by the misspending of money, and the frittering away of potentially useful lives. Indeed, despite the suggestion of optimism about the 'solution' to which Trafford and Marjorie talk their way in Labrador, the closing paragraphs reaffirm the condemnation of a wasteful society, with little hope that the Traffords will significantly alter it. The ship on which they return to London 'came in through the fog, very slowly, from that great wasteful world of men and women beyond the seaward grey'.[13] Wells himself, in the preface to the Atlantic edition, described the central problem of the novel as the inevitable waste involved in the marriage of two such differently motivated people, and denied that any lasting solution was possible within the existing framework of society.

In their several ways the three futuristic novels, *The War of the Worlds*, *In the Days of the Comet* and *The World Set Free*, all reinforce this impression of the inevitable disorder and waste which society will suffer until a new era of order shall have been instigated. Significantly, even in these cases where a new society does emerge triumphant, the reform process is described as being triggered by a stimulus external to the system since, *within* a sick society, it is virtually impossible for any individual or group of individuals to summon up sufficient spirit for the overthrow of the diseased system. In a real sense, therefore, this may be read as a tacit, perhaps an unconscious confession of failure by Wells to conceive of any widespread moral reform arising spontaneously among his contemporaries.

It is significant in this respect that there are almost no individual villains in Wells's books, no Uriah Heeps or Fagins, no Merdles or Murdstones even in the otherwise Dickensian *Kipps* and *Mr. Polly*. Wells's 'villain' is the disorganisation of society which prevents the 'little man' from finding self-fulfilment and which, more insidious than a single opponent, cannot be overcome merely by the individual's own efforts, however vigorous.

In *First and Last Things* Wells's nightmare vision sees misrule spreading to cover the whole earth:

> I see humanity scattered over the world, dispersed, conflicting, unawakened . . . I see human life as avoidable waste and curable confusion . . . I see gamblers, fools, brutes, toilers, martyrs. Their disorder of effort, the spectacle of futility, fills me with a passionate desire to end waste, to create order, to develop understanding. . . . All these people reflect and are part of the waste and discontent of my life.[14]

But, however acutely Wells was conscious of the immense spectacle of waste and disorder, inefficiency and misrule at every level of social and individual life, he was not, for most of his career, without a remedy to suggest. Even in *Tono-Bungay*, that litany upon the theme of waste, there is at least the suggestion of an answer to the problem, distasteful though that solution might be:

> Through the confusion something drives, something that is at once human achievement and the most inhuman of all existing things. Something comes out of it. . . . Sometimes I call this reality Science, sometimes I call it Truth.[15]

In so far as the remedy for disorder was a matter of government policy, the development of Wells's ideal from *Anticipations* through the utopian novels and the socialist propagandist works, to the 'world brain' concept, has already been discussed but it is worth considering also how Wells envisaged this new order as transform-

ing the life and outlook of the average citizen. Again *Anticipations* set
the pattern for the books which followed, for almost certainly its
popularity was the result primarily of its effort to deal with reform in
domestic measures and other facets of life which impinged on the
individual, and only secondarily of its proposed governmental
reforms.

In designing his utopian world-state, Wells was clearly torn
between two divergent ideals – the desire for order and efficiency on
the one hand and the desire to foster individual initiative on the
other. These two diverse ideals issue in subsidiary conflicts between
freedom of movement and desire for privacy, between socialism and
individualism, between devotion to the state and personal incentive, between state education and the encouragement of a
variety of motivating forces. It therefore seems most useful to
examine first the methods by which Wells hoped to increase the
order and efficiency of society and then to consider the means
whereby he attempted to mitigate the authoritarian element
involved in such reforms, and so avoid the jack-booted, totalitarian
conformity which has been the major subject of anti-utopian
literature and satires since his time.

In *Anticipations* Wells takes as his primary reform that of increased
facility of transport and communication networks. He then proceeds to show how this improved communication will affect land-
usage, a redistribution of population being consequent upon the
possibility of swift and flexible transport services. News of the latest
researches and ideas is transmitted quickly and cheaply throughout
the community, becoming readily available to all members, while
telegraphic communication provides free information for anyone
who cares to make use of the nearest 'listening-point'. Even this, of
course, falls far short of the ultimate stage in communication – that
of thought-transfer as practised by the citizens of *Men Like Gods*, for
this latter obviates the risk of misunderstanding at two levels – in the
formulation of a thought by one party and in the comprehension of
that expression by the recipient.

In the interests of the best and most economic use of the natural
resources, and to eliminate pollution of the environment, such as
that suffered by the Ravensbrook,[16] Wells presents his world-state as
being the sole landowner, with local governments holding land in
trust, like feudal landlords, responsible for its prosperity and
development. The state thus commands all the sources of food and
power, such as coal, water and atomic power.

Wells saw that, given an improved transport network, families would almost certainly become more flexible in their domestic arrangements, in their place of work and of residence. Working loyalties would break down, as would parish affiliations for, severed from the old ties, men would drift to areas where their work potential had currently the greatest value. The resulting state of social flux might easily become one of social chaos unless some check were kept on people's whereabouts. This problem led him to consider various methods of social organisation, including an international filing bank, with arterial branches which both recorded the changing distribution and particulars of this widely dispersed mobile population, and also functioned as a world-wide labour exchange, indicating the current concentration of maximum employment opportunities and channelling population flow to-' wards these areas.

War in a world-state is, of course, an anachronism, but if it should prove necessary during the period of the state's inception, then at least it should be conducted with maximum efficiency and the minimum brutality and bloodshed. Despite his pacifist theories, the idea of war elicited Wells's characteristic enthusiasm for well-designed machinery and the wars described in *War in the Air, Anticipations* and 'The Land Ironclads' betray his irrepressible delight in technical efficiency and ingenuity.

Even the human race itself was to be rendered more efficient by a dual programme of education and eugenics to select the qualities considered most desirable for proliferation in the community. Related to this was Wells's stress on a scheme for the endowment of mothers, who were to be subsidised by the state for their work in bearing healthy children. They would thus be financially independent of the child's father and free to devote themselves to bringing up their children, thereby performing with maximum efficiency a service to the whole community. On the other hand, a certain level of competence was to be demanded of those desiring to be parents. They must have proved their responsibility by holding a position of independence and solvency in their society, by being free from transmittable diseases and from a criminal record, and by having attained the required level of physical and mental development.

For the task of bringing about these sociological reforms, Wells in *Anticipations* dismissed democracy as being wholly incapable of coping with the ordering of society on the scale necessary in the future. His preference at this time for an authoritarian government led him to extend the principle to the local and even the individual level in conditions of emergency.

It is clear, therefore, that at this stage of his thinking Wells was still ruthless in his ideas concerning the duty owed by the individual to the state – at least in time of war, and hence, presumably, in any period declared an emergency by the government.

Even in the sphere of religious belief there is an element of somewhat forced ecumenism in the Wellsian scheme, presumably to ensure the most smooth-running system by eliminating sectarian antagonisms. In the chapter dealing with 'Faith, Morals and Public Policy in the Twentieth Century' he forecasts the emergence of a vaguely pantheistic humanism as the religion of all sane and educated men, who '. . . will have no positive definition of God at all. . . . They will content themselves with denying the self-contradictory absurdities of an obstinately anthropomorphic theology. . . .'[17] Their God bears a close resemblance to that of the nineteenth-century liberal tradition: '[God] is no moralist, God is no partisan; He comprehends and cannot be comprehended, and our business is only with so much of His purpose as centres on our individual wills'.[18] It cannot be accidental that these negative attributes are the ones least likely to arouse passions and antagonisms which might undermine the efficient running of the society.

Wells envisaged his new order not merely as being imposed from above on a submissive people, but as arising equally from the voluntary desire of each individual, yet it was inevitable that such a scheme should raise the question of how much freedom remained to the individual. In his desire for order and efficiency Wells represents the people of his utopia as being governed by reason to a greater extent than is usual, or perhaps even possible. Even when he does represent his ideal citizens as pursuing apparently irrational rituals expressive of instinctive urges (this is particularly so in the case of their religious observances), he justifies these habits intellectually, on the grounds that by these means the participants can accept and sublimate their basic drives and motivations in a manner which preserves rather than disrupts the ordered fabric of society.

Although at the time of writing *Anticipations* Wells clearly believed that the will of the individual should be subordinated to that of the society, nevertheless, in the later utopias, he was at pains to stress the fact that the individual in utopia was not unduly limited but rather had more freedom to develop than his counterpart in

Wells's own society since he did not waste time and energy contending at every turn with the frustrations of a disorderly system. Moreover Wells did in several crucial respects temper the ideal of strict efficiency to permit greater individualism.

If he endowed the world-state with power over all natural resources, he did not follow socialist dictates in the sphere of private property, but regarded certain possessions as a necessary part of the individual's freedom and as the basis of a sense of identity. Thus legitimate property may comprise, in his scheme, all that a man's toil, foresight or skill have honestly acquired, except in so far as these curtail the freedom of any other individuals. Clothes, jewels, tools, books, private household possessions, the privacy of his own home, as well as adequate means to ensure the upbringing of his children, are considered the inalienable rights of any individual who has had the initiative and ability to earn them.

Again, unlike many of the earlier utopians, Wells retained the usage of money, as well as of private property. Recognising how deeply rooted in man's evolutionary history are the basic motivations of self-interest, and the desire for private property as an inducement to individual effort and achievement, he endeavoured to make these instincts function in the service of the social order. Money was seen as both good and necessary in civilised life if used correctly, for it

> is the water of the body social; it distributes and receives and renders growth and assimilation and movement and recovery possible. It is the reconciliation of human independence with liberty. What other device will give a man so great a freedom with so strong an inducement to effort?[19]

However, the standard currency in his utopia is not an arbitrary one, such as gold, but the basic one of saleable productive energy, expressed in units of physical work. Such a standard appealed particularly to Wells because under his system it virtually eliminated the wastefulness of human potential through unemployment and unequal distribution of human labour with respect to resources.

This attempted reconciliation between individual independence and liberty on the one hand, and an efficiently run social organisation on the other, finds symbolic expression in *A Modern Utopia* in the question of personal appearance and dress, which

Wells treats not as a trivial matter but as a significant demonstration
of personal identity. Besides exemplifying his theory of aesthetics, it
stands also as a symbol of the relationship between the individual
and society. We have seen that Wells believed machinery could and
should be beautiful, and that it would in fact be most aesthetically
pleasing when it was most simple and most functional in design.
Similarly, in the realm of dress, the narrator expatiates at some
length upon the simplicity of the clothing worn by the utopians,
concluding that its beauty and grace reside in its simplicity which
allows expression of the individual's personality without competing
ostentatiously for attention. Thus although individual it also forms
part of an harmonious whole with the dress of others: 'Dress will
have scarcely any of that effect of disorderly conflict, of self-assertion
qualified by the fear of ridicule, that it has in the crudely
competitive civilizations of earth'.[20] As is emphasised by the terms
used – 'disorderly conflict', 'self-assertion' – this description of dress
clearly also stands as a symbol for an underlying moral attitude. It
thus becomes clear that throughout Wells's sociological novels and
treatises science provided him not only with his yardstick of social
organisation but also, by extension, with a guide for a personal ethic
which would be in harmony with the aims of the whole society.

But inevitably, however watertight his theories might be, there
were some awkward anomalies in his sociological novels. Wells
might categorically assert in the non-fictional works that the
individual's potential for self-fulfilment, as well as the improvement
of society as a whole, depended on the rigorous ordering of that
society, but in nearly all the novels, as in Wells's own life, such an
ethic is seen to chafe upon individuals – even enlightened, Wellsian
individuals. Again those characters who have, themselves, been
most critical of Victorian society for its waste and disorder are still
able to find a certain charm in the sprawling chaos of London and
even to regard human planners as pedantic, insignificant meddlers
endeavouring, ludicrously, to divert the course of Nature. In *The
New Machiavelli*, despite his reiterated pleas for order, Remington,
like Wells, undergoes a revulsion against the efficiency of the Baileys
(transparent representations of Sidney and Beatrice Webb, the two
most organisation-conscious Fabians of Wells's day).[21] He describes
an evening at the Baileys' house in Chambers Street with its intense
atmosphere of political power, as though the Baileys and those
whom they co-opted into their service had their 'hands on the very
strings that guided the world', and then contrasts his feelings on

emerging into the disorder of the London night. Clearly, there is a fascination in the scene for Wells as for Remington:

> And then with all this administrative fizzle, this pseudo-scientific administrative chatter, dying away in your head, out you went into the limitless grimy chaos of London streets and squares, roads and avenues lined with teeming houses, each larger than the Chambers Street house and at least equally alive; you saw the chaotic glamour of hoardings, the jumble of traffic, the coming and going of mysterious myriads, you heard the rumble of traffic like the noise of a torrent; a vague incessant murmur of cries and voices, wanton crimes and accidents bawled at you from the placards; imperative, unaccountable fashions swaggered trium-phant in the dazzling windows of the shops; and you found yourself swaying back to the opposite conviction that the huge formless spirit of the world it was that held the strings and danced the puppets on the Bailey stage. . . . You realized that quite a lot of types were under-represented in Chambers Street, that feral and obscure and altogether monstrous forces must be at work, as yet altogether unassimilated by those neat administrative reorganizations.[22]

The order which the Baileys try to impose on society is seen by Remington as being not merely ineffective, but also false, perhaps dishonest and certainly undesired, not only in the political arena but, more insidiously, in the sphere of personal relationships. The Baileys' attempt to bring about the marriage of Remington and Margaret is based solely on expediency – on what they see as being the most effective combination of her wealth and his political potential for their cause – rather than on an understanding of the emotions of the characters involved. Despite their marriage and their fundamental goodwill towards each other, Margaret and Remington prove in several vital respects to be incompatible, and it is significant that in the account of their tacit confrontation Margaret is, like the Baileys, identified with the forces of order, coolness and light, while Remington the protagonist is associated with the contrary elements of untamed passions:

> The chaotic and adventurous element in life was spreading upward and getting the better of me, over-mastering me and all

my will to rule and make. . . . And the strength, the drugging
urgency of the passion! . . .

Margaret shone at times in my imagination like a radiant angel
in a world of mire and disorder, in a world of cravings, hot and
dull red like scars inflamed. . . .[23]

Clearly, whatever Remington's rational mind may assert, these
latter forces have for him an attraction beyond that of peace and
order.

A similar inconsistency of attitudes is to be found in *The Dream*, in
which Sarnac, a citizen of a world 2000 years after the Age of
Confusion (nineteenth-century England), dreams the experiences
of a twentieth-century individual, Harry Mortimer Smith, passing
in sequence from Harry's boyhood in an impoverished shop at
Cherry Gardens to his rise to comparative wealth in a London
publishing firm. Of Cherry Gardens, Sarnac speaks with unmitigated horror, employing the characteristic Wellsian image of a
cancer to describe the evils of its society.[24] Yet although, when the
Smith family moves to London, his financial situation and consequent domestic arrangements are scarcely much improved,
Sarnac claims that the disorder and chaos of London has a real and
valid charm of its own:

> . . . the vast traffic of clumsy automobiles, and distressed horses
> in narrow unsuitable streets; I suppose your general impression is
> a nightmare of multitudes and a suffocating realization of jostling
> discomfort and uncleanness and of an unendurable strain on eye
> and ear and attention. The history we learn in our childhood
> enforces that lesson.
>
> But though the facts are just as we were taught they were, I do
> not recall anything like the distress at London you would suppose
> me to have felt, and I do remember vividly the sense of adventure,
> the intellectual excitement and the discovery of beauty I
> experienced in going there. . . . The aspects of this city's great-
> ness, the wonder of this limitless place and a certain changing and
> evanescent beauty rise out of the swamp that bears it.'[25]

The parallel between Harry's attitudes and Remington's, and
the similarity of both to Wells's own experiences, suggest a possible
autobiographical explanation of this apparent anomaly between
the censure of disorder in the counties, and the subsequent

celebration of disorder in London. Wells himself had hated and despised the confusion and slovenly muddle of his mother's disorganised household and came to regard this as an inevitable part of lower-middle-class provincial life. When his scholarship to study science at South Kensington 'rescued' him from this background and transported him to London, the vast size and sprawling confusion of the city offered the anonymity, the adventure and the opportunities necessary for self-fulfilment at a strategic point in his development. Its diversity and disorder appeared as the antithesis of the chafing restrictions on movement and thought imposed by his mother and, through her, the Establishment. Therefore in the novels, those who try to impose restrictions on the rich multiformity of London are tacitly regarded as allied, in this respect, with the Establishment, however radical their policies in other spheres. It would seem, then, that in the novels, and particularly those containing autobiographical elements drawn from his own boyhood and adolescence, Wells's personal experiences and the bias he had derived from them were strong enough to overcome his abstract principles and even to elicit some derision of them.

In the more theoretical utopias, however, the conflict between an individual's aims and the welfare of society is solved, apparently to Wells's satisfaction, by recourse to biology, for his theory of personal morality involves, as its major premise, the value of the submission of the individual to the good of the species, and in a world-state the state is, of course, quite literally equivalent to, and co-extensive with, the species. In the last analysis, despite his liberal emphasis on the rights and freedom of the individual, there is always, in Wells's mind, a prior allegiance to the rights of the race, and man the individual is to some extent at least, obscured by the shadow of *Homo sapiens.*

Wells seems to have rationalised his departure from the liberal tradition of individualism partly on the grounds of its inefficiency and partly by recourse to biological reasons. This prior allegiance to the species over and above the individual had appeared in Wells's thought before the utopias. Its first expression was a review article, 'The Novels of Mr. George Gissing', in which he wrote of

a change that is sweeping over the minds of thousands of educated men. It is the discovery of the insufficiency of the cultivated life and its necessary insincerities; it is a return to the essential, to honourable struggle as the epic factor in life, to children as the matter of morality and the sanction of the securities of civilization.[26]

Three years later it formed a central strand in the argument of *Love and Mr. Lewisham* where, after battling ineffectively to assert his individuality, Lewisham is represented as coming to his biological senses with the realisation that his wife is about to bear his child:

> '. . . it is almost as if Life had played me a trick – promised so much – given so little! No! One must not look at it in that way. . . . Career! In itself it is a career – the most important career in the world. Father! Why should I want more? . . . Yes, this is life. This alone is life. For this we were made and born. All these other things – all other things – they are only a sort of play.'[27]

Similarly, Trafford, whose acknowledged intellectual ability makes him a more likely candidate than the mediocre student, Lewisham, for personal ambitions in research, sounds the same note after the birth of his first child and does not afterwards revoke it:

> In this new light his passion for research and all the scheme of his life appeared faded and unworthy, as much egotism as though it had been devoted to hunting or golf or any such aimless preoccupation. Fatherhood gripped him and faced him about. It was manifestly a monstrous thing that he should ever have expected Marjorie to become a mere undisturbing accessory to the selfish intellectualism of his career.[28]

So too, Ann Veronica, despite her former academic aspirations, is shown as reaching the central meaning of her life in her marriage (significantly to a biologist, for this central meaning is itself biological) and in motherhood – that is, in the continuation of the species.

In the next two chapters some of the consequences of this relationship between the individual and the species will be considered in more detail, together with the closely-connected Wellsian concept of the 'mind of the race'. Basic to any such discussion of the individual is the question of free will and determinism, a question which Wells treated extensively with reference to what he believed to be its scientific foundations.

6 Free Will and Predestination: Freedom and Limitation

One striking result of the rise to pre-eminence of scientific materialism as a means of explaining and predicting phenomena, and particularly in the extension of this to the biological sciences, was a corresponding preoccupation with the question of free will in human behaviour.

Free will and determinism in human affairs are the correlatives of chance and design on the universal plane, and hence it might have been assumed that those who held to a belief in design throughout the universe at large would take a determinist stand on the question of human behaviour. In general, however, those who wished to see the universe as the finished design of a benevolent Creator were also most insistent, for moral reasons, on propounding a belief in free will. Darwinian theory further complicated the issue, for while the original chance variations which were the raw material for the evolutionary process were inexplicable before the establishment of the science of genetics in the twentieth century and therefore seemed to Darwin and his contemporaries arbitrary, they were acted upon by the apparently rigorous laws of natural selection governed by the joint arbiters of heredity and environment. It was this second stage of the process which, extended to the human realm, seemed to deprive man of the freedom of choice and ultimately, therefore, of moral responsibility for his actions and decisions. Thus evolutionary theory appeared to many people abhorrent on two virtually opposite grounds – firstly because it posited a universe of chance happenings and secondly because it seemed to stress the determination of human character by heredity and environment, thereby precluding free will. Darwin himself suffered mental turmoil over the questions of chance and purpose as seen in the evolutionary scheme. In a letter to Asa Gray in 1860 he wrote:

I cannot persuade myself that a beneficent and omnipotent God would have designedly created the Ichneumonidae with the express intention of their feeding within the living bodies of Caterpillars, or that a cat would play with mice. Not believing this, I see no necessity in the belief that the eye was expressly designed. On the other hand, I cannot anyhow be contented to view this wonderful universe, and especially the nature of man, and to conclude that everything in it is the result of brute force. . . . I feel most deeply that the whole subject is too profound for the human intellect. A dog might as well speculate on the mind of Newton. . . . The more I think, the more bewildered I become.[1]

In the popular mind science was, notwithstanding, the large element of chance in evolution, closely correlated with a mechanistic and hence a deterministic philosophy, and certainly the public utterances of Huxley and Tyndall, the spokesmen for biology, did little to discourage this association. Tyndall had asserted that though there was as yet no clear proof of a link between consciousness and molecular activity, nevertheless all the mysteries of nature would ultimately be explained in mechanistic terms.[2] Huxley too had claimed publicly that consciousness was reducible to a mere reflection of molecular movement, psychic events in the mind being caused solely by physical events in the nervous system. He thus virtually eliminated the mind in order to preserve the brain, since he saw no means of reconciling them and his desire for a precise and coherent relation between all phenomena would not allow him to accept a Cartesian dichotomy of the 'What is mind? No matter. What is matter? Never mind' type.

Among the major novelists of the late Victorian period, Hardy was perhaps the most influenced by Darwinism, deriving from his reading of evolution a rigorously determinist view of humanity. Wells, on the other hand, while also basing his thinking largely on Darwinism, reached a position almost contrary to that of Hardy with respect to the meaningfulness of human activity. Of all his work, the only book which proclaims a genuinely determinist viewpoint is *Mind at the End of its Tether*. The novels assume the need for choice and responsible action by human beings, while the sociological writings which deal explicitly with the question affirm a strong belief in free will.

The major reason for this divergence between Hardy and Wells is that while the latter saw a parallel between the continuing struggle for biological survival and the conflicts apparent in sociology and politics, he did not, like Hardy, see the struggle for existence as a universal principle, least of all in the moral realm. Hence he did not assume that the survival of the fittest was a valid basis either for ethics or for a theory of human behaviour. On the contrary, he followed Huxley and J. S. Mill in holding that the natural process must be curtailed, controlled and replaced by an ethical one. His position is thus similar to that of George Eliot, who also refused to take the step from determinism to necessitarianism. No character of hers is ever *compelled* to make a particular moral choice, for the 'self' of that character is one of the factors determining his choice and it is this element of 'freedom', however small, which in her view constitutes the basis of human responsibility and duty.

Several critics have regarded the desolate scene of the inevitable extinction of terrestrial life at the end of *The Time Machine* as evidence of Wells's basic adherence to a bleak determinism, which he later sought to conceal with a cheerful but insincere optimism. In fact, however, the 'exception' of *The Time Machine* in Wells's otherwise non-determinist approach provides a clue to his real train of thought, for while it describes vividly an unrelieved determinism on the cosmic scale – the dying earth and the consequent extinction of all life – it nevertheless affirms the possibility of, indeed the necessity for, voluntary action on the past of the individual. The Time Traveller's rescue of Weena, and his efforts to protect her, his struggle to regain his machine from the Morlocks, and above all his final decision to re-embark on another time journey, are decisive acts which mark him as a free spirit, undeterred by even the restrictions of time and the foreseen extinction of his species. At this theoretical level, Wells was thus able to espouse a long-term determinism in relation to evolutionary trends while holding equally firmly to the belief that at the level of individual action man must behave *as though* he were free, must make decisions and act responsibly. In the 'Epilogue' of *The Time Machine* the narrator emphasises this dichotomy, affirming, even in the face of the Time Traveller's experiences, his belief in the necessity for human responsibility:

He, I know – for the question had been discussed among us long before the Time Machine was made – thought but cheerlessly of the Advancement of Mankind, and saw in the growing pile of civilization only a foolish heaping that must eventually fall back upon and destroy its makers in the end. If that is so, it remains for us to live as though it were not so.[3]

Wells returned to an explicit consideration of this anomaly between thought and action in several of the non-fictional works.

In *Anticipations* he imputes his own beliefs about predestination and free will to his ideal New Republicans[4] in terms which he was later to expound *in propria persona* in *First and Last Things*. Here, in a section devoted entirely to a discussion of 'Free Will and Predestination', Wells distinguished between the theoretical plane of causality which is the basis of science, and the practical everyday level of human behaviour. It is worth quoting the passage at some length as it remained his clearest and most extensive statement on the subject:

> On the scientific plane, one is a fatalist, the universe a system of inevitable consequences. But . . . it is quite possible to accept as true in their several planes both predestination and free will. If you ask me, I think I should say I incline to believe in predestination and do quite completely believe in free will. The important belief is free will.
>
> But does the whole universe of fact, the external world about me, the mysterious internal world from which my motives rise, form one rigid and fated system as determinists teach? . . . as a provisional assumption it underlies most scientific work. . . . *For me as a person* this theory of predestination has no practical value. At the utmost it is an interesting theory. . . .
>
> I am free and freely and responsibly making the future – so far as I am concerned. You others are equally free. On that theory I find my life will work, and on a theory of mechanical predestination nothing works.
>
> I take the former theory therefore for my everyday purposes, and as a matter of fact so does everybody else. I regard myself as a free, responsible person amongst free, responsible persons.[5]

Thus Wells's working philosophy is essentially similar to the 'solution' proposed rather less subtly by the Metaphysical Society on the vexed question of free will – namely that 'if free will does not exist, we must and do act as if it did'.[6]

Clearly this view is related, in Wells's case at least, to the psychological need to feel that what he did had some significance;

that he, as a person, mattered in some abiding sense. In *First and Last Things* he stated this explicitly:

> My most comprehensive belief about the external and internal and myself, is that they make one universe in which I and every part are ultimately important. This is quite an arbitrary act of my mind. It is quite possible to maintain that everything is a chaotic assembly, that any part might be destroyed without affecting any other part . . . I dismiss the idea that life is chaotic because it leaves my life ineffectual, and I cannot contemplate an ineffectual life patiently . . . I assert therefore that I am an important part in that scheme.[7]

This apparent inconsistency in Wells's thought, whereby he attempted to maintain a deterministic philosophy of the universe and of life processes, while insisting on active freedom of will in the circumstances of the individual's everyday life, is related in turn to his beliefs about the dual nature of man. Biologically, man has inherited all the limitations of bodily function, physical circumstances and intellectual development, as well as all the instincts, inherited responses and neuroses which link him firmly with his prehuman ancestors. This much was a matter of indisputable biological fact. But Wells also believed that man could transcend many of these limitations through the full development of his intellect, if only the latter could be dissociated from selfish, petty aims and narrowminded superstitions, and focused instead on a larger, altruistic ideal. This too derived largely from Huxley's emphasis on the need to influence the evolutionary process rather than emulate or be subdued by it, and shows the close relationship in Wells's thought between the physical and moral bases for action.

It also elucidates the link between his ideas of determinism and his belief in a developing 'mind of the race', for this latter concept was, I believe, first invoked, and later extended, chiefly in order to reconcile his apparently contradictory beliefs of predestination and free will, the importance of the individual and the impossibility of personal immortality. On the one hand he seemed to think in terms of the species where other men thought of individuals; thus in his doctoral thesis he stresses the fact that the *unit* is the *species*, and that men must 'return to the essential', to the collective experience of struggle, if any evolutionary progress is to be made. In discussing the question of immortality he renounced completely any belief in a personal immortality:

> I do not believe I have any personal immortality. I am part of an
> immortality perhaps; but that is different. I am not the continu-
> ing thing. I personally am experimental, incidental, . . . I am a
> temporary enclosure for a temporary purpose; that served, and
> my skill and teeth, my idiosyncrasy and desire, will disperse, I
> believe, like the timbers of a booth after a fair . . . I shall serve
> my purpose and pass under the wheel, and end. That distresses
> me not at all.[8]

On the other hand, and this is particularly true in the utopian
writings, he repeatedly gave evidence of despising the masses, the
crowd mentality, stressing instead the need for unique individuals
who should develop to the utmost their own particular talents and
aspirations in order to stimulate initiative and variety within the
society.

In endeavouring to harmonise these diverse ideas Wells affirmed
the importance of individual freedom together with the pre-
eminence of the species over the individual by the simple expedient
of assuming that the individual is free, in any meaningful sense, only
in so far as he voluntarily contributes all his powers to the
developing life of the species. In the short term he is free – either to
waste his gifts in short-sighted and self-centred actions or to act
selflessly for the good of mankind; but whereas the former course of
action will ultimately lead nowhere, the latter will in the long term
achieve significance by enriching the life of the species. Thus, in this
scheme the individual can attain to a kind of immortality by
subordinating himself to the race. Such a theoretical framework was
capable of supporting also a doctrine of predestination on the
evolutionary scale – the scale on which Wells felt bound to accept
it – for he saw the sweep of evolutionary development proceeding
inevitably whether the individual within the species contributed to
it or not.

Within the human predicament as portrayed in the scientific
romances and the novels, and particularly in the comic novels, the
dichotomy between the determinism of circumstances and the need
for active choice as an assertion of free will is expressed most
frequently in terms of a character's relation to his environment. A
tentative balance is reached between his subjection to his circumstances and his escape from the bonds of family background,

education, social position and all the conventions thereby imposed. Usually the romance or the novel opens with a statement of the protagonist's impotent subjection, but ends with his transcendence and consequent sense of personal freedom and renewal. In the scientific romances the escape from circumstances frequently takes the form of a transition from the known world to another unknown one which, although it may be terrifying, never fails to evoke a feeling of deep personal satisfaction. The Time Traveller's preliminary journey fills him with a 'kind of hysterical exhilaration'; Gottfried Plattner, Filmer and Davidson and the characters who achieve liberation in 'In the Abyss', 'Under the Knife', 'The New Accelerator', 'The Argonauts of the Air', Cave in 'The Crystal Egg', Bessel in the 'Stolen Body', the Diamond Maker, Lionel Wallace in 'The Door in the Wall', and even, in a humbler way, Coombes in 'The Purple Pileus', all experience a kind of ecstasy when they achieve a certain degree of freedom from the bondage of everyday circumstances and humdrum existence.

A fuller consideration of the determinism of character by heredity and environment in Wells's novels will be given in Chapter 8, but it should be noted here that in *Kipps*, *Tono-Bungay* and *Mr. Polly*, the escape motif is primary although there are variations in the solution proposed to the human craving for liberation. Kipps is at first apparently trapped in the drab life of a draper's assistant. His fellow-apprentice, Minton, asserts the deterministic view of their circumstances: 'I tell you, we're in a blessed drainpipe and we've got to crawl along it till we die'.[9] Kipps's escape from the drapery business is the triumph of chance and freedom over this deterministic outlook and the straitjacket of social convention. He is saved from Minton's fate partly because of his own strength of character which refuses to submit to the fatalist view but chiefly, after the appearance of the Bohemian Chitterlow, by chance occurrences which he is flexible enough to seize upon for his advantage. His final emancipation from the perhaps worse fate of sterile gentility and marriage into the upper middle class is an assertion that only by the full acceptance of one's own character and personality can genuine freedom of the self be attained.

A similar escape from the double prison of circumstances and false values is achieved by Polly and, to a certain extent, though in a very different setting, by Ann Veronica. Wells was not deluded into believing freedom synonymous with irresponsibility, and both these characters have to distinguish a true from a false liberation. Polly's first attempts to escape are spurious – daydreaming and the reading of travel and adventure stories feature prominently among his efforts to escape from the real world. Similarly, Ann Veronica's first escape to a rented room in London is purely negative; she is technically free from her father's restrictions, but has no immediate purpose for which to use her freedom; hence she drifts into unworthy causes and situations dangerous to her integrity until she finds her real (in Wells's terms, 'biological') purpose, whereupon her freedom assumes its full meaning and validity.

In *Kipps*, *Ann Veronica* and *Mr. Polly* this lesson is somewhat blurred, for the exuberance of the first escape scenes – Kipps's 'night out', Ann's stormy defiance of her father and Polly's experiment in arson – tends in each case to outweigh the more subdued endings, certainly in dramatic effect and perhaps also in literary merit. But in *Love and Mr. Lewisham* and in *Tono-Bungay* the moral is firmly stressed that a seeming escape may be only a delusion and hence false – merely escapism. Wells had portrayed this, with the starkness of allegory, in *The Invisible Man*. Griffin, having achieved invisibility, the goal of his research, experiences an intense elation almost tantamount to a religious rebirth as he triumphantly sets fire to his lodgings and hastens into the city. In this real world, however, the limitations of physical circumstances press upon him and show that his freedom is illusory. Ultimately his own insane paranoia forces the issue, and death is the inevitable result of his own originally free choice.

In *Love and Mr. Lewisham* and in *Tono-Bungay* the lesson is more subtly expressed, as befits a realistic novel, but it is present none the less. Lewisham's detailed 'schema' for his life is a grandiose plan to escape from the circumstances of his birth, but it is destined to fail for two reasons: it takes no account of Lewisham's actual abilities and it is basically irresponsible since it is aimed primarily at the glorification of self rather than service to society. Hence this way of escape eludes Lewisham; he feels repeatedly baulked by external circumstances although it is clear to the reader that these spring largely from his own deficiencies of character and the inappropriateness of his aims. His final escape is the only genuine one – escape from his own illusions about himself: 'This will be my work now. The other . . . it was just . . . vanity! Yes, it was vanity. . . . A boy's vanity. For me – anyhow. I'm too two-sided. . . . Two-sided? Commonplace! Dreams like mine – abilities like mine. Yes – any man.'[10]

This sense of delusion is still more explicit in *Tono-Bungay*. Indeed, Uncle Ponderevo's whole life is a pageant of delusion – deception of others about the merits of his quack remedies, but also, more tragically, self-deception at every turn. His belief in his supposed financial genius which finally ruins him, belief in his newly acquired gentility which he expects to assume with his new top hat, even belief in his own patent products, belief that he is basically good at heart and had never intended to rob his nephew or make his wife wretched, belief in the power of wealth and ostentation to buy anything, belief in the permanence of his youth – all these crumble, one after another; but unlike Lewisham, Uncle Ponderevo is never enlightened. His whole life has become such an immense illusion that even at the end there is no possibility of self-realisation. George, after his uncle's death, muses on the essential unreality of the whole performance, on the escape that was only escapism:

> I felt as I sometimes feel after the end of a play. I saw the whole business of my Uncle's life as something familiar and completed. It was done, like a play one leaves, like a book one closes. . . . Before and after I have thought and called life a phantasmagoria, but never have I felt its truth as I did that night. . . . He had died a dream death, and ended a dream, his pain dream was over. It seemed to me almost as though I had died too. What did it matter, since it was unreality, all of it, the pain and the desire, the beginning and the end? There was no reality except this solitary road, this quite solitary road, along which one went rather puzzled, rather tired.[11]

Seen together, Lewisham and Edward Ponderevo exemplify the true and the false escape, the true and the false freedom of will. Lewisham is finally free, not because he escapes from material circumstances – indeed there is every indication that his life will continue to be a financial struggle – but because he comes to accept his own limitations and thereby transcends them, envisaging a new and different kind of fulfilment appropriate to his real capabilities. Edward Ponderevo, on the other hand, escapes for a time from penurious circumstances but his freedom is essentially spurious because it is not based on a valid assessment of his own abilities and external circumstances.

In Wells's work, these complementary concepts of freedom and predestination, escape and imprisonment are intimately related to his own oscillation between optimism and pessimism about the human predicament, an oscillation which has continued to perplex readers who demand a consistent viewpoint from him. Until recently it was customary to regard Wells as an exuberant optimist, busily planning man's glorious future development, to pass quickly over the difficult *Mind at the End of Its Tether*, and to ignore altogether the significance of the grim picture of terrestrial desolation in *The Time Machine*. However, Anthony West, extending his analysis of Wells's nominalism, has more recently asserted the extreme opposite:

> [Wells] was by nature a pessimist, and he was doing violence to his intuitions and his rational perceptions alike when he asserted in his middle period that mankind could make a better world for itself by an effort of will. . . . [His] progressive writing represents an attempt to straddle irreconcileable positions, and it involved a perpetual conflict of a wasteful character. In all too much of his work he is engaged in shouting down his own better judgment.[12]

Bergonzi too sees Wells in the tradition of *fin de siècle* malaise, preoccupied with an end-of-the-world myth and strongly influenced by Max Nordau's *Degeneration*.[13]

These attempts to demonstrate Wells's innate pessimism about human nature, about contemporary society, and indeed about the entire universe, contain an element of truth which needed stressing. The generation after Wells's death had tended to dismiss him as a shallow late-Victorian liberal, a devotee of progress, who refused to see the evils so manifestly present in the world; but the contrary view has also been falsely exaggerated by those who have attempted to make Wells intellectually respectable to a generation for whom anything approaching optimism is usually regarded as gross superficiality, and a preoccupation with existential *Angst* the only criterion of profundity. Thus West and Bergonzi regard the *fin du globe* scenes of *The Time Machine* as amongst the few genuine expressions of the Wellsian disposition. It should, however, be remembered that the first version of *The Time Machine* contained no such sequence (which indeed ill accords with the Time Traveller's original enthusiastic vitality).[14] Wells's vivid evocation of the dying world is less the involuntary product of a mind obsessed with morbid fantasies, than an example of the usual relish with which he extrapolated from known scientific data to expound an entirely credible picture of future conditions.[15]

Wells's increasing optimism during his middle period about the future of technology, the emergence of a world state and improvement in the quality of life was symptomatic of his changing attitude to the universe in general and, like much in his philosophy, has a basis in his personal experience. It was when his success as an author brought concomitant financial security and social status and thus freedom from the imprisoning circumstances of his own early years, that an escape motif emerged explicitly in his work and a corresponding optimism became dominant. This is less the result of a determination to suppress his 'own better judgment', than a further example of Wells's self-preoccupation – the reflection in his work of a natural exuberance at his sudden accession to wealth and position. In 1911, he himself described the way in which literary success had changed his outlook and circumstances by providing a passport to social flexibility:

> The literary life is one of the modern forms of adventure. Success with a book, even such a commercially modest success as mine has been, means in the English-speaking world not merely a moderate financial independence, but the utmost freedom of movement and intercourse. One is lifted out of one's narrow circumstances into familiar and unrestrained intercourse with a great variety of people. One sees the world.[16]

The terms used here – 'adventure', 'freedom', 'narrow circumstances', 'the world' – would seem to imply that this is the personal counterpart and, I suspect, a major cause of a recurrent theme in his work – the need to transcend given conditions in order to attain to freedom of self.

At first this urge to overcome limitations was expressed in mechanical terms – the surmounting of physical boundaries of time and space constitutes one of the central themes of the early scientific romances – and only later did Wells come to see it as a universal longing, equally applicable to the psychological and sociological novel. Besides the 'small souls' discussed above, who almost unwittingly break loose from a life of rigid forms, there are the would-be heroic figures, Griffin and Moreau, who deliberately set out to defy the limitations of nature, and those who, like the characters of 'The Door in the Wall', 'The Beautiful Suit' and *The*

Sea Lady, seek to escape to a beauty beyond the world of everyday existence. Also in this company of freedom-seekers are the social reformers, consciously detaching themselves from the comfortable niche society has assigned them, and trying to awaken their contemporaries to a higher sense of social purpose. In all these cases the decision as to whether the escape is realistic and feasible, that is, endorsed by the author, depends on the same criterion as that applied to Lewisham, Kipps and Polly: namely, whether the desire for escape is based on genuine self-knowledge and acceptance of the inevitable limitations of human and individual nature or whether it is fundamentally escapist and ignores these limitations.

So too, once Wells had attained a position of literary eminence, it became feasible for him to plan his future in a way which would have been unrealistic before. His autobiography vividly describes the realisation, almost the revelation, that he was now in a position to build a house, to have a family and to expect things from life.[17] *Anticipations*, the utopian novels and *The Open Conspiracy* are an extension of this realisation made respectable by its application to the data of biology and sociology.

Later still, at the end of the thirties, when Wells's optimism began to decline, there is again an autobiographical factor involved: his own failing health. In *The Fate of Homo Sapiens*, in the chapter entitled 'Estimating Hope', he writes:

> It is well to remind the reader that though all that follows is written as objectively and truly as I can, it is overshadowed by . . . misadventures of my generation and mental type. . . . A consideration he must bear in mind in weighing what I am putting before him is the possibility that there is a kind of egotistical intolerance in every definitely elderly mind. That is almost inevitable.[18]

If these related themes of escape from limitations and the confident prediction of the future have their roots in Wells's own personal experiences, they are certainly also consistent with Huxley's reading of evolutionary theory; for if Huxley's belief in the inevitability of mechanical laws operating in natural selection led to his assertion of an automatist biology and resulted in his 'cosmic pessimism', his stress on the possibility and indeed the necessity for man to militate against these laws, at least in the moral sphere, presupposed an equally powerful optimism.

It would seem, then, that Wells's own career and his understanding of biology combined to produce in him a strong core of optimism which might be expected to falter under severe opposition, but which nevertheless remained the basis of his views on the nature of man and society. This optimism is not a facile one; he never at any stage believed that the outcome, either for man the individual or for man the species, would *inevitably* be favourable. The possibility existed for man to achieve freedom and fulfilment, but these would never be won without struggle and effort; they were no automatic birthright to be thrust into languid hands.

The large number of pamphlets and books which Wells produced cajoling and inciting men to instigate social reforms, improved education systems and world understanding, would be inexplicable had he held either a pessimistic view of man or an optimistic necessitarianism, for his work explicitly presupposes the value of effort and struggle in producing a new society. Kagarlitsky holds that

. . . the aspect of the future which appealed most to Wells was its capacity to illuminate the present. His science fiction novels were primarily satirical and in them everything of the present is seen as from the perspective of the future.[19]

There are certainly elements of truth in this contention, and especially in Kagarlitsky's assertion that Wells showed, as no one else had done, that only the future could adequately judge the present. But the spate of novels and articles which Wells later produced detailing the plans for an 'open conspiracy' throws retrospective light on the utopian novels and indicates an alternative view – namely that the imperfections of the present drove him to devise a better system for the future in the hope that man might reform first himself and then his world.

Such a hope does not necessarily preclude despair. Man is free to strive for a better society, but he is equally free to ignore the challenge and to decline to make any such effort. He is thus free to bring about his own extinction, either through ignorance of the issues involved or by choosing to retain the evils of the present system. This is the choice presented starkly in *The Fate of Homo Sapiens*:

If *Homo sapiens* is such a fool that he cannot realize what is before

him now and set himself urgently to save the situation while there
is still some light, some freedom of thought and speech, some
freedom of movement and action left in the world, can there be
the slightest hope that in fifty or a hundred years hence, . . . he
will be collectively any less of a fool. . . . In spite of all my
disposition to a brave-looking optimism, I perceive that now the
universe is bored with him, is turning a hard face to him, and I see
him being carried less and less intelligently, and more and more
rapidly, suffering as every ill-adapted creature must suffer in gross
and detail, along the stream of fate to degradation, suffering and
death. . . . Adapt or perish, has always been the implacable law
of life for all its children.[20]

Chapter 71 of *A Short History of the World*, as revised for the 1945
edition, was entitled 'From 1940 to 1944. Mind at the End of its
Tether'. Section i of this chapter describes the course of the Second
World War in 1940 and 1941, while sections ii to viii give a
recapitulation of biological evolution, presenting the same
alternatives – adapt or perish. These sections were re-used in a
slightly expanded form, as Chapters 4 to 8 of *Mind at the End of its
Tether*, concluding with the hope that the descendants of *Homo
sapiens* will in fact have adapted sufficiently to continue their
evolutionary dominance. Yet the tone of the first half of *Mind at the
End of its Tether* is utterly inconsistent with any such hope, for it
states categorically that a new element has entered into the history
of the universe and that the world is rapidly approaching an end
from which no escape is possible, thereby rendering any effort by
mankind useless. Wells claims that this is not, as one might expect,
the consequence of man's failure to educate himself and to reform
his base and selfish progress; rather it is because '. . . a frightful
queerness has come into life. . . . This new cold glare mocks and
dazzles the human intelligence. . . . There is no way out or round or
through the impasse'.[21] That is, the new element is not the result of
anything man has done or failed to do; nor can it be prevented. This
is determinist philosophy at its most uncompromising and it is
entirely alien to all that Wells had hitherto been promulgating,
since it precludes any call for responsible judgment or action. In this
it differs not only from the utopian writings of Wells's middle years,
but also from the early scientific romances, even those which
portray the overthrow of mankind, for there the disasters are seen as
emanating from man's own stupidity.

It would seem, then, that in the whole sequence of Wells's thought, the single anomalous section is the pessimistic opening of *Mind at the End of its Tether*, and not the optimistic period of the utopias which involved his major output, and which were intimately linked with his earlier work. Indeed, the very inconsistency inherent in *Mind at the End of its Tether*, between the pessimism of the first section and the recapitulation of hope in the second half, constitutes a strong argument against attributing too much weight to this final work, and should certainly counsel against accepting it as a negation of the whole corpus of Wells's previous work. In this connection it should also be remembered that on Wells's desk at the time of his writing *Mind at the End of its Tether*, and in a similar state of incompleteness at his death, was the fundamentally optimistic work, I came to a *Happy Turning*, which reaffirms his hope for mankind. This must be read as further evidence against the view that the pessimism of the last book is an indication of a latent, deterministic despair throughout Wells's work. Perhaps, after all, the best 'explanation' is that of Wells himself, as voiced in *The World Set Free* thirty-one years earlier. In this novel Marcus Karenin, one of the inspirational figures of the new world-state, about to die in hospital, warns his secretary not to remember his last hours which may be rent by pain or numbed by anaesthetic:

I do not see why life should be judged by its last trailing thread of vitality . . . I know it for the splendid thing it is . . . I know it well enough not to confuse it with its husks. Remember that, Gardener, if presently my heart fails me and I despair, and if I go through a little phase of pain and ingratitude and dark forgetfulness before the end. Don't believe what I may say at the last. If the fabric is good enough, the selvage doesn't matter. It can't matter. So long as you are alive, you are just the moment, perhaps, but when you are dead then you are all your life from the first moment to the last.[22]

It would seem then that Wells contrived to maintain two apparently contrary sets of propositions and, by showing the fundamental relation between them, to attain more closely to a basic truth than would have been possible through a rigorous devotion to either one alone. He holds that, although determinism may operate on the cosmic scale, nevertheless, at the level of human behaviour we must and should act as though we were free; he also holds that at the minute particle level, while each entity is in fact unique, we must and should reason as though it were possible to classify and group similar entities for the purpose of making causal predictions about them.

Thus Wells does not despair of finding order and causality in the universe nor does he deduce that intelligence can have no function in the cosmos because matter is essentially chaotic. Had he done so, it would indeed have been feasible to conclude that his position was conducive only to despair – the despair voiced in *Mind at the End of its Tether*. But, on the contrary, he derived from his innate belief in the uniqueness of every entity a mysticism which provided him with a faith and a hope for mankind, and one which he thought he could reconcile with the principles of science and rationality.

7 Science as Myth and Mysticism

Samuel Butler, who commenced writing from a Darwinian position, fully aware of current mechanistic interpretations of the universe, came eventually to adopt a vitalistic position bordering on mysticism, whereby he renounced '. . . the present mindless, mechanical, materialistic view of nature . . . to insist on the presence of a mind and intelligence throughout the universe to which no name can so fittingly be applied as God'.[1]

Ironically Wells, who began by espousing the scientific method even more rigorously than Butler, also came finally to propound the concept of a 'mind of the race' which was comparable to Butler's 'race memory' and, like this latter, essentially mystical. A similar development is observable in the work of Aldous Huxley and leads to interesting speculations upon the effect scientific enquiry may have on the mind which attempts to combine it with literary expression.

It is well to note here that this strand of mysticism in Wells's work arises directly from his scientific thought and has no connection with his so-called 'religious' phase during the First World War, a phase which has already been well documented in relation to *Mr. Britling Sees it Through* and *God, The Invisible King*[2] and which will not be discussed here since its relevance to his scientific background is minimal. It is perhaps significant that Wells himself later regarded this religious period as 'a falling back of the mind towards immaturity, under the stress of dismay and anxiety',[3] while he never disavowed his belief in a 'mind of the race'.

Two major and closely related aspects of Wells's mystical thought are relevant here. One is the teleological element whereby he came increasingly to believe in a guiding Mind and Purpose active in the affairs of mankind and directing men's lives towards a greater and more fulfilling development. The second, which is actually a development of this, is his concept of a Mind of the Race in which individual aims and wills become submerged for the greater glory and development of the species *Homo sapiens*. It is best to trace the emergence of these two strands of thought before attempting some assessment of their scientific validity.

In Wells's early work there is no evidence of any belief in a mystical element in the universe although there is the necessary prerequisite for this, namely the affirmation of a sense of mystery and unpredictability at the centre of all things. But there is certainly at this stage, no clear assertion of a guiding purpose, such as was associated with orthodox christian theology or with Lamarckism. The germinal idea for the increasingly teleological trend of his thought seems to have come, like so many of Wells's beliefs, from Huxley, whose stress on the concept of an 'Ethical Process' as running counter to the amoral process of biological evolution, and, ideally, inspiring men to a new directing role in evolution, had so strong an influence on Wells. The whole body of his utopian thought, for example, presupposes the value of purpose and moral effort. Indeed Wells implicitly associates the evolution both of his ideal individuals and of his ideal society with a teleological principle. His 'Modern Utopia' is confessedly the result of 'a great and steadfast movement of will', for 'Will is stronger than Fact, and it can mould and overcome Fact'.[4]

Thus, contrary to his original intentions, and probably without his perceiving it, Wells through his vacillation between the fatalistic 'chance' of Darwin's scheme and a native teleological optimism, seemed to arrive at a belief in a creative will almost indistinguishable from the teleological message of those Lamarckists like Butler and Shaw, who preached a vision of life as purpose, will and effort.

In *The Science of Life* Wells firmly asserts the Darwinian view that any apparent purpose in evolution is an illusion, that 'Life . . . is not the arbiter of its own destiny',[5] yet the whole imaginative and moral basis of the utopias resides in the contrary view – namely that in man at least there is a purpose, a will and a power to strive for a 'better' life.

This apparent anomaly however does not necessarily involve a negation of Wells's biological training. He makes no claims for any teleological evolution in the past, as Lamarck had done, but only urges a moral purpose as the incentive for the future – as Huxley had done before him. We have seen that Wells was already fully aware of the two fundamentally different kinds of evolution, biological and cultural, and of their diverse characteristics. There is ample scope for ethical purpose and drive in cultural evolution, which became operative with the advent of man on the biological scene, and thus Wells's emphasis on the need for a purposeful development of society, and for a moral and intellectual evolution of mankind in the future, does not necessarily entail a tacit capitulation to Lamarckism. His position is not dissimilar to that expressed by the eminent twentieth-century biologist, Julian Huxley:

> In the light of evolutionary biology, man can now see himself as the sole agent of further evolutionary advance on this planet, and as one of the few possible instruments of progress in the universe at large. He finds himself in the unexpected position of business manager for the comic process of evolution. He no longer ought to feel separated from the rest of nature, for he is part of it – the part which has become conscious, capable of love and understanding and aspiration. He need no longer regard himself as insignificant in relation to the cosmos.[6]

It is interesting that Julian Huxley stresses, as a necessary part of man's purposeful role in evolution, the fact that he 'no longer ought to feel separated from the rest of nature, for he is a part of it . . .', for like much mystical thought, Wells's concept of a Mind of the Race implies a sense of man's oneness with the universe at large, or at least with a significant part of it. Yet by temperament and upbringing he began his career as an individualist, and the effect of his scientific training was at first merely to reinforce this attitude by encouraging him to justify his belief in individualism as scientifically as possible. The scientific romances are, almost without exception, stories about individuals, often glorifying the exceptional skill or daring of a single man. The Time Traveller, Moreau and Griffin are the prototypes but there are many other lesser figures who distinguish themselves by endeavouring more or less successfully to escape the limitations imposed upon ordinary men and women. The early novels are a continuation of this attitude – Lewisham embarks on a solitary quest while *Kipps, Ann Veronica* and *Mr. Polly* are fundamentally stories of individuals set in relief against the background of their uncomprehending society.

Of the non-fictional works in this period, *Anticipations*, also, is still basically individualist in outlook, still couched in the traditional nineteenth-century terms of personal struggle in a *laissez-faire* society, with the added dimension of a personal biological survival –

defined as the largest number of offspring who can be reared in
health and well educated. The typical New Republican is described
as being

> . . . a father of several children, I think, because his scientific
> mental basis will incline him to see the whole of life as a struggle to
> survive; he will recognize that a childless, sterile life, however
> pleasant, is essentially failure and perversion, and he will
> conceive his honour involved in the possession of offspring.[7]

The stress on a more community-based and correspondingly less
individualistic attitude seems to have arisen concurrently with
Wells's interest in the Fabians' programme for social reform. In *New
Worlds for Old*, one of his several efforts to promulgate socialist ideals,
he envisages 'The Mind of the Civilized State', a bank of ideas to
which all citizens would contribute and to which they would then
voluntarily subdue their own individualistic and short-term aims.[8]
It would seem to have been chiefly from this 'Mind of the Civilized
State' concept that Wells evolved his more mystical 'Mind of the
Race' theory. An idea which began as a practical and definable
programme – the organisation of the existing body of knowledge –
gradually swelled to assume for him almost limitless proportions
while Wells, quite unjustifiably, continued to attribute to it
virtually the same substance and feasibility as had attached to his
original social programme. It is the fallacy of misplaced concreteness on a grand scale.

There is also perhaps a subsidiary factor involved in the evolution
of the Mind of the Race concept, namely the extension of one of
Wells's favourite analogies – that of the insect community.
Numerous references are made throughout the scientific romances
as well as in *The Sleeper* and *The First Men in the Moon* to insect
communities as being parallel to human societies. At least two of the
short stories, 'The Empire of the Ants' and 'The Valley of the
Spiders', describe the defeat of human civilisation by an insect
species which is more fitted to survive because it practises cooperation and thus presents a united front unlike the sporadic efforts of
self-seeking, individualistic humans. Nor can it have been by
chance that the Selenites, allegedly more advanced on the evolutionary scale than man, are organised on lines closely resembling a
bee community. As Cavor (who, significantly, is kept by the
Selenites in a hexagonal cell) reports with approval: 'All sorts and

conditions of Selenites – each is a perfect unit in a world machine. . . . Every one of these common Selenites is exquisitely adapted to the social need it meets'.[9] It is relatively easy for the unwary thinker to regard the purely instinctive behaviour of insect communities as the direct analogue of human altruism and then by assuming that the latter also is instinctive, attribute an innate biological urge towards perfection, a 'Mind of the Race', to mankind. Wells nowhere draws such an analogy explicitly but it would seem there is sufficient evidence to suggest that this, or a similar consideration, may have been a contributory factor in the development of his 'Mind of the Race' concept.

Whatever the actual precedents it is surely not accidental that *First and Last Things*, the book in which Wells first confessed explicitly to a sense of mysticism, was also the place where he first fully expounded his belief in a sense of community embracing all mankind, perhaps the whole of life. There could scarcely be a more thoroughgoing expression of mysticism, and it is characteristic of such a position that no real attempt is made to justify or explain what is ultimately an intimate and personal conviction. Wells merely states it categorically as a fact of his own experience that

> . . . at times I admit the sense of personality in the universe is very strong. If I am confessing, I do not see why I should not confess up to the hilt. At times, in the silence of the night and in rare lonely moments, I come upon a sort of communion of myself and something great that is not myself. It is perhaps poverty of mind and language that obliges me to say that then this universal scheme takes on the effect of a sympathetic person – and my communion of a fearless worship. These moments happen, and they are the supreme fact in my religious life to me, they are the crown of my religious experiences.[10]

No overt correlation is drawn here between this confession and his assertion of a 'Being of Mankind' but the relation between the two seems to be not merely arbitrary, for the second is also described as a religious tenet encountered under the same conditions of immediate personal awareness, rather than derived by any logical process of thought. Wells expresses it in explicitly religious terms.

> I will boldly adopt the technicalities of the sects . . . and declare that I have been through the stresses of despair, and the

conviction of sin, and that I have found salvation.

I believe in the scheme, in the Project of all things, in the significance of myself and all life. . . .

The essential fact in man's history to my sense is the slow unfolding of a sense of community with his kind . . . between us and the rest of mankind there is *something*, something real, something that rises through us and is neither you or me, that comprehends us, and that is thinking and using me and you to play against each other.[11]

In the preface to the 1914 edition of *Anticipations* Wells again attempted to clarify his expression of this mystical awareness, which he here designated the 'Collective Mind':

I saw then [i.e. during the period in the Fabian Society] what hitherto I had merely felt, – that there was in the affairs of mankind something unorganized which is greater than any organization. This unorganized power is the ultimate Sovereign in the world. . . . It is something transcending persons just as physical or biological science or mathematics transcends persons. . . . This Collective Mind is essentially an extension of the spirit of science to all human affairs, its method is to seek and speak and serve the truth and to subordinate oneself to one's conception of a general purpose.[12]

To compensate for the vagueness of such a concept, Wells tried to adduce more tangible biological evidence by demonstrating the common ancestry of all men. *First and Last Things* expounds in considerable and somewhat tedious detail the commonness of our genetic inheritance:

Disregarding the chances of intermarriage, each one of us has two parents, four grandparents, eight great-grandparents, and so on backwards, until very soon, in less than fifty generations, we should find that but for the qualification introduced we should have all the earth's inhabitants of that time as our progenitors. For a hundred generations it must hold absolutely true; everyone of that time who has issue living now is ancestral to all of us.[13]

So too, in the future, 'in less than fifty generations . . . all the population of the world will have my blood',[14] and this future mixing of the hereditary pool, as much as common ancestry, unites each individual in a continuing stream of being:

> It is not the individual that reproduces itself, it is the species that reproduces through the individual and often in spite of his characteristics. The race flows through us, the race is the drama and we are the incidents. . . . Insofar as we are individuals, insofar as we seek to follow merely individual ends, we are accidental, disconnected, without significance, the sport of chance. Insofar as we realize ourselves as experiments of the species for the species, just insofar do we escape from the accidental and the chaotic. We are episodes in an experience greater than ourselves. . . . We signify as parts of a universal and immortal development.[15]

This passage attempts to interweave a would-be scientific rationale with a mystical philosophy, not only in its thought but also in the language used. Its mystical content is apparent in the stress on the nothingness of the individual except in the purpose of another higher being. Wells explicitly reiterates the paradoxical assertion of the mystics that they, like every entity, are simultaneously of no account and of infinite importance in the universe. Yet the phrases 'accidental . . . sport of chance', 'the accidental and the chaotic', are as reminiscent of Darwinian phraseology as of mystical philosophy, while the metaphor, 'experiments of the species for the species', appears to provide a credible, and at first reading a suitably biological, prelude for the groundless assertion of 'a universal and immortal development'. In his endeavour to justify his position scientifically, Wells repeatedly uses such phrases as, 'Let me point out that this is no sentimental or mystical statement. It is hard fact as any hard fact we know . . .' and 'While I am being thus biological . . .' and even 'This is not any sort of poetical statement, it is a statement of fact'.[16] The attempted biological basis becomes most tenuous in the discussion of personal immortality, for here Wells seems to reason that because mankind is identifiable biologically, as one species, therefore the individual personality is necessarily also part of a group consciousness. In his descriptions of this alleged stream of personality his language becomes increasingly mystical:

> . . . I believe in the great and growing being of the species, from which I rise, to which I return, and which, it may be, will

ultimately even transcend the limitation of the species and grow into the conscious Being of all things. . . . . What the scheme as a whole is I do not clearly know; with my limited mind I cannot know. There I become a Mystic.[17]

Even his programme for the socio-political 'Open Conspiracy' includes as one of its seven articles of faith the assertion that 'our immortality is conditional and lies in the race, not in our individual selves'.[18]

For the next decades the theme on which Wells was to concentrate most of his literary energies was this belief that individuals and particularly states and nations were essentially, if not entirely, subsidiary to the continuing stream of the race. This is the basis of his utopias and political novels; it is the justification for his theory of morality and social conscience, and even underlies his determination to write a history of the world which should be as free as possible of any national bias, and hence acceptable everywhere as a common textbook. The following affirmation from *First and Last Things* might adequately serve as the text for most of his work for the next thirty-four years:

> Our individualities, our nations and states and races are but bubbles, clusters of foam upon the great stream of the blood of the species, individual experiments in the growing consciousness of the race.[19]

In *The World Set Free* there is, side by side with the emphasis on science, an affirmation of a mystical element in life. Karenin, discussing the novelists of the new era, comments:

> Our later novelists give a vast gallery of individual conflicts in which old habits, and customs, limited ideas, ungenerous temperaments and innate obsessions are pitted against this great opening out of life that has happened to us. . . . The clearer their vision and the subtler their art, the more certainly do these novelists tell of the possibility of salvation for all the world. For any road in life leads to religion for those upon it who will follow if far enough.[20]

A few pages later, Karenin explicitly associates this attitude with the Mind of the Race and further identifies it with the concept of science in the abstract; again the relation is simply asserted without any attempt at justification.[21] In this novel, too, the characteristic ending recurs, when Karenin, dying in body but not in spirit, cries defiantly:

> 'And you, old Sun . . . beware of me . . . I shall launch myself at you and I shall reach you and I shall put my foot on your spotted face and tug you about by your fiery locks. One step I shall take to the moon, and then I shall leap at you . . . Old Sun, I gather myself together out of the pools of the individual that have held me dispersed so long. I gather my billion thoughts into science and my million wills into a common purpose'.[22]

Once again the feasibility of a body of common knowledge – 'gather my billion thoughts into science' – is taken to justify, by extension, the assertion of a common will in some undefined but supposedly concrete sense – 'my million wills into a common purpose'.

A year later, in *Boon*, Wells returned to another justification of the Mind of the Race. Here again he merely states, as though it were axiomatic, that this Mind of the Race *does* exist and *will* merge with a mystic god-mind; he cannot justify his belief. But there is an interesting variation in this novel. Wilkins and Boon are both identifiable with facets of Wells's own personality, Wilkins representing the rigorously disciplined, intellectual mind which Wells wanted to be, while Boon is closer to Wells the creative dreamer and myth-maker. It is significant that Wilkins's scepticism about the idea is never finally answered by Boon. Wilkins says:

> 'I want to suggest that the Mind of the Race may be just a gleam of conscious realization that passes from darkness to darkness.'
> '*No*,' said Boon.
> 'Why not?'
> 'Because I will not have it so,' said Boon.[23]

Thus, ironically, the view of man which Wells had derived from Huxley and evolutionary theory, led him finally to his least scientific and most mystical extremes of thought.

In *The Dream* Wells succeeded in using his principle of a continuing consciousness within which all individual experiences are subsumed, as an integral part of the narrative fabric, and this permits a discussion of some interesting extensions of the theory. Sarnac, from a civilisation some two thousand years in advance of Wells's own, relates a dream in which he lived through the experiences of Harry Mortimer Smith, an individual of the early twentieth century. Harry's first wife, Hetty, is seen as a prefiguration of Sunray, Sarnac's own chosen companion, and in the epilogue Sarnac and his audience discuss the implications of this similarity:

> 'It was very dreamlike, the way Hetty grew more and more like this dear lady, and at last dissolved altogether into her.' . . .
> 'That tale,' said the guest-master stoutly, 'was no dream. It was a memory floating up out of the deep darkness of forgotten things into a living brain – a kindred brain.'
> Sarnac thought, 'What is a personality but a memory? If the memory of Harry Mortimer Smith is in my brain, then I am Smith.' . . .
> 'When children have dreams of terror, of being in the wild with prowling beasts, of long pursuits and hairbreadth escapes, perhaps it is the memory of some dead creature that lives again in them? . . . Maybe life from its very beginning has been spinning threads and webs of memories. Not a thing in the past, it may be, that has not left its memories about us . . . I can well believe, without any miracles, that Sarnac has touched down to the real memory of a human life that lived and suffered two thousand years ago.'
> '. . . in everything he said and did, even in his harshest and hardest acts, Smith and Sarnac were one character. I do not question for a moment that Sarnac lived that life.'[24]

In *William Clissold* Wells tried again with doubtful success to expound his philosophical beliefs through his protagonist. Reviewing the novel, D. H. Lawrence remarked:

> What has got him [William Clissold] into such a state is a problem, unless it is his insistence on the Universal Mind, which he, of course, exemplifies. The emotions are to him irritating aberrations. Yet even he admits that even thought must be preceded by some obscure physical happenings, some kind of confused sensation of emotion which is the necessary coarse body

of thought, and from which thought, living thought, arises or sublimates.

This being so, we wonder that he insists on the Universal or racial *mind* of man as the only hope of salvation.[25]

Lawrence is of course partially justified in accusing Wells of excessive intellectualism; it is arguable that a preoccupation with rationalistic science had dulled his aesthetic and emotional senses, just as long concentration on biology had atrophied Darwin's early appreciation of poetry.[26] But Lawrence has misunderstood Wells's meaning of 'Mind', and has assumed it to be associated with that sterile intellectualism of which he was the implacable enemy, whereas Wells used the phrase 'Mind of the Race' to include not only the intellect, but art and consciousness as well – all the facets of life embraced by such a term as 'civilisation'.[27]

Even in *The Science of Life*, written in conjunction with Julian Huxley and G. P. Wells, Wells continued to promulgate a mystical approach to biology by preaching the submergence of the individual within the species. Here, as would seem appropriate, he asserts that his view can be biologically justified, though he does not actually give any reasons for this claim. Discussing the means whereby man has endeavoured to reconcile himself to the certainty of his death as an individual, Wells first dismisses any belief in a personal immortality and then turns to an elaboration of his concept of a mind of the race as the alternative and superior form of immortality:

> It is remarkable how closely the biological analogy of individuality brings us to the mystics. The individual, according to this second line of thought, saves himself by losing himself. But in the mystical teaching he loses himself in the Deity, and in the scientific interpretation of life he forgets himself as Tom, Dick or Harry, and discovers himself as Man. . . . Western mystic, and Eastern Sage find a strong effect of endorsement in modern science and in the everyday teaching of practical morality. Both teach that self must be subordinated; that self is a method and not an end.[28]

The following year in the companion volume, *The Work, Wealth and Happiness of Mankind*, Wells again stated in somewhat extravagant terms the possibility that mysticism was at least not inconsistent with a scientific approach,[29] but his most explicit attempt to correlate his search for the Mind of the Race with mystical religious experience occurs at the end of his *Experiment in Autobiography*. Here he not only classifies together the widest range of beliefs, from his own Open Conspiracy and positivist science to the mysticism of Christianity, Islam and Buddhism but at the same time elucidates the fundamental differences between them in an effort to demonstrate the intellectual respectability of his apparently mystical approach, by comparing it with modern materialistic modes of thought.[30] In the essay 'Religion and Science' Wells again specifically associates the scientist with a religious pursuit:

> The scientific worker, whatever his upbringing may have been and whatever sectarian labels he may still be wearing, does in fact believe in Truth – which is his God – in a God who is first and foremost Truth and mental courage. His life business is unfolding the divinity in things, and the real conflict is between the Truth as he unfolds it and the priests and exploiters of the false Gods who still dominate most men's lives.[31]

The fictional advocates of this assertion are Trafford and George Ponderevo, who also explicitly identifies science with truth: 'Sometimes I call this reality Science, sometimes I call it Truth'.[32]

Even in his doctoral thesis Wells seemed determined to expound his belief in the need for the individual to subdue his own immediate and personal aims to the ongoing development of the race. In a scientific thesis it was obviously necessary that such a concept should not merely be affirmed, but that the maximum amount of biological proof should be adduced in its support. Again he returns to the point that the differences between men of different races are slight when set against the background of evolutionary development, and argues that since all races are capable of interbreeding the unit is, by definition, *Homo sapiens*.

> The integrality of the human individual is illusory and does not sweep aside the continuity from life. The individual belongs to his species. . . . The biological reality is that while he can interbreed with every variety of human being, he goes on as a unit in the whole species and, whatever frame of community he adopts, it can, from the eschatological point of view, have no narrower

boundary than the species. Every individual is in the nature of an experiment.[33]

As evidence for his assertions, this marks little advance on the would-be biological 'proofs' cited thirty-four years earlier in *First and Last Things*, and its scientific merit is negligible.

It would seem then, that Wells's belief in a Mind of the Race arose as an extension of his proposal for a 'mind of the civilised state', itself, in turn, an expression of his socialist desire for a wider community awareness; and that the concept of the Mind of the Race began to assume, in his thinking, a concreteness which rational argument and logical deduction could not justify. This process of ascribing concreteness to an idea because it has been given a name is reflected in the way he expressed his beliefs in the novels. So far we have considered chiefly his non-fictional assertions of a Mind of the Race, but a parallel development can be seen in the imagery in which he clothed his metaphysical beliefs.

In the scientific romances the imagery suggestive of a mystical element of experience is minimal. The nearest approach to it is the recurrence of star imagery to suggest remoteness and idealism, and of escape imagery to suggest a mental and sometimes spiritual release from the bonds of custom and social circumstances.

In Wells's first full-length novel, *Love and Mr. Lewisham*, the suggestion of a more metaphysical level of experience, transcending the individual's own personal sphere, is introduced only at the conclusion of the novel and its expression, as befits Lewisham's character, is vague and inarticulate. Reflecting upon his aborted scientific career, and upon his child-to-be, he muses: 'Come to think, it is all the Child. The Future is the Child. The Future. What are we – any of us – but servants or traitors to that?'[34] Here 'the Future' is a vague term, apparently intended to convey the amorphous entity which Wells was later to designate as the Mind of the Race, but at this stage the vagueness was almost certainly Wells's as well as Lewisham's.

In *The Food of the Gods*, written four years later, the mystic ongoing force has become identified with 'growth', of which the whole story is a parable. At the end of the novel young Cossar addresses the other Giant children in these terms:

'Tomorrow, whether we live or die, the growth will conquer through us. That is the law of the spirit for evermore. To grow according to the Will of God! . . . Greater . . . greater, my Brothers! . . . growing. . . . Till the earth is no more than a footstool. . . .' For one instant he shone, looking up fearlessly into the starry deeps. . . . Then the light had passed and he was no more than a great black outline against the starry sky, a great black outline that threatened with one mighty gesture the firmament of heaven and all its multitude of stars.[35]

This passage shows the extent to which the star imagery of the early scientific romances has been extended to suggest a metaphysical element. Apparently the symbol appealed strongly to Wells for he repeated it almost verbatim several times, not only in the fictional works but also in the documentary works where it seems to have assumed, in Wells's mind, an objectivity equivalent to that of the more mundane facts surrounding it. Indeed he first used it in 'The Discovery of the Future', his lecture to the Royal Institution:

A day will come . . . when beings, beings who are now latent in our thoughts and hidden in our loins, shall stand upon this earth as one stands upon a footstool, and shall laugh and reach out their hands amidst the stars.[36]

Again, in *Marriage*, Trafford muses on his future in similar terms:

Logic and language, clumsy implements, but rising to our needs . . . thought clarified, enriched, reaching out to every man alive – some day – presently – touching every man alive, harmonizing acts and plans, drawing men into gigantic co-operations, tremendous co-operations. . . . Until man shall stand upon this earth as upon a footstool and reach out his hand among the stars.[37]

The image recurs, in almost the same words, at the conclusion of the 1920 edition of *The Outline of History*, which again relegates the Earth to a mere footstool and stresses the need to reach out toward the stars.[38] And again in *Man Like Gods* where, in Barnstaple's vision: 'The sons of Earth also, purified from disease, sweetminded and strong and beautiful, would go proudly about their conquered planet and lift their daring to the stars'.[39]

This imagery can be interpreted on two levels – the biological sense of continuity with future generations whose achievements will almost certainly include space-travel,[40] and a more mystical sense of some intrinsic life-force flowing through all generations of men (and indeed through the whole universe) to which they reach out their hands. Wells's plausibility depends on leading us to the second level of meaning through our acceptance of the first, this being, in all probability, the sequence of his own thinking.

If Wells's concept of the Mind of the Race was to be effective in his literary work, it was necessary that it should find valid expression not merely in flights of imagery, however vivid, but also in the characters in whom he chose to embody it, and here an apparent anomaly exists. Even those Wellsian heroes who are allegedly awakened to a sense of their potential fulfilment in the Mind of the Race remain, for the most part, staunch individualists standing apart from their fellows and regarding them with indifference if not contempt. Trafford, William Clissold, Benham and Remington are closer to traditional heroic figures, individualists to the core standing above and apart from their lesser contemporaries, than to Wells's theoretical men of the future who allegedly see themselves as part of the evolutionary stream.

This apparent contradiction is partly removed when it is recognised that one may in practice support individuals, as opposed to labelled movements, while offering allegiance to the ideals of mankind, as opposed to the limited aims of individuals. More importantly though, in Wells's view, is the fact that his individual characters who are aware of the wider vision must be seen as signposts pointing the way forward to the future evolution of mankind. They cannot, and should not, become submerged in the mass of average men, for the masses are yesterday's men, living in the chaotic past and ignorant of the possibilities of the future. Remington, Trafford, Karenin and the eventually enlightened Barnstaple, are the models for tomorrow's men. Every mutant in the history of evolution is an apparent misfit at the time of its first appearance, for it is produced by chance and not in answer to an environmental change; only later, under different conditions, may its progeny be selected as the spearhead of the evolutionary advance. These Wellsian heroes of the present have to struggle to maintain their vision in the face of their hostile environment. Only in the utopias of the future will the values they perceive and cherish be fully vindicated and accepted by all.

It remains to consider whether Wells's concept of a Mind of the

Race was in any sense a scientifically based one. It is customary to consider the early works as being the product of Wells's scientific thinking, and the later works as representing an abstrusely metaphysical, certainly an unscientific, aspect of his thought. We have already seen that in one sense at least the Mind of the Race concept is unscientific because it precludes experimental examination. It is a purely inductive line of thought, and Wells's few attempts to justify it biologically are at best unconvincing and at worst intellectually dishonest. However, there is another sense in which the Mind of the Race concept can indeed be considered as a scientific one. In defining the two divergent ways of thought involved in the scientific and the literary approach to experience Aldous Huxley comments:

> For Science in its totality, the ultimate goal is the creation of a monistic system in which – on the symbolic level and in terms of the inferred components of invisibly and intangibly fine structure – the world's enormous multiplicity is reduced to something like unity, and the endless succession of unique events of a great many different kinds gets tidied and simplified into a single rational order. . . . The man of letters, when he is being most distinctively literary, accepts the diversity and manifoldness of the world, accepts the radical incomprehensibility on its own level, of raw unconceptualized existence, and finally accepts the challenge which uniqueness, multifariousness and mystery fling in his face and, having accepted it, addresses himself to the paradoxical task of rendering the randomness and shapelessness of individual existence in highly organized and meaningful works of art.[41]

In this sense Wells's Mind of the Race theory tends towards the scientific rather than the literary end of the spectrum for characteristically he over-simplifies in the interests of bringing a single explanatory theory to bear upon the heterogeneous data of the senses. His Mind of the Race represents for him just such 'a monistic system in which . . . the world's enormous multiplicity is reduced to something like unity'.

Again, if his thought tends towards mysticism, this too is not necessarily unscientific. The physicist Heisenberg describes modern science in terms which are certainly not inconsistent with Wells's mysticism:

Modern science shows us that we can no longer regard the building blocks of matter, which were considered originally to be the ultimate objective reality, as being things 'in themselves'. . . . Knowledge of atoms and their movements 'in themselves', that is to say, independent of our observation, is no longer the aim of research; rather we now find ourselves from the very start in the midst of a dialogue between nature and man, a dialogue of which science is only one part, so much so that the conventional division of the world into subject and object, body and soul, is no longer applicable, and raises difficulties. For the scientist of nature, the subject matter of research is no longer nature in itself, but nature subjected to human questioning, and to this extent man once again meets only with himself.[42]

Part III
Science and the
Approach to Characterisation

8 Wells's Concept of the Individual

Before Wells embarked on the study of science he was already well acquainted with such diverse social settings as the unprofitable china-shop in Bromley, Up Park, the gracious home where his mother was housekeeper, two drapery shops and a chemist's shop, where he served aborted apprenticeships, and Midhurst Grammar School, where he spent a year as a student teacher. All these scenes were later to feature in the novels of his middle period, described with great vividness and peopled with vigorous life-like characters presumably modelled on Wells's former acquaintances. Yet such scenes and characters formed no part of his early writing.

The scientific romances, as we have seen, are concerned with character only as a secondary interest if at all, and indeed this was almost inevitable if they were to succeed in their purpose of focusing the reader's attention and interest on impersonal considerations. Edmund Crispin writes of science fiction in general that:

> The characters in a science fiction story are usually treated rather as representatives of their species than as individuals in their own right. They are matchstick men and matchstick women, for the reason that if they were not the anthropocentric habit of our culture would cause us, in reading, to give altogether too much attention to them and altogether too little to the non-human forces which constitute the important remainder of the *dramatis personae*.[1]

Wells apparently held a similar view. It therefore becomes relevant to ask whether his intervening years as a science student and the writing of scientific romances affected his perspective and attitudes when he came to reconsider his earlier acquaintances as the subject of fiction, or whether they are rendered with the freshness of a first impression.

One's immediate reaction is to assert that such characters as Hoopdriver, Kipps and Polly are untouched by the harsh light of scientific investigation, that they spring from the page, like Dickens's characters, with all the freshness of immediate obser- vation, and at least one critic has dwelt at length on the similarities between Wells's comic characters and those of Dickens.[2] However, closer analysis shows that there are several important ways in which Wells's approach to characterisation had been modified by his training in science. None of these is, in itself, unique to Wells's work, but seen together their cumulative effect indicates very strongly the scientific influence.

First and perhaps most noticeably there is the stationary attitude in which so many of his characters are presented – as though anaesthetised for dissection or frozen into tableaux. His habit of looking at the world as if through a microscope or through the art of the taxidermist has already been discussed in relation to a number of the scientific romances where the actual image of the microscope or telescope appears explicitly in the story. The same attitude often underlies the presentation of character even in stories where the explicit mention of such instruments would be out of place. Frequently his actors are introduced in a characteristic pose, like exhibits against their appropriate backgrounds. We move up to them and examine them from all sides, and are told the necessary supporting details about their family and background, while they themselves remain immobile. Uncle Ponderevo is seen in a whole series of such tableaux against backgrounds which suggest them- selves as correlatives of the hoardings proclaiming 'Tono-Bungay'. From his first appearance in grey carpet-slippers outside the ill- fated Wimblehurst shop, through the periods of silk top hats and increasing flabbiness, to his final demise, he is visualised on the grand scale. The frequent epithet of 'Napoleonic' is not accidental, for this little man strikes poses through every situation until the last. In the early stages of his acquired wealth he postures memorably in his first silk hat, so memorably that the chapter title records this detail – 'The Dawn Comes and My Uncle Appears in a New Silk Hat'. Later, as the financial assets accumulate still further, his progress is charted by changes in stance and gesture:

> There was, I seem to remember, a secular intensification of his features, his nose developed character, became aggressive, stuck out at the world more and more; the obliquity of his mouth I

think increased. From the face that returns to my memory projects a long cigar that is sometimes cocked jauntily up from the highest corner, that sometimes droops from the lower; it was as eloquent as a dog's tail, and he removed it only for the more emphatic modes of speech . . . he preferred silk hats with ample rich brims, often a trifle large for him by modern ideas, and he wore them at various angles to his axis.[3]

To the end, even after his uncle's death, George can still scarcely believe that the whole episode of Edward Ponderevo's life was anything more than a series of theatrical events. He records, 'I felt as I sometimes feel after the end of a play'.[4]

Love and Mr. Lewisham opens with the stage-setting of an attic study bedroom, a scene which is carefully planned and constructed to tell us a great deal about the essential Lewisham; indeed the novel is virtually a series of such settings appropriate to critical points of the protagonist's career and connected mainly by the continuing presence of Lewisham himself.

This manner of visualising characters as fundamentally static, spread like specimens awaiting examination, has its counterpart in the kinds of characters whom Wells chose to consider. Here he displays the bias of the scientific mind which is comparatively uninterested in the multifarious differences between human beings, and the uniqueness of individuals; he is interested, instead, in people as characteristic examples – examples of the laws of causality, or genetics, or sociology. Hence the majority of his character studies are unmistakeably average specimens of humanity, and Wells is at pains to stress their basic ordinariness, as though to guarantee the randomness of his sample and hence the validity of his conclusions about the human species. Hoopdriver, Lewisham, Kipps, Aunt Susan Ponderevo, Polly, Willie Leadford and his mother, and Britling, are all such unmistakeably 'little' people and even Uncle Ponderevo's apparently vivacious personality is shown to be a façade behind which the 'real' character is small and frightened, trying desperately to lose itself in escapist fantasies of its own importance. Bert Smallways's mediocrity is stressed several times, apart from his name. We are told that he

was a vulgar little creature, the sort of pert limited soul that the old civilization of the early twentieth century produced by the million in every country of the world. . . . It was as if Heaven was experimenting with him, had picked him out as a sample from the English millions to look at him more nearly and to see what was happening to the soul of man.[5]

Here Wells is doing precisely what he attributes to Heaven – experimenting with Smallways as a sample of the English millions and professing thereby to gauge what is happening to the soul of man.

Where Wells contrives to combine a real interest in a character as an individual with the awareness of his representative role, his success is undeniable. On the publication of *Kipps*, Henry James wrote to him:

> You have for the very first time treated the English 'lower middle' class, etc., without the picturesque, the grotesque, the fantastic and romantic interference of which Dickens, e.g., is so misleadingly, of which even George Eliot is so deviatingly, full. You have handled its vulgarity in so scientific and historic a spirit, and seen the whole thing in its *own* strong light. And then the book, has, throughout, such extraordinary life; everyone in it, without exception, and every piece and part of it, is so vivid and sharp and raw.[6]

Yet with his minor characters Wells's desire to create a typical representative often degenerated into mere caricature. This appears to result less from an objective viewing of society than from an intention to vilify certain aspects of social tradition and convention. Thus several of his minor characters are little more than embodiments of the more unattractive traits of the Victorian age as Wells chose to imagine it, distorted representatives of a system seen through the eyes of one prejudiced against almost everything inherited from the past. Mr Stanley, Ann Veronica's father, and Mr Pope and Mr Magnet, Marjorie Trafford's father and first suitor respectively, are such scape-goats. Even amongst the major characters there is often a suspicion of caricature; indeed Wells himself later admitted that he was not averse to type characters provided they served his purpose. Of *Love and Mr. Lewisham*, *The Sea Lady*, *Kipps*, *In the Days of the Comet*, *The New Machiavelli*, *Marriage*, *The Passionate Friends*, and *The Wife of Sir Isaac Harman*, he wrote that:

In all these novels, the interest centres not upon the individual character, but upon the struggles of common and rational motives and frank enquiry against social conditions and stereotyped ideas. The actors in them are types, therefore, rather than acutely individualised persons. They could not be other than types.[7]

This is because to Wells, at least in theory, the species *Homo sapiens* was both more interesting and more important than the individuals who comprised it. If the human species as a whole was a cumbersome topic for literature, the nearest manageable approximation was a panoramic view of society as a whole, and hence the social novel was the form to which Wells turned with increasing frequency, often with the tacit but clear assumption that one society was very similar to another, so that the study of a 'typical' member within his natural milieu might serve as a reasonable statement of the species as a whole.

The practical outcome of this tendency is that many of Wells's novels begin with a panoramic view of society before focusing on its individual members. *The War of the Worlds* opens with the widest possible panoramic sweep – the earth as seen from Mars. That mankind is being viewed as a specimen is emphasised beyond doubt by the comparison with the infusoria under the microscope:

> As men busied themselves about their affairs, they were scrutinized and studied, perhaps almost as narrowly as a man with a microscope might scrutinize the transient creatures that swarm and multiply in a drop of water. With infinite complacency men went to and fro over this globe. . . . It is possible that the infusoria under the microscope do the same.[8]

The alleged author of *In the Days of the Comet*, the 'man who wrote in the tower', in order to describe the lives and events of individuals, elevates himself to a situation which enables him to look down upon them from afar and from above, and even then he surveys the scene below not directly but in a concave, and hence distorting, mirror.[9] The situation is reminiscent of the Martian astronomers with their telescopes trained on earth to note the effects as the star passes.[10] In all cases the human characters are diminished to the status of specimens. Similarly, *The World Set Free* commences with a panoramic sweep in time – man's development since the dawn of his history – while *Tono-Bungay* begins with a broad survey of social classes as George reviews his experiences in a cross-section of settings and then proceeds to a description of Bladesover which is explicitly stated to be a 'complete authentic microcosm . . . a little working model – and not so very little either – of the whole world'.[11] All this before any individual characters are introduced; indeed Wells himself later wrote of *Tono-Bungay*:

> It was an indisputable Novel, but it was extensive rather than intensive. That is to say it presented characters only as part of a scene. It was planned as a social panorama.[12]

If Wells's scientific training thus influenced the kinds of character he chose to study and his approach to them, it affected his presentation of individual characters even more profoundly.

Because he tended to view characters as specimens arranged or posed for his inspection, he tended also to record what he observed in firm clear outlines analogous to dissection-diagrams in a laboratory manual. Typically, Wells's character novels proceed through an accumulation of these fine details, not set down randomly but correlated and patterned to produce a coherent picture. He had employed this method with considerable success in novels of the future where he was concerned to make real a scene hitherto outside the reader's experience or imagination. Here his technique was to erect a massive edifice of detail until the reader seemed to step into the scene. Thus in 'A Story of the Days to Come' and in *The Sleeper* we follow Denton and Graham through an unfamiliar city, observing one detail after another until a credible, three-dimensional structure has been realised for us and becomes the background for the subsequent events of the story. It is significant that Wells uses, in these cases, precisely the same technique as he had used in his article, 'The Things that Live on Mars': the careful building-up of an unfamiliar background and then the gradual extrapolation from this to a scientifically credible picture of the conditions and population of Mars.

When this analytic gaze is turned upon the characters themselves, there is again the careful enumeration of external details – the clothing worn, the stance, the stature, the characteristic gestures or expressions, the normal background, a particular manner of speaking. This desire for the clearest and most accurate accounts of characters and their environments led Wells to stress the need for the utmost realism in presentation, and links him at this point not only with the English realist novel, but also with the French naturalist tradition. He himself wrote that *Tono-Bungay* was 'planned as a social panorama in the vein of Balzac' and there is little doubt that he would have been in accord with Zola's conception of the novelist as a scientific experimenter operating on 'the characters, the passions as the human and social data'.[13] This accumulation of numerous background details, was typical of many of Wells's novels, particularly the early novels of character, and several contemporary critics who abhorred this method of amassing detail cited with derision the fact that so many of his novels began with a painstaking description of a room and its contents.[14] Indeed no less than ten of the novels contain such a description.[15]

So important did Wells consider the exact and truthful rendering of such details that he often conformed to the most stringent standard of fidelity, namely that of authorial experience. The Emporium where Hoopdriver works, Bladesover in *Tono-Bungay*, and the chemist's shop of George Ponderevo's apprenticeship, the Bromstead of *The New Machiavelli*, Polly's ill-fated shop, Lewisham's term as a student-teacher, even the room he occupies and his years at South Kensington, Capes the biology demonstrator entering into an affair with Ann Veronica, a girl student whom he later marries, and much of Britling's background, are all confessedly drawn from Wells's own experiences, while George Ponderevo and Remington read almost exactly the same selection of books in their programme of self-education as Wells himself had done.[16]

A further outcome of Wells's preoccupation with ordinary characters was the necessity of drawing upon backgrounds which were at least humble, often squalid, if realism were to be retained. This tendency again links Wells with the Naturalist tradition, although he never descended to the depths of squalor portrayed by many of the French novelists. At least one reviewer saw *Love and Mr. Lewisham* as similar in mood to Gissing's novels of financial distress and struggling, chronically unsuccessful characters. Wells however differed markedly from Gissing in the attitudes which he ascribed to characters sunk in poverty, and rejected as a breach of realism the implied idea that happiness was dependent upon wealth. In an article, 'The Depressed School', which begins as a critique of Gissing's novel, *Eve's Ransom*, he wrote:

No doubt Mr. Gissing's spiritual anatomy and physiology are correct, and his perspective is right; but is his colouring true? Is this harsh greyness really representative of life, even the life of the lower middle class? Or is it that Mr. Gissing is colour-blind, that he has the distinctive fault as well as the distinctive precision of photography? For our own part, we do not believe that any social stratum is so dull as this melancholy world of his. Happiness is, after all, mainly a question of physical constitution . . . the true Realism, we hold, looks both on the happy and on the unhappy.[17]

Thus Wells maintained, with some truth, that his lower-middle-class characters were in fact more accurate pictures of reality, more truthfully and objectively drawn, than many of the same stratum as depicted by the naturalist writers. This difference lay less in the material presented than in the interpretation of personality and in the authorial attitude towards the characters. Wells understood that although novelists themselves might find the exigencies of straitened circumstances intolerable and impute their own despair to all who experienced poverty, nevertheless those members of the working class whose cultural demands were less exacting might be genuinely cheerful.

The effect of this stress on individuals as units of a society is to set each character very firmly in his social *milieu*, and indeed this was intentional. Wells believed that few people had either the chance or the inclination to change their station in life and hence remained predictably within the niche which heredity and early environment had carved out for them. *Tono-Bungay* opens with George Ponderevo's meditation upon this theme:

> Most people in this world seem to live 'in character'; they have a beginning, a middle and an end, and the three are congruous one with another and true to the rules of their type. You can speak of them as being of this sort of people or that. They are, as theatrical people say, no more (and no less) than 'character actors'. They have a class, they have a place, they know what is becoming in them and what is due to them, and their proper size of tombstone tells at last how properly they have played the part.[18]

Thus, in the majority of Wells's novels there is a definite suggestion of the determinism of circumstances. The emporia where Hoopdriver and Kipps are apprenticed, the stifling trivialities of Polly's domestic arrangements, are made to seem physically and mentally inescapable, and on the whole the majority of Wells's characters are shown as being so shaped by their family and education that few have even the wish to break away from the pattern laid down in their formative years.

The general change of emphasis from heredity to environment as the major deterministic factor in the novel during the last decades of the nineteenth century reflects the belief that since biology had been so successful in explaining the physical nature of individuals, psychology would soon explain behaviour also in scientific terms. Wells, who was temperamentally sympathetic to such an attitude, fell naturally into a similar procedure in his novels. Even those characters who succeed in surmounting their given circumstances, are enabled to do so only because some external force impels them or encourages them to abnormal effort. It is Kipps's unexpected inheritance and the impact of Chitterlow's personality on him, Polly's 'successful' experiment in arson and Leadford's experience of the euphorious gas, which temporarily galvanise these characters to take some initiative in directing their lives. Essentially they remain passive. George Ponderevo is lifted out of his drifting, impecunious existence only by his uncle's sudden accession to the ranks of the wealthy through the expanding prospects of Tono-Bungay; Lewisham, on the other hand, fails to change his social circumstances precisely because no external factor forces him to do so, and his own efforts fail to achieve any significant results other than reconciliation to his lot.

Thus, in Wells's novels, the very occasions on which social determinism appears to have been overcome are themselves instances of a further deterministic element. The agency which jolts a character out of his habitual rut and motivates him to surmount his circumstances, is itself unpredictable and apparently arbitrary; hence as far as the individual is concerned, it is as much beyond his control as the original state of affairs.

Wells's desire to create characters as complete as possible made him try to explain them at the subconscious level as well, for his analysis of thoughts and motives, of heredity and environment, is part of his effort to incorporate each observation into a consistent world view. This approach is further emphasised by his tendency to introduce characters didactically, explaining them and admonishing the reader in a Thackerayan manner, like a demonstrator at the blackboard – in fact, like the young Wells, science master at Henley House School. Perhaps unwittingly he has extended into the province of psychology that emphasis on causality which was basic to the success of the scientific romances. The whole conception of the utopias also involves an underlying assumption of psychological conditioning. It is utopian policy continually to perfect environment and education, precisely because these factors are seen as operating to shape character and thus, in the long-term view, inevitably to produce an harmonious society. Thus Wells's aptitude for meticulous background descriptions and for the habit of analytical thought led him to show operating on his characters a level of determinism which he elsewhere explicitly disavowed.[19]

This same preoccupation with external details and descriptions has led to the frequent charge that Wells omitted all spiritual and religious values from his characters' make-up. Whereas Julian Huxley wrote of Wells that 'his intensely human nature and broadly humanist interests kept him from any narrowness of scientific or intellectual approach',[20] critics with a humanities background were less tolerant. Odette Keun blamed the influence of Huxley upon an impressionable student for what she regarded as the destruction of all spiritual and mystical values in Wells's thought.[21] However, the limitations allegedly deriving from his religious scepticism have been exaggerated. The absence of orthodox religious forms from any one novel is frequently made to appear more heinous by the observation that a large number of his other novels are similarly deficient in religious awareness, whereas within the confines of each individual novel this may not be unrealistic, for Wells wrote in and of an age when formal religion was commonly treated with indifference if not with disdain. The religious turmoils which followed the publication of *The Origin of Species* had subsided and, for many, questioning had given way to a tacit agnosticism. The very word 'agnosticism' was coined, significantly, in the latter half of the nineteenth century to describe the attitude of a generation which found that atheism, no less than orthodoxy, involved a level of commitment it was unwilling to profess. If Wells chose to portray characters who did not undergo the spiritual struggles of the previous generation, or suffer mental tortures for their defiance of orthodoxy, his sample is not necessarily atypical.

Nor is it valid to assume that because Wells showed little but contempt or indifference towards orthodox religious attitudes he was therefore totally lacking in spiritual or even religious awareness. For him, as for many of his contemporaries, a social conscience was replacing religion as the arbiter of morality. While some traditional values came to be considered redundant by him, particularly the sanctions governing sexual relations, he viewed other moral questions with increasing stringency, notably the often hypocritical attitudes of Victorian and Edwardian society in politics, in business dealings and social responsibility. His professed faith demanded, at least in theory, a rigorous, even ascetic, code of behaviour which, being based on altruistic principles, was to inspire selflessness and a spirit of evangelism in its followers. Consequently the social reformers in the novels and utopias of Wells's middle period, before his work became explicitly didactic, display some or all of these virtues or are prevented from a more devoted pursuit of this ideal only by the blindness of a society which will not permit them the necessary freedom. Remington enters upon his political career as an idealist whose views Wells describes in religious terms. Trafford pursues his research into crystals with a similar devotion and his account of his work comes close to the language of mysticism:

> The sense one has of exquisite and wonderful rhythms – just beyond sight and sound! And there's a haunting suggestion of its being all there, displayed and confessed if one were only quick enough to see it. . . . It takes me like music. . . . Is there anything else so rich and beautiful in the whole world? . . . a different scheme of harmonies . . . as if the whole world was fire and crystal and a-quiver – with some sort of cotton wrappers thrown over it.[22]

while George Ponderevo sees his proposed dedication to research in religious terms, as the pursuit of an ultimate reality.[23]

From this we might expect Wells to appear as a religious writer, at least in the broad Tolstoyan sense of religion as devotion to life. But in fact, although not devoid of religious symbolisim, his novels are not deeply religious in any accepted sense of that word. This failure to realise artistically his intellectual belief in a metaphysical dimension is at least partly attributable to his scientific training, although not as directly as Odette Keun and others have assumed. There are several other contributory reasons involved, notably his preoccupation with the passage of time and the sense of urgency which this involves. His characters live and move in a world of limited time; they hasten to press forward their ideas or to implement their plans before it is too late; the awful warning of the dying world of *The Time Machine* seems to hang over them. There is no sense of grace or eternity to impart a religious meaning or depth to this spectacle of busy creatures hastening to reform their society by their own efforts.

Again, like the majority of his contemporaries, Wells was brought up in a home where lip-service at least was paid to religious orthodoxy, and along with many of his generation, he trod the well-worn path from Evangelical fundamentalism to pantheistic rationalism; but whereas for Hale White, Edmund Gosse and countless other searching souls the experience was a traumatic one involving deep heart-searching, for Wells the transition appeared so inevitable a part of his education as to be barely worth recording. His position is not dissimilar to the final state of mind of those who, having discarded their faith in revealed religion, found a viable substitute in social activism, but by omitting the intermediate stages of the struggle, he leaves us with semi-autobiographical characters who appear over-confident, free from self-doubt, and consequently superficial. Thus although his plans for social reform were often more explicit, detailed and coherent than those proclaimed by the ardent protagonists of Kingsley, Mrs Humphry Ward and their followers, Wells fails to convince us of either his own or his characters' total commitment to them. The proposed reforms remain a theory, carefully evolved and clearly set out, but a theory nonetheless, and his characters seem, in this respect, tainted with the 'academic' vice of non-commitment. Trafford, for all his alleged adoption of a social mission, fails to evince the zeal of the reformer.

However the major reason for the failure of Wells's characters to suggest any religious dimension in their lives results from the very clarity of their delineation. Basically they lack a religious dimension not because they fail to embrace an orthodox faith but because such a possibility is precluded by the apparently exhaustive analysis of these characters into other components. They are complete without it.

Wells's preoccupation with external details in characterisation has issued in a further and more widespread criticism – namely the deficiency of subconscious depth in his work. Compared with the characters of the major nineteenth- and twentieth-century novelists his protagonists seem lacking in any suggestion of an inner life as surely as they lack a religious dimension. But it is important to realise that he was writing from a different starting-point. Whereas the earlier novelists had, through their own intuition and acute observation, been able to show the range and depths of human nature, Wells was probably one of the first novelists consciously to use current psychological theories. He had become interested in psychology while at South Kensington although it was not then regarded as an independent science, but only as fragments of philosophy, physiology, psychiatry and biology. Characteristically, the few psychological questions treated in his early writings are drawn chiefly from the work of Darwin[24] and Galton,[25] and thus his approach at this stage was more biological and deterministic than it was to become later when he was attracted to the behaviourist school of psychology. Havelock Ellis had apparently introduced Wells to the comparative psychology of the sexes,[26] and he later became interested in the work of Jung, but the major influence on his view of psychology was the work of William James, whose *Principles of Psychology* he described as 'that most wonderful book'.[27] The attractions of James's approach to psychology for a young science graduate of the 1890s are manifest. James stressed the alternating processes of analysis and synthesis as the key to understanding the workings of the mind, and these same processes were the very basis of the scientific romances.

Not only did Wells himself come to portray his characters in terms of analysis and synthesis, but his more intellectual and articulate protagonists pursue a similar method in attempting to analyse their surroundings and fellow-characters. George Ponderevo is prone to analyse his uncle at frequent intervals and his system of 'social anatomy' whereby he endeavours to explain London, and indeed England, by analogy with the Bladesover hierarchy, involves both analysis into component units and a boldly synthetic plan of sociological prediction. Again, Wells's conscious attempts at psychoanalysis are frequently reducible either to physiological considerations or to a study of socio-economic factors. Wells clearly believed in the validity of this latter approach for in his outline of the psychology to be practised in Utopia he writes:

Many problems that we should regard as economic come within the scope of Utopian psychology. My Utopians make two divisions of the science of psychology, first the general psychology of individuals, a sort of mental physiology, separated by no definite line from psychology proper, and secondly the psychology of the relation between individuals. This second is an exhaustive study of the reactions of people upon each other and of all possible relationships.[28]

Apart from the more socially-oriented areas of psychology, there is much evidence to suggest that Wells was aware of most of the fundamentals of psychoanalytic theory. As a contemporary of Freud he must inevitably have imbibed many of the same germinal ideas and current modes of thinking which inspired Freud, and on some points Wells's own expression of psychoanalytical principles predates Freud's formulations. Because of his background Wells inevitably approached psychoanalysis from a biological viewpoint, his earliest appreciation of the potential developments of the science being formulated in the essay 'The Limits of Individual Plasticity', where he not only accords hypnotism the dignity of treating it as a science, a relatively new conception,[29] but also shows a familiarity with the concepts of sublimation and psychotherapy. In 'Human Evolution, an Artificial Process', published the following year, Wells made suggestions which anticipated Jung's theory of the civilising process and its effects upon the 'persona' and the 'shadow' of personality, while in his autobiography, published twenty-three years after Jung's work, Wells attempted to analyse himself in specifically Jungian terms.[30] In his early work, when he was far less confident in his understanding of the unconscious (which, at this period, he called half jocularly 'the back of the mind'), Wells was tentative about ascribing glimmerings of subconscious thought to so humble a character as Hoopdriver, but by the time of writing *Kipps* he was prepared to acknowledge the unconscious as universal. Nevertheless he does seem to have distinguished at least four distinct aspects, appropriate to characters with different levels of self-awareness. Kipps is a simple soul, aware of an inner self only spasmodically and, even then, uncomprehendingly. After his engagement to the formidable Helen Walshingham, he '. . . conversed, as it were, out of his superficial personality, and his inner self lay stunned in unsuspected depths within'.[31] Later, after discovering his proper *milieu*, in marriage with Ann, his 'inner life' again reasserts itself, impinging briefly and inarticulately upon his conscious self:

[Kipps] had ceased from rowing and rested on his oars, and suddenly he was touched by the wonder of life – the strangeness that is a presence stood again by his side.

Out of the darkness beneath the shallow weedy stream of his being, rose a question . . . of the wonder, of the beauty, the purposeless inconsecutive beauty, that falls so strangely among the happenings and memories of life. It never reached the surface of his mind, it never took to itself substance or form; it looked up merely as the phantom of a face might look out of deep waters, and sank again into nothingness.[32]

On the other hand, for Remington this 'mental and spiritual hinterland' is largely cultural, certainly wholly intellectual, and is not, therefore, strictly subconscious.

This back-self has its history and phases, its crises and happy accidents and irrevocable conclusions, more or less distinct from the adventures and achievements of the ostensible self. . . . In the life of the individual it takes the role that the growth of philosophy, science and creative literature may play in the development of mankind.[33]

For Trafford it has more emotional overtones, as he accumulates a reservoir of resentments against his wife:

If Trafford was a faithful husband he was no longer a happy and confident one. There grew up in him a vast hinterland of thoughts and feelings, an accumulation of unspoken and largely unformulated things in which his wife had no share. And it was in that hinterland that his essential self had its abiding place.[34]

For Stephen Stratton, communing with the silence, the unconscious is identified with a wider consciousness which appears to be almost identical to Wells's 'Mind of the Race' since it urges him from his personal, individual problems to a wider, international involvement in life:

You are not only Stephen Stratton who fell into adultery; in these silences he is a little thing and far away; here and with me you are Man – Everyman – in this round world in which your lot has fallen. . . .
   'But who are you?' I cried out suddenly to the night. 'Who are you? . . . This is just some odd corner of my brain,' I said. . . . Yet – How did I come to have this odd corner in my brain? What is this lucid stillness? . . .[35]

It should be noted in this connection that whereas the unconscious or subconscious self which Freud and his followers were defining was characteristically less 'noble', less laudable by current social standards, than the *persona* of the conscious, civilised self, the 'inner self' of Wells's characters is almost invariably seen as being more elevated, more morally sound than the conscious self. This relationship with an inner self which is intrinsically 'better' is given physical form in *A Modern Utopia* where the narrator encounters an idealised *alter ego*:

> The idea of an encounter with my double, which came at first as if it were a witticism, as something verbal and surprising, begins to take substance. The idea grows in my mind that after all this is the 'someone' I am seeking, this Utopian self of mine . . . between us there will be a strange link of essential identity, a sympathy, an understanding. . . . That I have come to Utopia is the lesser thing now; the greater is that I have come to meet myself.[36]

Apart from this general cognisance of an inner self, Wells was certainly also aware of the fundamental characteristics of the unconscious as they were known to Freud and his contemporaries. Although he did not refer to them in technical terms, he was conversant with several important aspects of psychoanalytic theory and with the close interconnections between them – with the dynamic aspect of the unconscious, reaction-formation, sublimation, symbolism, repression, hysterical conversion, parent complexes, inferiority complex and compensation, and the significance of dreams – for at times he portrayed them in his characters with the clarity of case-histories. Because of the many derogatory criticisms centring on Wells's supposed ignorance of psychology it is worth examining a few instances of these factors before considering how well this technical understanding of the principles of psychology is embodied in his actual characters.

Certainly, Wells was fully aware of the dynamic nature of the unconscious for he referred to the multiform, kaleidoscopic patterns and juxtapositions of subconscious thought and motive as 'mental landslides'. Trafford, one of his most articulate protagonists, describes this vividly as

> a new set of riddles filling my mind. Now thought swings about thought . . . now the waves of motive and conviction sweep through the crowd, and all the little drifting crystallizations of

spirit with spirit, and all the repulsions and oddities and difficulties that one can catch in that turbulent confusion.[37]

Like Lawrence, Wells had no interest in the 'old stable ego' of character, and his awareness of a perpetual state of flux at the unconscious level of personality was doubtless contributory to this, although the influence of Darwinism with its emphasis on non-static forms and on continual development and change must not be discounted. The excitement of living in a growing, ever-changing society is the external equivalent for Wells of a fluid unconscious level of experience.

Reaction formation is the process wherein the energy generated by an impulse which is unacceptable either to the individual or to his society, is channelled towards emphasising the opposite behaviour. This may be seen most clearly in Wells's female characters. Ann Veronica wishes to envisage herself as a modern emancipated woman, and hence her behaviour is flagrantly aggressive, not only towards her father, against whom she is consciously rebelling, but also towards Manning and Ramage, the suitors whom she does not wish to marry. However, when she finally commits herself to Capes, it becomes apparent that her real nature is, by contrast, clinging and submissive, and she shows a strong wish to be dominated. In one extraordinarily revealing scene her desire to be submissive is seen to extend almost to fetishism:

> She slid her cheek down the tweed sleeve of his coat. 'Nice sleeve,' she said, and came to his hand and kissed it. 'I say,' he cried, 'Look here. Aren't you going a little too far? This – this is degradation – making a fuss with sleeves. You mustn't do things like that.'
>
> 'Why not?'
>
> 'Free woman – and equal.'
>
> 'I do it – of my own free will,' said Ann Veronica, kissing his hand again. 'It's nothing to what I will do!'[38]

In *Tono-Bungay* there is a humorous but nonetheless penetrating discourse by George's friend Ewart on what is now often cited as the classic case of such reaction formation – excessive prudery produced by strong but suppressed sexual desires. Ewart gleefully expounds in detail and with variations, his theory that Mrs Grundy does not exist, only Mr Grundy![39]

Sublimation, a closely related phenomenon, may also be seen operating in many of Wells's major characters, although with various degrees of success. Thus Stephen Stratton finally channels the energy of his futile passion for Mary Justin into literary and publishing ventures; Benham strives to sublimate his unconscious desire for a perfect wife, patterned on his mother, in his 'research magnificent', and Trafford attempts unsuccessfully to redirect his passion for pure research towards the world of business before achieving a satisfying compromise in the pursuit of sociology. George Ponderevo expresses his pent-up drives, generated at least in part by his unsatisfied desire for Beatrice, in the building of flying machines and torpedo boats. Remington's attempts to suppress his love for Isabel are perhaps the most conspicuously doomed to failure, for Remington, like Wells, remains unconvinced that sublimation is either desirable or possible. The very concept implies to him an inadequacy either in the individual or more probably, in the society which requires it. Thus in *The New Machiavelli* authorial condemnation falls more heavily on the society which rejects Remington's alleged political gifts because of his moral nonconformity, than on the lovers themselves.

Symbolism, also, although relatively rare in Wells's work, is sometimes used to convey a subconscious psychological meaning, usually referring to relations between the sexes. Thus in *Marriage*, Magnet, the undesirable suitor, makes two attempts to propose marriage to Marjorie, both occasions being associated with artificial settings – once near the stylised lily-pond at Lady Petchworth's pretentious garden party, and once in the artfully planned excursion to the church tower during an elaborate picnic. By contrast, Trafford's encounters with Marjorie are uncontrived, at least on his part. Once he drops, literally, from the sky, while their second encounter, again outdoors and hence in a 'natural' setting, is associated with unpretentious donkey carts. This latter occasion imports a second reinforcing element of symbolism – the interlocked wheels of the carts caught in the narrow lane prefigure the interlocking futures of the two drivers.

The attempted proposal in Lady Petchworth's garden entails further symbolism in Magnet's suggestion that he and Marjorie should go to look at the aviary for he thinks of Marjorie as a beautiful bird to be ensnared, and preserved by the cage of wedlock for his entertainment, while Marjorie's disinclination for such a view of marriage is emphasised by her reply that she hates to see birds in cages.[40]

Ann Veronica, too, symbolises her ambivalence about her formal engagement to Manning and her as-yet-unconscious desire to give herself instead to Capes, when she takes off Manning's ring and hands it to Capes to examine.[41] The most striking example of such symbolism occurs in *Tono-Bungay*. George is practice-gliding when Beatrice's horse gallops directly in the path of his low-flying plane, just as Beatrice herself had deliberately forced her presence upon him. In this emergency George decides to soar over her, and the ensuing imagery is startlingly reminiscent of the Leda myth, with all the reinforcement of the final Yeatsean phrase:

> She had almost got her horse in hand when I came up to her. Her woman's body lay along his neck, and she glanced up as I, with wings aspread, and every nerve in a state of tension, swept over her.
>
> Then I had landed, and was going back to where her horse stood still and trembling. We exchanged no greetings. She slid from her saddle into my arms, and for one instant I held her. 'Those great wings,' she said, and that was all.[42]

Repression is closely related to reaction formation and also to sublimation, but in so far as it may be considered separately there are several distinct examples of this condition in Wells's work. Again the most obvious and sustained treatments are to be found in the realm of sexual relationships for, like Freud, Wells regarded sexual relations as exerting the greatest effect upon the individual's personality. Miss Miniver in *Ann Veronica* evinces a strongly repressed attitude towards men whom, at the conscious level, she despises and avoids, on the rationalisation that she has never yet found a man intellectually worthy of her. The inevitable tension produced by this conscious behaviour and her unconscious physical drives, is clearly evident both in her evasion of the subject and in her final outburst when Ann Veronica questions her about 'love and the facts of love'.[43]

A more humorous, though no less valid, example of repression is to be found in Kipps's awkwardness at table, culminating in his desire to avoid teacups and all afternoon tea gatherings. This phobia clearly derives from the scenes of his childhood humiliation when his aunt and uncle repeatedly criticised his table-manners if he did not 'eat properly',[44] and, although repressed, the fear erupts at critical points throughout his life. Wells was also acutely aware of the far-reaching effects of parent complexes, some form of which occurs in nearly all his novels, although he denied the existence of any such emotional disturbance in his own life.[45] Apart from sheer economic dependence upon parents, he describes a whole range of dependent and rebellious relations between parent and child. Ann Veronica suffers from an overbearing father whose authoritarianism she strongly resents, but even when she has rebelled physically and socially against this by leaving her parental home, there remains a strong bond of self-imposed moral obligation which renders her, in a very real sense, dependent upon his approval. At the end of the novel, after she and Capes have married and achieved worldly success, she is still deeply affected and emotionally tense about the first visit from her father and aunt since her elopement. Her real independence begins only when she can view them as social equals, whereupon she finds them 'smaller . . . even physically smaller':

'To think that is my father! Oh, my dear! He stood over me like a cliff; the very thought of him nearly turned me aside from everything we have done. He was the social order; he was law and wisdom. And they come here, and they look at our furniture to see if it is good; and they are not glad, it does not stir them, that at last, at last, we can dare to have children!'[46]

In the same novel Capes voices Wells's theory of the major difficulties inherent in parent-child relationships:

'It's a perpetual trouble,' he said. . . . 'There's a sort of instinct of rebellion . . . it's a sort of home-leaving instinct.'
    . . . 'There's another instinct, too,' he went on, 'in a state of suppression, unless I'm very much mistaken; a child-expelling instinct. . . . I wonder. . . . There's no family-uniting instinct, anyhow; it's habit and sentiment and material convenience hold families together after adolescence. There's always friction, conflict, unwilling concessions. Always! I don't believe there is any strong natural affection at all between parents and growing-up children.'[47]

Wilbur Cross commented of Wells's 'small souls', that 'some of them had acquired an inferiority complex years before amateur psychologists had picked up the phrase'.[48] Hoopdriver, Kipps, Bert Smallways, Uncle Ponderevo and Polly all display, at some stage, diverse symptoms of an inferiority complex – indeed Kipps, Uncle Ponderevo and Polly might almost serve as case-studies of such a condition. Hoopdriver, the simplest character sketch of the timid 'little man', provides an outline for the more elaborate studies of Kipps and Polly which followed and, of all Wells's apprentices, Hoopdriver is certainly the most conditioned to his station and employment – his shop gestures and phrases have become so deeply ingrained in his nature that he uses them unawares. Yet he too has his pride and aspirations to self-respect, and spins a highly-coloured tale of his supposed South African exploits to compensate for his servility and deeply-felt humiliation.

Kipps also, through his limited education and his apprenticeship, has had a sense of his own inferiority deeply ingrained upon his native exuberance and when, in an effort at self-improvement, he attends evening classes in wood-carving, he feels like

> a creature of outer darkness blinking in an unsuspected light . . . an inexcusable intruder in an altitudinous world. When the epigram happened, he first of all smiled to pretend he understood, and instantly suppressed the smile to show he did not listen. Then he became extremely hot and uncomfortable, though nobody had noticed either phase.[49]

Wells describes many such agonies endured by his socially inept characters – situations which, though insignificant to others, become magnified into enormous public trials for those possessed by an inferiority complex. Kipps suffers a similar though more prolonged humiliation when staying at the pretentious Royal Grand Hotel and endeavouring to obtain a meal under the eyes of the socially adept company. The whole episode, beneath its humour, is a fine and subtle study of the diverse interpretations given to each trivial incident by Kipps and by those whose confidence springs from an easy familiarity with their circumstances.

Polly indulges in the escapist daydreams characteristic of the introvert suffering from a deep sense of inferiority, but they are more all-encompassing and more subtly rendered than Hoopdriver's hasty attempts to conceal his identity on the spur of the moment.

Incapable of adapting to the world about him because, in that world, he can never, with his muddled thinking and ineffectual actions, hold any position of importance, Polly lives increasingly in a dream world where his daring, knowledge and wit mark him as a leader among men. His response to literature is that of a starving man to food, for it furnishes him with the raw materials for his daydreams and provides virtually the only source of beauty available in the squalor and drabness of the village-shop situation. Later, at the Potwell Inn, where natural beauty abouds, Polly's sense of inferiority vanishes, and so, significantly, do his escapist reveries.

Uncle Ponderevo represents the extrovert equivalent of Polly. Lacking Polly's essential idealism and inarticulate response to beauty, he has the extra drive necessary to convert his dreams to reality until the odds against him become too immense. His escapism is basically a moral one, for having once deluded himself about the merits of Tono-Bungay, he has no scruples about promoting it to all possible lengths.

As an extrovert, Uncle Ponderevo repeatedly parades his would-be social superiority, one manifestation of an inferiority complex, in his appurtenances. The first indication of his new social position, his silk hat, is partly a status symbol, partly a prop to compensate for his short stature, and the hat symbol recurs throughout the days of success in the Tono-Bungay venture until it is finally replaced, in the last hours of ignominious flight, by a humble tweed cap.[50] He is repeatedly compared to that more famous historical extrovert who also allegedly suffered from short stature and an inferiority complex, Napoleon, partly because the comparison has become part of his own thinking about himself. Even when his dubious business transactions begin to recoil upon him, he contrives to view his dyspepsia as a further indication of his similarity to Napoleon.[51] The explicit identification of Uncle Ponderevo with Napoleon both emphasises his comparative smallness, hence rendering the more ridiculous his attempts to emulate his hero, and also, by implication, demonstrates his psychological sense of inferiority by the very fact of his needing such identification.

Ponderevo's most grandiose declaration of his would-be superiority is the vast, ugly and useless mansion which he insists upon building at fantastic expense, and which is named, significantly, 'Crest Hill', with its 'marble staircase and my aunt's golden bed, the bed that was facsimiled from Fontainebleau'.[52] The Napoleon image is several times coupled with the Crest Hill motif and reinforces it. George writes of his uncle:

> I found him there one day, most Napoleonic, on a little Elba of dirt . . . he also enraged her [Aunt Susan] by giving each bedroom the name of some favourite hero – Clive, Napoleon, Caesar, and so forth – and having it painted on the door in gilt letters on a black label.[53]

Uncle Ponderevo is Wells's most sustained and vivid portrait of a character seeking compensation for an inferiority complex, but even amongst his minor characters there are instances of a similar psychological state. Ann Veronica's father, and Marjorie Pope's father, are not merely stylised, irate father-figures, but are shown in retrospect as essentially 'small men' assuming an air of exaggerated authority in order to convince themselves and others of their importance as individuals. Mr Stanley, in particular, is finally won over to accept his daughter's marriage through the Achilles' heel of his social vanity. His eagerness to profess himself a critic of modern drama and to patronise successful playwrights leads him unawares to flatter his son-in-law, who has assumed a *nom-de-plume*, while his essentially materialistic values render him readily susceptible to the now-wealthy and socially-competent Capes.[54]

Perhaps the most striking example of inferiority compensation in Wells's work is that of Preemby in *Christina Alberta's Father*. His story is almost a classic case-history of a small personality seeking grandeur in the belief that he is a reincarnation of Sargon, the King of Kings; indeed Jung himself considered Wells's portrayal of Preemby as a scrupulously accurate statement of such a condition.[55]

In the nineteenth-century novel the use of dreams as a revelation of character was already known before the publication of Freud's *The Interpretation of Dreams*, although usually the interpretation was left vague and implicit, a technique appropriate to both a realistic approach and the generation of an effective element of mystery. Wells, however, made comparatively little use of the dream motif either as an instrument of psychological exploration or as a means of describing subconscious motives, although he can scarcely have been unfamiliar with Freud's essay, which appeared in English translation in 1900. In *The Wheels of Chance*, Hoopdriver's dream shows that Wells was already aware of the power of the unconscious in dreams to reconsider and deal with sense impressions which have already been forgotten, ignored or suppressed by the conscious mind. Bechamel's behaviour towards Jessie, which Hoopdriver's own embarrassment at the encounter had obscured in his conscious thought, reasserts itself in his dream, is reconsidered, and finally leads to the conclusion, still within the framework of the dream, that Bechamel is not in fact the brother of 'The Young Lady in Grey', as had been declared, but is abducting her. On waking, Hoopdriver forgets the details of this dream, but not the main point – 'the curious dream conviction that the girl was not really the man's sister'.[56] The extravagant Marjorie Pope's dream following her engagement to wealthy Magnet and her newly aroused feelings for Trafford, indicates that Wells was fully aware of the main postulates of this area of Freud's work – indeed the symbolism of Marjorie's dream plane failing because of her unpaid bills and falling down into the arms of the smiling Magnet is rather too obvious.

It would seem, however, that if Wells was fully conversant with current progress in the study of dreams, he nevertheless remained somewhat sceptical of its validity. In *The Food of the Gods* he shows subconscious states, which the waking person suppresses, becoming dominant in fairly predictable dreams, and simultaneously pokes gentle fun at the excesses of dream interpretation.

. . . as a general rule it is not, I think, at all interesting for people to tell each other about their dreams.

By a singular coincidence, Redwood also had a dream that night, and his dream was this:

. . . Ridiculous of course, but that too shows –

That either dream is to be regarded as in anyway significant or prophetic beyond what I have categorically said, I do not for one moment suggest.[57]

A more interesting use of the dream is that which besets the obsessed Hapley in the short story, 'The Moth'. He believes that the moth which torments him, alike in his waking hours and in his dreams, is the ghost of Pawkins, once his competitor in entomological research, so that 'while he was awake he longed for sleep, and from sleep he awoke screaming'.⁵⁸

Wells seems to have been most intrigued by dreams resulting from unusual psychic experiences. In 'The Stolen Body' Vincy has cooperated in an experiment of psychic research involving his friend Bessel's attempts to project an apparition of himself through space to Vincy's apartment by sheer force of will. Vincy later dreams twice, in rapid succession, that Bessel is in great distress and is trying to contact him. This premonition is found to have been justified and hence the dream is seen as having conveyed a genuine psychical message. Again, in 'Under the Knife', the narrator, on the eve of a major operation, dreams of Regent's Park as a cemetery on the day of Resurrection. However the most original of the dreams in Wells's fiction is the magnificent sweep of the same narrator's dream experiences while under chloroform during his operation. This vision of a disembodied soul journeying forth through the solar system to the 'Outer Universe' and beyond, is as powerful in its impact as the vision of the dying world in *The Time Machine*. Indeed, in its cosmic scope and philosophical overtones it is more reminiscent of Chaucer or Dante than of anything in modern literature. Moreover, even within the immense sweep of such a sequence, Wells succeeds in keeping the dream integrally related to the narrator's state of mind prior to his operation, so that the whole experience impresses us as being fundamentally 'true'. The protagonist's first thought on being told of the need for an operation is that few of his acquaintances would regret his death or consider it as more than a minor inconvenience. He has long felt remote from, and emotionally uncommitted to, the few friends remaining from his youth and the 'dream' under the chloroform echoes and expands upon this scheme on a cosmic scale: throughout his vast dream-journey, as the earth and all recognisable places fade and become insignificant in the immensities of space, the feeling that assails and chills him is that of his isolation from any social intercourse – the terrible loneliness.

Suddenly feeling came back to me – feeling in the shape of overwhelming terror; such a dread of those dark vastitudes as no words can describe. Were there no other souls, invisible to me as I to them, about me in the blackness? or was I indeed, even as I felt, alone? Had I passed out of being into something that was neither being nor non-being?⁵⁹

This is the most intricate dream sequence in Wells's writing since it actually elucidates the subconscious levels of the character involved. Unlike the other examples, it also involves a therapeutic element, for the dream experience of terrifying solitude removes the emotional block which has hitherto held the narrator back from commitment to personal relationships. On returning to consciousness after his operation, he finds that 'the dull melancholy of half a year was lifted from my mind'.[60]

Apart from his treatment of the general aspects of the science of psychology, as outlined above, Wells was also deeply interested in theories of sexual conduct and here too his approach is that of the scientist eager to propound a general theory from his observations and predict future behavioural patterns at both the personal and the social level. Freud's theories placed a very great, even, many believed, a disproportionate emphasis on sex as the primary motivating force in determining behaviour, but although Freud's germinal work on the subject, *Three Contributions to the Theory of Sex*, was first published in German in 1905, and translated into English in 1910, it was long before its influence on the English novel was seen directly. Wells's writings show a progressive awareness of sex as a primary motivating force, but it would seem from his autobiography that the increasing preoccupation with sexual problems in his novels was less the result of an acquaintance with Freudian psychology than the reflection of his own personal relationships which he was beginning to analyse with much interest. Looking back on his life, he wrote:

> The second main system of motivation other than the intellectual in the working out of my personal destiny, has been the sexual system . . . I suspect the sexual system should be at least the second theme when it is not the first, in every autobiography, honestly and fully told. It seizes upon the essential egoism for long periods, it insists upon a prominent role in the dramatizations of the *persona* and it will not be denied.[61]

and of his writings about sex:

> [They] arose very directly out of my own personal difficulties. They were essentially an eversion, a generalization, an attempt to put my case in the character of Everyman.
> In my earlier writings the topic of sex is conspicuously absent, I

felt then that I knew nothing about it that could possibly be communicated.[62]

The scientific romances avoid the subject of sexual relations without too great a sense of sidestepping the issue, but in the early novels the omission of such discussion is noticeable as a deficiency. In *A Modern Utopia* he again avoided posing sexual problems, this time not by ignoring them altogether but by assuming them to have been already 'solved'. Like Plato he took the purely intellectualist solution, and described a utopia in which sexual attractions were freely accepted and freely satisfied at least between the Samurai, without arousing any inconvenient personal or social tensions. Only gradually did he come to understand the primacy of fixation, possessiveness, dominance and jealously, not merely as artificially imposed social taboos but as innate instincts in the human psyche. *In The Days of the Comet* has as its major theme a study of jealousy and the evil passions it spawns in the lives of individuals and of society, but again Wells knows of no means to overcome it by an act of will. He can only juxtapose the portrait of a new society where such passions no longer exist – a restatement of the utopian situation – and sexual relationships are treated with a sensitive casualness epitomised in the *ménage à quatre* which is the solution offered to Nettie and Leadford's simultaneous love for each other and for two others.

In *Ann Veronica* Wells made a more realistic attempt to deal with the sexual situation as it was, rather than merely with an 'ideal society'; indeed this, together with the element of libel, was the reason for the scandal it occasioned amongst Wells's contemporaries. The aspects of Ann's character which caused most offence to supporters of the conventional picture of womanhood were, firstly, her frank confession of curiosity about sex itself and, secondly, her role as aggressor in the relationship with Capes. Not only does she declare her love before she has any indication of his feelings towards her, but this attraction has been triggered by frankly physical stimuli:

> She looked down at him and saw the sunlight was gleaming from his cheeks and that all over his cheeks was a fine golden down of delicate hairs. . . . She became aware of his presence as she had never been aware of any human being in her life before. She became aware of the modelling of his ear, of the muscles of his

neck. . . . She found she was trembling at his nearness and full of
a thrilling dread that he might touch her. . . . Then he got up
and left her. She had a feeling at his departure as of an immense
cavity, of something enormously gone; she could not tell whether
it was infinite regret or infinite relief. . . .

But now Ann Veronica knew what was the matter with her.[63]

Besides Ann's realisation and acceptance of such physical attraction, Wells notes also the ambiguous emotion which such a
realisation elicits – 'infinite regret or infinite relief'. More interesting, and almost certainly unique for its time, is Wells's clear
indication of the presence of a male principle in his heroine's
personality. Immediately after this scene in which she finds herself
so attracted by the 'fine golden down of delicate hairs' on Capes's
cheek, and the 'muscles of his neck', there follows a vignette of Ann
Veronica both delighting in and wondering at her own physical
characteristics, principal among which are 'the soft flow of muscle
under her skin' and on 'the back of her arm . . . the faintest down of
hair'.[64] Later, in prison, and genuinely repentant for what she sees
as her 'smirched innocence', she admits explicitly to an element of
maleness in her character:

'I'm not a good specimen of a woman. I've got a streak of male.
Things happen to women – proper women – and all they have to
do is to take them well. They've just got to keep white. But I'm
always trying to make things happen. And I get myself
dirty. . . .'[65]

Here Wells is certainly formulating the now accepted but then
highly unorthodox principle of the combined active and passive,
male and female, elements within any individual personality.

The New Machiavelli adds little in terms of insight into sexual
relationships and, despite the descriptions of Remington's childhood, ignores any element of infantile sexuality. The novel does
reassert strongly, however, the primacy of sex as a motivating force
in adult life, even at the cost of ideals, intellectual principles and
social rules. But despite his own flouting of social conventions, Wells
also shows in this novel a perceptive realisation of the need for social
sanction which lies deep in the nature of the sexual drive itself.
Before the liason between Remington and Isabel has become

publicly known, they consider the opposing values involved in their relationship:

> We wanted quite intensely to live together and have a child, but also we wanted very many other things that were incompatible with these desires. . . . It wasn't as if we could throw everything aside for our love and have that as we wanted it. Love such as we bore one another isn't altogether, or even chiefly, a thing in itself – it is for the most part a value set upon things. Our love was interwoven with all our other interests; to go out of the world and live in isolation seemed to us like killing the best parts of each other; we loved the sight of each other engaged finely and characteristically, we knew each other best as activities . . . we wanted to share a home and not a solitude.[66]

When, eventually, they do decide to ignore the opinions of their society, their defiance emphasises both the strength of their passion for each other and its subsequent failure, for once forced into premature retirement in Italy they lose their previously dominant concerns and interests, and hence all that held them together intellectually. Their two-level love has been tragically reduced to a one-level relationship.

In *The World Set Free* Wells suggests that the comparative freedom of the world-state is but a first step in the evolution of a more distant and more ideal future state in which men and women will be freed altogether from the traumas imposed by their sexuality. Karenin, one of the intellectual leaders of the new world-state, expounds this hope that sexual excitement will come to be seen merely as a part of growing up, and sexual differences rendered unimportant.

> Humanity is not only overspecialized in these matters, but all its institutions, its customs, everything exaggerate, intensify this difference. I want to unspecialize women . . . I do not want to go as we go on now, emphasising this natural difference; I do not deny it, but I want to reduce it and overcome it. . . . Men and women have to become human beings.[67]

Thus, although Wells seems to have read little of Freud's work at the time of writing his major novels, he apparently arrived independently at many of the ideas held by European psychologists about sexual motivation and behaviour. In his autobiography (written later than the major novels) he analyses as objectively as possible his own sexual motivations and, as a result of this self-scrutiny, reaches the conclusion that human beings oscillate between fixation upon an individual and promiscuity.[68] But he never succeeded in portraying this oscillation convincingly in his characters – possibly because the character novels were all written before his own views were clarified.

With this exception, Wells's novels present sexual relations primarily as he understood, or was aware of them, from his own personal experiences and direct observation of life, rather than as the direct outcome of his reading of Freudian psychology. It is therefore some measure of his perceptive and scientific approach to the subject that the analogues of so many of Freud's ideas may be traced in Wells's work.

Whatever his shortcomings may have been in the portrayal of emotions, there remains one area of psychological study in which Wells's novels cannot be considered deficient – the description of intellectual activity. This preoccupation with the conscious self as it develops during intellectual activity is most apparent in the extent to which his characters continually meditate on, soliloquise about, or debate issues. Wells was particularly concerned with the formative effect of problems on character, and those protagonists who do not debate within themselves or discuss with others, do not grow or develop – indeed, in Wells's opinion, they scarcely live. In his autobiography he explains this concentration on debate as follows:

> There is no satisfactory device I knew for exhibiting a train of reasoning in a character unless a set of ideas similar to those upon which the character thinks exists already in the reader's mind. . . . I could not see how, if we were to grapple with new ideas, a sort of argument with the reader, an explanation of the theory that is being exhibited, could be avoided. I began therefore to make my characters indulge in impossibly explicit monologues and duologues.[69]

Thus Ann Veronica develops as a person when she begins to consider problems intellectually – both her own personal situation and wider social issues – and, whatever we may feel about the appropriateness of her over-long soliloquies, it is chiefly through these that we know her as a lively and developing personality.

Ann Veronica is an educated young woman and hence her extensive periods of cerebration are not incredible, but in portraying his 'little men' Wells had first to solve the problem of presenting the motivations of the conscious self without exceeding the bounds of realism. In *Kipps* he did not reach a wholly satisfactory solution, and Kipps is therefore seen too much from the 'outside', almost wholly through his words and actions. Indeed from the outset we are warned that 'by nature of his training he was indistinct in his speech, confused in his mind and retreating in his manners'. Five years later, however, in *Mr. Polly*, Wells achieved a brilliant and unique presentation of the mental processes of a non-intellectual character. The richness of Polly's mental activity and his intellectual growth to a realisation of certain fundamental values, are accounted for by his wide and avid reading, yet rendered credible by the unconventional vocabulary and whimsical turns of phrase which are the legacy of his particular background. As he passes from a state of chronic agitation and dyspepsia to one of tranquillity and fulfilment, his thought patterns follow a corresponding path, expressed in the change from near-unintelligible exclamatory outbursts and heated irrelevant interjections to the calm and meditative tone epitomised in his final discussion with the Fat Woman on the subject of sunsets.

Many of Wells's later characters are required to voice explicitly their author's views on the importance of rational procedures, both for the individual and for the race, and are therefore necessarily represented as being, themselves, intellectuals prone to exposition. Remington pins his hopes for socio-political reform on a return to 'fine thinking' and writes interminable essays whenever he is not orally expounding his political views. The Traffords spend six months in Labrador discussing their own situation and their potential social role, until Trafford finally returns to England to propound his own equivalent of Remington's 'fine thinking'. *The Research Magnificent* is largely a discussion and monologue by the ostensible writer about Benham's quest; *Mr. Britling Sees It Through* begins as a factual narrative but ends in dialogue and monologue, while *The Soul of a Bishop* is even more expository. *Joan and Peter* lapses into dialogue towards the end, and in *The Undying Fire*, Wells reverts frankly to the form of a Platonic dialogue with characters who are the clearly recognisable counterparts of those in the Book of Job, and who recite their arguments almost liturgically along the pattern laid down by their Old Testament predecessors.

There are several reasons for this apparently undue emphasis on cerebration and exposition in Wells's novels. Partly it would seem that he saw a clear causal link between mental processes and behaviour, the aspect of character in which he was most interested, and therefore he was concerned to trace the lines of thought which resulted in certain actions; but also, like many of the Behaviourist School of his time, he was not prepared to dabble extensively in the workings of the unconscious. Despite his acknowledgment of its existence, Wells believed that an undue preoccupation with the subconscious mind could lead only to a stultifying introversion, an opting out of social responsibilities. In *The New Machiavelli* Remington meditates upon the relative concern which should be accorded the physical activities of life and the motivations of the subconscious or pre-conscious self – the 'mental hinterland'. He concludes:

> No man can abolish his immediate self and specialize in the depths! If he attempts it he simply turns himself into something a little less than the common man. He may have an immense hinterland, but that does not absolve him from a frontage. That is the essential error of the specialist philosopher, the specialist teacher, the specialist publicist. They repudiate the frontage; claim to be pure hinterland.[70]

In making this criticism, Wells seems to have foreseen in part the effect which a preoccupation with the unconscious would have upon the novel under the influence of Virginia Woolf, Dorothy Richardson and James Joyce. Concentration on the subconscious mental processes of a few characters produced a different kind of novel – one in which the characters were studied in depth as individuals, usually in comparative isolation from their background and from society. Although Wells later became interested in the work of these writers,[71] he would scarcely have considered writing such a novel himself for his aims were utterly contrary to theirs – his stress was upon the role of the individual in *society*, not in isolation, and on the individual as he might become rather than as he was at present. In so far as he was concerned with complexes, repressions, and phobias, it was not for their own sake but rather to overcome them as speedily as possible. Indeed Wells apparently had no great faith in the progress of psychology, even in its own sphere, condemning what he considered its failure to follow the experimental method, and its propensity to produce, instead, elaborate theories based on insufficient evidence. Later study has tended to support this verdict, for in the early years of the century, psychology undoubtedly was bedevilled by copious theories which made predictions too vague and too ambiguous to admit of clear experimental support or disproof.

The major reason, however, for the apparent psychological limitation of Wells's characters lies in his confessed propagandist purpose. In his autobiography he admitted:

The general reader to whom I addressed myself cared no more for finish and fundamental veracity about secondary things of behaviour than I. I did not want to sweep under the mat for crumbs of characterization, nor did he want me to do so. What we wanted was a ventilation of the point at issue.[72]

Necessarily then, Wells was concerned primarily to show his characters as thinking their way conclusively to some particular conviction which he himself wished to propound. Like Shaw, the other great literary reformer of this period, he was not content merely to describe psychological principles at work in his characters, but was more interested in using such understanding to manipulate and convert his readers to his own particular sociological beliefs. By making his characters think, discuss and actually develop their ideas during the course of the novel, he induced his readers to follow the same intellectual process, often without their realising or resisting it. Above all, he wanted to stimulate his readers to think, not merely to sweep them along on a surge of emotional response. Inevitably therefore his characters seem often to be correspondingly poor in emotional appeal. If this is a flaw in his art – and it must to some extent be considered so – it must also be seen within the perspective of his overall purpose as expressed in his non-fictional works.

It would seem, then, that Wells brought to the characterisation of his novels a concept of mankind and of individuals which arose directly from his scientific training and which, other things being equal, was such as to militate against the description of an individual's emotions and to concentrate instead on wider social issues. Of psychology as a theoretical study Wells seems to have been as aware as any novelist of his time, and allusions, either direct or implicit, to many of the concerns of twentieth-century psychology may be found throughout his novels; but in general he fails to realise his characters sympathetically and emotionally because this was neither his ambition nor his interest. With few exceptions his characters are subsidiary to his sociological purpose, as he himself freely conceded:

> In effect in my hands the Novel proved like a blanket too small for the bed, and when I tried to pull it over to cover my tossing conflict of ideas, I found I had to abandon questions of individuation. . . . I had very many things to say and . . . if I could say one of them in such a way as to get my point over to the reader I did not worry much about finish.[73]

We may well criticise this as a basis for literature, but given his avowed intention Wells's characterisation is more than adequate and often rises to considerable heights. Almost never are his characters totally flat, even when they are little more than mouthpieces for his own theories. Here again he capitalises, whether consciously or unconsciously, on his familiarity with science which could usually be relied upon to produce a novel perspective, an added dimension or an unexpected comment and insight into an otherwise predictable passage of propaganda.

9 The Scientist as a Literary Character

Apart from these general aspects of Wells's characterisation, there was one class of character whose conception was particularly influenced by Wells's scientific background – the figure of the scientist – and it is worth tracing the development of his portrayal of scientists in some detail since previous studies of the scientist as a figure in literature had, in the main, been rudimentary.[1]

Wells's early attempts at describing scientists were not entirely successful either. Dr Nebogipfel of 'The Chronic Argonauts' seems at first to be merely an exaggerated alchemist figure, his face that of the sunken-eyed fanatic, his demeanour reminiscent of Frankenstein:

> His aquiline nose, thin lips, high cheek-ridges and pointed chin, were all small and mutually well-proportioned; but the bones and muscles of his face were rendered excessively prominent and distinct by his extreme leanness. The same cause contributed to the sunken appearance of the large, eager-looking grey eyes, that gazed forth from under his phenomenally wide and high forehead. . . . It seemed to be great beyond all preconceived ratio to the rest of his countenance. Dimensions, corrugations, wrinkles, venation, were all alike abnormally exaggerated. Below it his eyes glowed like lights in some cave at a cliff's foot. It so overpowered and suppressed the rest of his face as to give an *unhuman* appearance almost to what would otherwise have been an unquestionably handsome profile. The lank black hair that hung unkempt before his eyes served to increase rather than to conceal this effect, by adding to unnatural altitude a suggestion of hydrocephalic projection, and the idea of something ultra human was furthermore accentuated by the temporal arteries that pulsated visibly through his transparent yellow skin.[2]

Only from Wells's later work do we realise that this description of
Nebogipfel whose name, as Bergonzi points out, means 'Promised
Land'[3] – in this case the land or time of the future, for he specifically
refers to himself as 'a man born out of his time' – is really closer to
Wells's concept of man of the future than to a figure from the past.
In 'Man of the Year Million' he describes imaginary, more highly
evolved members of the species, the increase in whose brain
development has demanded a greater proportion of brow and
cranium to house it:

> Eyes large, lustrous, beautiful, soulful; above them, no longer
> separated by rugged brow ridges, is the top of the head, a
> glistening hairless dome, terete and beautiful; no craggy nose rises
> to disturb by its unmeaning shadows the symmetry of that calm
> face, no vestigial ears project; the mouth is a small, perfectly
> round aperture, toothless and gumless, jawless, unanimal, no
> futile emotions disturbing its roundness as it lies, like the harvest
> moon, or the evening star, in the wide firmament of the face.[4]

The mention of the harvest moon is a reminder that the description
is not inapplicable to the Grand Lunar, also of a more highly
evolved species, in the Wellsian canon, than twentieth-century
man, or to the Martians of *The War of the Worlds*.

Apart from his physical appearance, Nebogipfel embodies
another traditional characteristic of the scientist – devotion to his
research at the expense of physical comfort and social discourse. He
is a recluse, like the mediaeval alchemist in his cave, arousing the
suspicions of his neighbours who believe he is a 'war-lock'; he guards
his secret not, as did the alchemists, for financial gain, but in order to
find in a future age the fulfilment which his benighted contemporaries deny him.

In Wells's later development of 'The Chronic Argonauts', *The
Time Machine*, Nebogipfel is modified almost beyond recognition.
The Time Traveller, far from being the exotic figure of the earlier
draft, has become the epitome of ordinariness, so much so that he
lacks even a name to identify him as an individual, as he shuffles in
his carpet slippers around his cosy drawing room or devotes himself
with relish to his dinner and cigar. There are at least two possible
reasons for this change. In the interim between 'The Chronic
Argonauts' and *The Time Machine* Wells apparently decided that
the brief glimpse of a man of the future was worthy of further

development, for, two years before *The Time Machine*, he published 'Man of the Year Million'; presumably he may have felt that he could not exploit this same theme yet further in *The Time Machine*. However a more forceful reason for the change was probably his realisation that one of the most effective methods of inducing a suspension of disbelief in his reader was to people an incredible story with the most ordinary characters and, where possible, to enclose an improbable happening within an envelope of the most mundane setting. After 'Man of the Year Million', Wells's scientists become closer to the commonplace than those found in almost any earlier writings. In *The Time Machine* the sense of wonder is reserved for the events which befall the Time Traveller; he himself remains, apart from his having designed the machine, almost a passive spectator, provoked to action only in self-defence. He is thus predominantly the scientist-as-observer or the traveller to whom things happen, in the tradition of Verne's scientists.

In *The Wonderful Visit*, Wells's next novel, we have a third kind of scientist, different from both the mysterious alchemist and the passive observer. Crump typifies the worst aspects of scientific pretension; indeed he is almost a parody of the bigot, ignoring whatever does not fit into a preconceived theory, and brutally chopping data to fit his Procrustean system. The vignette of Crump's confrontation with the angel's wing is a classic example of his obstinate prejudices and preconceptions:

> 'Spinal curvature?' muttered Dr. Crump. . . . 'No! abnormal growth. . . . Curious. . . . Reduplication of the anterior limb – bifid coracoid . . . curious integumentary simulation of feathers. Dear me. Almost avian . . . curious malformation this is!'[5]

That Crump should have been modelled on Huxley, whom Wells continued to admire, seems highly unlikely. What does seem probable is that he embodies Wells's resentment against the two professors who succeeded Huxley as his teachers at South Kensington. In his autobiography, comparing Judd, the professor of geology, with Huxley, Wells writes:

> That flame of interrogation which kept Huxley's biological course molten and moving, burnt not at all in the geological course, and except for the bright moments when our own individual curiosity lit up a corner – and went out again, – we

were confronted by a great array of dark, cold assorted facts, lifelessly arranged and presented.[6]

Such an attitude is both the cause and effect of Crump's approach.

Between *The Wonderful Visit* and *Dr. Moreau* came the volume of short stories, *The Stolen Bacillus and other Incidents*. Most of these stories add little to any developing portrayal of the scientist; the bacteriologist of the title story is an amiable eccentric who turns out to have more presence of mind than seemed at first probable, but he is basically only a variation of the comic figure. The astronomer at the Avu observatory who is attacked, apparently by some unknown species of bat, is even less distinguished, for he is of interest in the story only as the object of the strange creature's attack. His reactions do change from interested curiosity to fear, to an expression of helpless rage and finally to a 'curious sinking sensation' as he regains consciousness, but these potentially interesting experiences are not explored in any psychological depth, and the characterisation as a whole remains shallow. 'The Diamond Maker' returns to the idea of the scientist as a fanatic, disregarding personal comfort, even necessities, and social relationships for the sake of his experiment, but unlike Nebogipfel, his motives are not untainted by avarice, and in the unexpected difficulties which attend his scientific 'success', we have a foretaste of *The Invisible Man*, published two years later. In 'The Remarkable Case of Davidson's Eyes', also in this volume, there is a brief but interesting juxtaposition of two contrasting attitudes found among scientists. On the one hand is the narrator who has learnt and assimilated a certain systematic view of the universe and refuses to consider anything which seems to be at variance with such a picture. This attitude seemed to Wells a wholly unscientific approach for it rejected as superstition any observation which appeared to conflict with its world view. Contrasted with him is the mentally flexible Professor Wade, who is not seen directly but whose views are relayed to us by the disapproving narrator. Wells contrives to play off one attitude against the other and to elicit our sympathy for Wade, despite our inherent impulse to question his assertions. In the narrator, as in the character of Crump, Wells is satirising the pseudo-scientific attitude which he believed he had encountered in the rote-learning and water-tight classifications of Professor Judd's geology classes.

'The Moth', in this same collection, pinpoints a more dangerous trait of the false scientist – the desire for glory, and the concomitant rivalry, extended to the point of obsession, between colleagues. However small the rewards of publication and recognition amongst one's co-workers may seem to the uninitiated, to the scientist the desire for such fame can become a ruling passion, directing, and perhaps ruining his life. 'The Moth' is one of the few instances in which Wells explicitly considered the psychological effect of circumstances on his characters. Hapley is motivated not only by his desire for esteem amongst entomologists but, and this is by far his major concern, by hatred of his rival, Pawkins. Science becomes for him a means to his one end of destroying the reputation of Pawkins, and his apparent devotion to research is in fact only his way of providing ammunition for his antipathy.

> For twenty years he had worked hard, sometimes far into the night, and seven days a week, with microscope, scalpel, collecting net and pen, and almost entirely with reference to Pawkins. The European reputation he had won had come as an incident in that great antipathy.[7]

Pawkins's death leaves Hapley's life with a void which nothing can fill – nothing, that is, except Pawkins himself, and in Hapley's deranged mind Pawkins does indeed return to fill the gap. All attempts to divert Hapley's attention by amusement fail dismally, until finally Pawkins assumes for him the guise of a rare, perhaps unique, moth whose capture becomes an obsession, even as he teeters on the brink of realising, with half his mind, that the moth is an illusion. His awkward reply to the vicar who, naturally, fails to see 'his' moth is more illuminating than he knows: 'The eye of faith is no better than the eye of Science'. Wells seems to have been deeply aware of the danger to the mind when science, or indeed anything, assumes the status of a fanatical obsession, but in 'The Moth' much of the effect of this potentially important study is lost through the humorous telling which detracts from its seriousness, until one suspects that Wells is virtually only playing with the idea. None of these early portrayals of the scientist has the depth which he was to achieve in his later work, but they hint at the studies of the perverted scientist which followed.

In *Dr. Moreau*, the picture of a scientist is given in much greater length and depth. This novel has already been discussed with reference to its mythical qualities, and it has been seen that Moreau is portrayed not only as a man, but also as an allegorical figure, representing in part the process of evolution itself. As a scientist he displays that devotion to science for its own sake which Wells believed to be the only true scientific attitude and on which he later tried to pattern his ideal societies. Moreau has no thought of financial gain or even of fame; he is motivated solely by the desire to succeed for his own satisfaction in the experiment he has conceived. However he is also the scientist untouched by ethical considerations; his experiment is his religion and his only morality is that dictated by the material he observes; emotional considerations carry no weight in determining his behaviour. It is because his ethics have become in fact those of the evolutionary process that he succeeds as a symbol as well as a person; he embodies all the violence and arbitrariness of a 'nature red in tooth and claw', 'so careful of the type she seems, so careless of the single life'.[8] It is tempting to regard Moreau as the type of the scientist in this novel – and indeed this has induced some critics to see the novel as a criticism of Huxley and all biologists – but such an assumption ignores the importance of the contrast which Wells has deliberately contrived within the novel by the juxtaposition of Prendick and Moreau. Prendick is also a scientist, significantly, like Wells, a past student of Huxley, and it is his relatively objective appraisal of the scenes on the island which balances the excesses of Moreau and Montgomery. Prendick is the type of the earnest, self-effacing research worker whose original ideas are few and limited, who in fact may fail to grasp a new concept at first, but who considers it and weighs it, not merely in isolation but in relation to the rest of life – to morality and humanity and the dictates of social conscience. Moreau, on the other hand, is still the scientist-as-alchemist, not only in his physical appearance, which is reminiscent of Nebogipfel, but also in his secretiveness and isolation. He thus embodies the attitude which Wells was later to denounce explicitly as being most detrimental to both science and society.

Before leaving this succession of 'bad' scientists, Wells portrayed one more example. Griffin, the invisible man, is his most complete study of the pretension of 'false science'. Like Moreau, Griffin is larger than life both as a character, and in his allegorical role. He is a modern Faustus, whose career he follows in some detail, and in his invisibility he also partakes of the aura of folk story and myth, standing as a whimsical inversion of 'The Emperor's New Clothes' fable, in that his clothes are visible but he is not. Like Faustus, Griffin apparently began as a conscientious student, but soon desired too eagerly the material benefits which he believed his researches would bestow. The language in which he relates these aspirations to Kemp is characteristically Marlovian:

'To do such a thing [become invisible] would be to transcend magic. And I beheld, unclouded by doubt, a magnificent vision of all that invisibility might mean to a man – the mystery, the power, the freedom.'[9]

Almost immediately these aspirations beget a selfishness, a bourgeois mania for financial gain which degrades the would-be pure-minded scientist. Already he has ceased to serve science and wants it to serve him; his common humanity has become deadened by a megalomaniac desire for power and profit. Like Faustus, Griffin fails to realise that his supposed superiority has begun to diminish him by humanitarian standards, just as, believing that his desire for power is justified because the lives of common people are purposeless, he fails to see the barrenness of his own life. Contempt becomes his habitual attitude towards others, and what he regards as their stupidity provokes his rage yet further:

'By Heaven, Kemp, you don't know what rage *is*! . . . to get some fumbling, purblind idiot messing across your course. Every conceivable sort of silly creature that has ever been created has been sent to cross me.'[10]

Again like Faustus, his unspecified but grandiose plans for exploiting his invisibility give way to cheap conjuring tricks; the scene with the tramp Marvel resembles nothing so much as that of Faustus at the Pope's banquet. He promises Marvel, 'I will do great things for you. An invisible man is a man of power', but is soon reduced to gloating over petty theft:

'I could take my money where I found it. I decided to treat myself to a sumptuous feast and then put up at a good hotel and accumulate a new outfit of property. I felt amazingly confident.'[11]

When these proposed triumphs fail to eventuate, his rage becomes a mania. As with Faustus, the corruption of the best in him (his genius) leads directly to the worst, and he becomes a ruthless and virtually inhuman madman, whose only goal is to institute a reign of terror. However, unlike Marlowe, Wells does not trust to a supernatural scheme of punishment; Griffin's nemesis springs inevitably from his own actions and attitudes. The things he reaches for recede before his Tantalus-like grasp; cold, hungry, pursued, and in dire danger of being run over, he remains unrepentant even at death. But Wells wreaks a further and perhaps more severe punishment on Griffin, one which Faustus was not forced to endure. Unlike Moreau, Griffin is, from the first, presented as faintly absurd and the suspicion of this is never fully overcome even in the scenes of his 'reign of terror' and the final brutal chase. It is not easy to be sure how far this was intended by Wells as a further level of meaning in the story and how far it resulted from his exuberant inability to pass by an opportunity for the vivacious situational humour which the particular circumstances of this story offered, but it seems reasonable to see it as an extension of the warning already inherent in 'The Moth' – the insanity to which obsession with an evil motive potentially leads. To condemn Griffin out of his own mouth is damning enough, but to render him, as well, a semi-comic figure is a greater and more humiliating indictment. In this story, too, as in *Dr. Moreau*, there is a foil to Griffin. Kemp is the counterpart of Prendick – though he carries more authorial approbation. He is the capable and humane man of science, alert, open-minded, and conceding that his moral and social responsibilities are primary considerations. His cunning and what, in other circumstances, might seem rank brutality – the decision to spread powdered glass on the roads in order to catch the bare-footed Griffin – are tempered, within the context of the story, by the urgency of the situation, and made to appear justified.

Up to this point in his work, Wells's scientist-protagonists, with the exception of the Time Traveller, who is not fully individualised, have been increasingly reprehensible characters. Griffin stands as the nadir of any concept of a scientist and it would appear therefore that at this juncture the young Wells had scant respect for the profession. One might question how sincere was his avowed admiration for Huxley when he repeatedly portrayed scientists as immoral, inhuman sadists who are ultimately seen to be as mean and foolish as the most petty of mortals. What must also be realised though, is that in all these cases where scientists are reviled, Wells's condemnation is evoked precisely because they are *not* acting as 'true' scientists, but are prostituting their scientific knowledge for other purposes. They act from greed, from hatred or from a desire for self-aggrandisement but never in the selfless and responsible pursuit of truth and certainly never in the attitude which Huxley advocated – that of sitting down humbly before the facts like a little child.[12]

Having thus castigated the false practitioners, Wells turned to the glorification of the true scientist; but first there came two intermediate studies, interesting because of their ambiguity.

In one sense Lewisham can barely be considered a scientist at all since he never attains to the heights of research or even to his first degree, but he is the first of Wells's science students, modelled on his own days at South Kensington, and as such he was hailed in *Nature*.[13] Lewisham's story resembles Wells's own experiences in several details, apart from the basic setting of his student years – the conflict between his studies and an incipient romantic entanglement, membership of a student debating society, and the attractions apparently offered by the humanities to truant science students who frequented the Dyce and Foster Reading Rooms instead of attending practical classes.[14] Lewisham is interesting here, in a discussion of Wells's scientists, chiefly in a negative sense; he supplies the type, not of the evil scientist, but of the student who lacks the necessary drive and single-mindedness to qualify. His most outstanding characteristic is his unmitigated ordinariness and thus his early aspirations, as embodied in the Schema, are from the beginning rendered powerless by the commonplace elements of his personality. His succumbing to the first diversion which offers any real interest, his inability to cope in encounters with attractive members of the opposite sex, are ill omens for the years of more serious temptations at university and he duly falls before them. However the surprising, and hence the most interesting, feature of the novel is Wells's ambivalence about Lewisham's final situation. Having eventually relinquished his grandiose ambitions for a career in research, Lewisham comes to see his mission in life in terms of his child-to-be, his contribution to the future of the race. As he weighs the alternatives:

His eyes came back to the Schema. His hands shifted to the opposite corners and he hesitated. The vision of that arranged Career, that ordered sequence of work and successes, distinction and yet further distinctions, rose brightly from the symbol. Then he compressed his lips and tore the yellow sheet in half, tearing very deliberately. He doubled the halves and tore again, doubled again very carefully and neatly until the Schema was torn into numberless little pieces. With it he seemed to be tearing his past self. 'Play,' he whispered after a long silence. 'It is the end of my adolescence,' he said, 'the end of my empty dreams.'[15]

This final action by Lewisham is recorded without authorial comment and the question therefore arises as to how far Wells endorsed his character's decision. On the one hand it seems an abrogation of any belief in the validity of a scientific career. Yet the chapter is entitled decisively 'The Crowning Victory', and in fact we have never been led to believe very strongly in Lewisham's aspirations. Does Wells reject a career in science for Lewisham because of Lewisham's own deficiencies in intellect and character, or because he has deeper doubts about the benefits of such a career *per se*? After the series of novels and short stories in which the scientist figure is never portrayed in a wholly favourable light, and often in quite the reverse, we might well suspect that we are intended not only to endorse Lewisham's decision but even to feel that he may be too noble for such a dubious profession. Yet later in his career Wells came to regard scientists as being almost the only hope for the future of an otherwise benighted mankind.

The anomaly is continued in Wells's next novel, *The First Men in the Moon*. One of the most successful scientific romances, it anticipates many of the hopes and fears of the space age. The study of Cavor, the man who discovers how to make and use the revolutionary substance, cavorite, would seem to imply an ambiguous attitude, still common today, towards the scientist and his role in society. As a character, Cavor displays nearly all the virtues of the scientist – devotion to his work for its own sake (Cavor, one of the first 'absent-minded professors' in literature, is, to Bedford's disgust, untainted by any desire for financial gain), sacrifice of time, money and bodily comfort, even the ultimate sacrifice of his life, for his research. Yet although this cheerful Cavor, with his apparently harmless eccentricities of behavour, seems far removed from the sinister Moreau or the vicious Griffin, he is potentially more dangerous to society than they, for, unsuspected behind this naïve façade, there lurks an attitude quite as ruthless as theirs. Cavor is prepared to sacrifice not only himself but others too, if necessary, for the success of his experiment. After the explosion at his house during the first attempts to produce cavorite, he merely remarks of his assistants, presumed dead:

> 'My three assistants may or may nor have perished. That is a detail. If they have, it is no great loss; they were more zealous than able, and this premature event may be largely due to their joint neglect of the furnace.'[16]

Later in the novel, the irresponsible and avaricious Bedford betrays a similar attitude towards the unfortunate boy who has disappeared in the cavorite sphere. The parallelism of the two incidents cannot be accidental. A moral question is being posed: is Cavor's callousness, albeit arising from his single-minded devotion to the pursuit of science, any less reprehensible on that account than Bedford's, which is obviously unprincipled, and if not, what are we to think of a science which apparently encourages, if it does not directly induce, such behaviour by Cavor?

Cavor also epitomises the trained scientific observer, recording accurately and without emotional bias. Even when he is being hunted by the Selenites he does not cease to record with a stub of pencil on a fragment of paper: '. . . a different sort of Selenite altogether. . . . They have larger brain cases – much larger. . . .'[17] Such an attitude, which is presented as an integral part of Cavor's scientific training, seems at first brave and admirable, but concerning this trait too Wells raises an unanswered query. Cavor observes the social organisation of the Selenites and reports on the methods whereby the young Selenites are conditioned so subtly and completely for their preordained careers as to be completely unaware of the fact. Yet his only apparent emotion while describing this system, which cannot but seem abhorrent to the reader, is the most naïve wonder at its ingenuity and efficiency:

> So also he [the conditioned Selenite] loves his work and discharges in perfect happiness the duty that justifies his being. And so it is with all sorts of conditions of Selenites – each is a perfect unit in a world machine.[18]

Wells can hardly be endorsing an attitude which extends tolerance and objectivity to the point where no moral judgments at all seem appropriate, for this was Moreau's position; when Cavor does admit to some instinctive distaste at the sight of the conditioning process as practised amongst the Selenites, he immediately apologises for this lapse from scientific objectivity and expresses a hope that he will learn in due course to appreciate these methods.[19] Thus Cavor may be seen in one sense as Wells's most subtle and complete attack on the scientist, for while few scientists would willingly identify themselves with Moreau or Griffin, many might fail to detect in Cavor anything other than a wholly admirable scientific approach to life.

The Food of the Gods, Wells's next major novel to include a study of a scientist, is also the first to suggest whole-hearted approval of such a figure. Bensington and Redwood, the two scientists who stumble upon the secret of Herakleophorbia, retain, for much of the novel, the initial impression we have of them as faintly ridiculous little men, who have had greatness thrust upon them because of their esoteric research into apparently irrelevant topics. Despite their research ability, they are accurately and succinctly assessed by Cossar as:

'Clever chaps . . . but no initiative whatever. I shall have to spend the whole night seeing they do what they know perfectly well they ought to have done all along. I wonder if it's research that makes 'em like that?'[20]

On the other hand, Cossar himself, an engineer who stands for the practical as opposed to the purely theoretical scientist, is wholly endorsed throughout. It is he who sees the potential of the 'food' and, while fully aware of its possible dangers, refuses to yield to the small-minded reactionaries who wish to prevent its production and to enslave the giant children. Nevertheless it is Redwood and his son who, at the end, are permitted the vision of a better world under the leadership of the young giants, and such a vision is granted only to those whom Wells considered the pure in heart, the trusted prophets of the future. The final comment on Redwood is clearly an approving one. Young Cossar, the leader of the gaints, acknowledges his wisdom:

'We are here, Brothers, to what end? To serve the spirit and the purpose that has been breathed into our lives. We fight not for ourselves – for we are but the momentary hands and the eyes of the World. So you, Father Redwood, taught us.'[21]

It is not until *Tono-Bungay* that, for the first time, a scientist becomes the protagonist of a full-length realistic novel. Although the novel has been valued chiefly for its commentry on the social and intellectual climate of late-Victorian and Edwardian England, the treatment of George himself marks a new event in the growth of the novel – the inclusion of science and the scientist as the central subject of serious literature.

It is interesting that, for most of the novel, George does not function as a scientist at all, and this may partly justify the apparently chaotic conglomeration of material in the novel; yet, at the end, he is held up to us as the dedicated pursuer of scientific truth. Where and why does the change take place and does it reflect a corresponding change in George's character? As a student, George resembles Wells himself in his somewhat dilettante approach to study once the first flush of enthusiasm has died down. Like Wells he lacks the earnestness and application to endure sheer routine, and casts around for other interests. However, after a period of immersion in his uncle's financial exploits, he turns to research in physics and aeronautics in order to understand and perfect his glider. The reason for this renewed interest in science is not.that George has changed, but rather that the subject is now sufficiently related to his main interest to secure his disciplined attention in a way that the abstract syllabus of his student days had not done. George's career thus follows a familiar pattern – the diligent fervour of the young, adolescent student, striving to attain university entrance, the slackening of self-discipline when the new freedom and varied interests of a university environment are encountered, the subsequent falling away from his studies and the belated return of the mature man who can summon self-discipline at will, since, having tasted most possible diversions, he can forsake them without difficulty. Wells himself trod the same path; Lewisham had followed it although he failed to take the final step – indeed George's penultimate stage is almost identical with Lewisham's university career: '. . . London took hold of me and Science which had been the universe, shrank back to the dimensions of tiresome little formulae compacted in a book.'[22]

But at this stage George begins to realise that the faults of the system lie in the teaching methods rather than in the subject.

If I had been *trained* in research – that ridiculous contradiction in terms – should I have done more than produce additions to the existing store of little papers with blunted conclusions, of which there are already too many?[23]

When he returns to scientific research, he brings with him something of the spontaneity and zest for work which are his uncle's chief assets. Science is no longer merely a disciplined curbing of all other interests and a dogged attention to duty, but a highly desirable 'mistress' to be pursued with passionate devotion. George develops this simile at length, in terms reminiscent of a classical invocation of the Muses:

> Scientific truth is the remotest of mistresses. She hides in strange places, she is attained by tortuous and laborious roads, but *she is always there!* Win her and she will not fail you; she is yours and mankind's for ever. She is reality, the one reality I have found in this strange disorder of existence. . . . Things grow under your hands when you serve her. Things that are permanent as nothing else is permanent in the whole life of man. That, I think, is the peculiar satisfaction of science and its enduring reward.[24]

This passage is almost certainly intended as a prelude to that in the last chapter where George contrasts the ephemeral material world with the enduring reality which he identifies with science:

> Sometimes I call this reality Science, sometimes I call it Truth. But it is something we draw by pain and effort out of the heart of life, that we disentangle and make clear. . . . I see it always as austerity, as beauty. This thing we make clear is the heart of life. It is the one enduring thing. Man and nations, epochs and civilizations, pass, each making its contribution. I do not know what it is, this something, except that it is supreme.[25]

This assertion seems at first wholly sincere – Wells's unreserved admiration for the values of science thus conceived; surely here at least there can be no ambiguity. Yet there is also a cold shaft of irony at the heart of the passage, for the symbol of this penetrating drive is wholly inhuman, bereft of any moral consideration – it is George's destroyer, 'stark and swift, irrelevant to most human interests'. George's own description of its passage down the Thames is fraught with ambivalence. While seeming whole-heartedly to approve, he simultaneously sows seeds of doubt and condemnation: 'Through the confusion something drives, something that is at once human achievement and the most inhuman of all existing things'.[26] Nor should we ignore the stress on the very name, 'destroyer'; it is not merely a battleship, or a submarine, but quite definitely a *destroyer* and Wells was surely aware of the symbolism, for Marion, who had virtually destroyed George's early career, rejoiced in the family name of Ramboat.

Wells's next qualified scientist is Capes in *Ann Veronica*, but Capes never becomes a major figure in the novel, and what we do know of him bears little relation to his career as an FRS. Eventually Wells, perhaps unable to visualise with any great conviction how the life of a research biologist might significantly contribute to his society, causes Capes to shrug off his scientific career, apparently without regret, and follow in his author's own steps to discover a literary vocation.

Wells's last major novel to portray a scientist as protagonist is *Marriage*. Here he explores the problems of Trafford, one of his most idealised scientists, in the sphere of personal relationships. Whereas George Ponderevo had remained basically a detached figure, Trafford is a warm personality, involved in close relationships, enjoying friendships and devoted to his family. His difficulties arise not from any incompetence or boredom with his research, but from the conflict between his work and his social obligations which he fully acknowledges. At the beginning of the novel he is already more mature than Lewisham or George Ponderevo, and finds his research fascinating and fulfilling. If, after the birth of his first daughter, he seems to waver in his career and wonders whether he has deprived his wife Marjorie unduly of his time, this doubt arises from his affection for her and not from any disenchantment with his research. Wells describes in some detail the ways in which tensions build up between Trafford, dedicated to his work, and Marjorie, who fails to understand why the demands of his research should not be always subsidiary to her claims upon his time. Her amazement when Trafford first comes home late from the laboratory is vividly and perceptively described.[27] A cumulation of such scenes and tensions begins to undermine Trafford's formerly placid nature:

It is only in romantic fiction that a man can work strenuously to the limit of his power and come home to be sweet, sunny and entertaining. Trafford's preoccupation involved a certain negligence of Marjorie, a certain indisposition to be amused or

interested by trifling things, a certain irritability. . . . But while
Marjorie shrank to the dimensions of reality, research remained
still a luminous and commanding dream. In love one fails or one
wins home, but the lure of research is for ever beyond the hills.
Every victory is a new desire. Science has inexhaustibly fresh
worlds to conquer.[28]

When Trafford is finally forced by the financial pressures of
marriage and Marjorie's extravagance to abandon his research in
crystallography for a job in industry, it is a genuine sacrifice on his
part, engendering a feeling of resentment against Marjorie, and
leaving a void in his life which, only after long consideration of his
social responsibilities, is he enabled to fill. Thus even Trafford, one
of Wells's most mature scientists, is not permitted to find ultimate
fulfilment in scientific research. Yet both before and after this novel,
Wells continued to produce sociological works, often flagrantly
propagandist, advocating the innovation of a world state, under the
leadership and guidance, at least initially, of scientists.

This apparent anomaly is best resolved by reference to Wells's
three-phase time scale of past, present and future man. Trafford and
George Ponderevo represent perhaps the farthest development of
present man *qua* scientist, capable and efficiently idealistic, but
unable to resolve the inherent conflict between research and
personal relationships, between a pursuit which is essentially
oriented towards the future, and the claims of present-day society
with all its instinctive resistance to change and progress. Like
Remington in the political sphere, they are not permitted to achieve
their full development in isolation from their society. So, too, the
brief portrait of Holstein in *The World Set Free* depicts a man torn
between his belief in the validity of his research and his awareness of
the inadequacy of his society to cope with the new knowledge he has
gained. Holstein is the prototype of many scientists in modern
fiction – the scientist-hero returned to the novel as an ordinary man
but greatly enriched morally as he struggles to save his society even
against its own will. Only in the moral and social utopia of the future
will this conflict disappear, for then all men will have been educated
to appreciate and foster the development of research concurrently
with, and not in opposition to, their obligations to society as a whole
and to the individuals within it. Nor, in this future utopia, will there
be any division of interest between man-the-thinker and man-the-
father, the biological contributor to his race – the division which

torments Lewisham and Trafford. All members of Wells's future society will gladly contribute whatever talents they possess to the Mind of the Race, which is both a physical and a cultural concept.

From this chronological survey of the scientists portrayed in his novels, it would seem that the young Wells, fresh from three years at South Kensington, but embittered by the failures of his last two years there, and resentful of the teachers whom he blamed for these failures, was all too aware of the imperfections of scientists, and only too ready to mistrust the established scientific pundits whom he saw as typifying the closed mind and the water-tight system, intolerant of any opposing views. He was at this stage prepared to approve of science and its principles, but not to applaud its practitioners. However, with the widespread acclaim accorded his scientific romances, he himself began to enjoy a reputation as an authority in scientific matters, and his portraits of scientists become correspondingly more sympathetic, with special emphasis on the problems facing the young science student, and the difficulties of reconciling pure research and personal relationships. (Wells was perhaps attempting to explain away his own early failures and to excuse his present incapacity to undertake scientific research.) The study of sociological questions, with which Wells was himself preoccupied, is represented as being more important than pure research in this present, imperfect world, because it will usher in the day when such research will not conflict with the highest humanitarian aims. Thus in the utopian novels of the future, Wells was able to project an idealised picture of his own newly-won scientific respectability and to gloss over the intermediate problems which, perhaps unwittingly, he had uncovered in his scientists of the present. Whatever the reason for his changing attitude to scientists however, his treatment of Lewisham and of George Ponderevo, and particularly of Trafford, paved the way for the entry of the scientist into the realistic novel, no longer as the alchemist figure, but as a fully human personality.

Nevertheless it must be admitted that Wells often failed to imagine in significant detail, or to speculate with sufficient confidence on what a life of research would actually entail. His scientists are therefore shown only fleetingly at work. What mainly interests Wells, and thus what his characters discuss and think about at great length, is the application of science to society; hence those scientists who are treated in detail soon follow their author and leave their laboratories to become advocates of social reform. Capes becomes a controversial playwright and Trafford returns from Labrador with the express intention of producing journalistic essays on social questions. Their situation is parallel to that of Remington whose interests are channelled towards the writing of autobiography when Wells find himself lacking in sufficient knowledge or enthusiasm to describe the details of a political career.

There is another group of Wells's characters who, having had a scientific education, fail to pursue it, and they are certainly the first of their kind in English, perhaps any, literature – Wells's modern young women. In a very real sense, the development of the new science made the emergence of the 'new woman' a necessity. The beginnings of this process are seen as early as Elizabeth Gaskell's *Wives and Daughters*. Here Molly Gibson clearly has to be 'educated' by Roger Hamley if she is to become a suitable wife for him and hence he prepares her for her future by lending her scientific articles to read even before there is any hint of their betrothal. In *Middlemarch*, on the other hand, Lydgate's marriage fails largely because Rosamond, despite her social accomplishments, has no awareness or appreciation of her husband's work, nor had Lydgate foreseen the necessity for such interest.

The majority of Wells's new women are said to have studied science, although only Ann Veronica is actually seen in the laboratory. In the first section of the novel, her values and method of thinking are alleged to be those of science – objectivity, a desire for the experimental approach and for precise deliberation. She quickly classifies others according to these criteria and dismisses her instructress at the Tredgold College as being 'hopelessly wrong and foggy – it was the test of a good anatomist – upon the skull'.[29] Her surroundings as well as her speech are studded with the symbols of science – her room is decorated with a pig's skull and her refusal of Manning's proposal is couched in terms of a botanical simile: 'I feel . . . as though I was being shut in from the light of life, and, as they say in botany, etoliated. . . .'[30] Later, her courtship with Capes, the class demonstrator, is conducted in a setting of methylated spirits, scalpels and microscope sections, while their garden of romance is the Zoological Gardens where they study attentively the chimpanzees, wart-hogs and toucans.[31] Ann Veronica's interests, and to a lesser extent Capes's, are aggressively those which proclaim the strongest bond with other members of the animal kingdom. Thus, at the Zoological Gardens, they particularly admire the chimpanzees for 'the gentle humanity of their eyes – "so much more human than human beings" '.[32] Capes considers himself as a 'mixture of beast and uncle', while Ann Veronica regards the down on the back of her arm with some satisfaction as 'etherialised monkey'.[33] Further, she believes it a valid implication of her scientific creed that she should assert her right to live aggressively, not merely receptively, and to seek out the mate of her choice.

However, there are other aspects of Ann Veronica's character which seem, on closer examination, to be ill-matched with a scientific training in clear, logical thought. Her actions are, for the most part, singularly devoid of foresight or of calculation as to their consequences – this is particularly so in the episodes with Ramage, with Manning, and with the suffragettes. Moreover, although Wells clearly conceived of Ann Veronica as being in revolt against the traditional attributes associated with womanhood, he came, in his turn, to romanticise her schismatic values. Ann Veronica and Capes spend their honeymoon in the rarefied air of the Alps and experience a Keatsian mood of being 'half in love with easeful death', when Capes, semi-jestingly, contemplates a united suicide from the summit of their delight. In the final chapter describing their married life, Ann Veronica, having abdicated without any apparent regret from a career in biology, finds her ultimate fulfilment in entertaining as Capes's wife and in bearing his child – a strange capitulation to the Victorian domestic ideal.

Marjorie Pope too, has studied science, at Oxbridge, and when the novel begins has impressed Trafford with her understanding of his subject – crystallography; but her interest was apparently somewhat spasmodic – she has also dabbled in political theory – since the chief legacy from her student days seems to be a sheaf of bills. Once married and involved in a career of entertaining and interior decorating, she spares no further thought for the pursuit of science or indeed of any serious intellectual activity, and is unable to comprehend why Trafford should need to spend long hours away from her engaged in his research. Her first sympathy with Trafford's eagerness and love of his work,[34] a sympathy which contributed in no small measure to their immediate *rapport*, evaporates quickly after their marriage, and it is at this point that Marjorie ceases to be a credible character, the natural product of her background experiences; she becomes, instead, a foil for Trafford, a deliberately placed obstacle to his research and the type of the foolish, shallow woman with insufficient to occupy her time. Wherever she is contrasted with other women she emerges as credible and clear-headed again – Trafford is relieved to hear her reactions to the illogical outpourings of a gaggle of militant suffragettes, for she sees at once that the agitation for female suffrage is merely a symbol:

> To her the advancement of science, the progress of civilization and the emancipation of womanhood were nearly synonymous terms for different phases of one thing.[35]

But as soon as she is alone with Trafford again she reverts to being an embodiment of the wholly emotional, clinging female. When Trafford endeavours to reason with her, to make her understand why he feels it necessary to go away completely from London to Labrador, her instinctive response is merely to embrace him, so that he is moved to exclaim:

> 'My dear . . . my dear! Why do you always want to turn love into – into touches? . . . Stand up there and let me talk to you as one man to another. If we let this occasion slide to embraces. . . .'[36]

Thus Marjorie, although she has allegedly had a scientific training, joins the ranks of Wells's modern women who fail to find a viable outlet for their intellectual energies and become submerged in, or frustrated by, social inanities.

Lady Mary Justin's indictment of the social role of her sex stands equally well for Marjorie Trafford:

> 'Men invent, create, do miracles with the world, and we translate it all into shopping, into a glitter of dresses and households, into an immense parade of pride and excitement. We excite men, we stir them to get us and keep us. Men turn from their ideas of brotherhood to elaborate our separate cages.'[37]

Wells seems to have been unable to formulate any clear conception of what his ideal women should be. In *Men Like Gods* they are equal co-workers with men in scientific progress – Arden and Greenlake, the scientists who experiment in the F-dimension, are not differentiated in the novel, though one is a woman. In *A Modern Utopia* Wells put forward the prototype of his scheme for the endowment of motherhood, which was to free women from their position of financial dependence on men in order to devote themselves more completely to the rearing of children. Ironically, Wells had himself criticised Grant Allen's similar proposal to abolish the family and provide support for women, who might then have children at the expense of the State. In a review of *The Woman Who Did*, Wells claimed:

> Now Mr. Grant Allen knows perfectly well that amorous desires and the desire to bear children are anything but overpowering impulses in many of the very noblest women. The women who would inevitably have numerous children under the conditions that he hopes for, would be the hysterically erotic, the sexually incontinent.[38]

Yet Ann Veronica's impulses are very little different, and in Isabel's cry for the right to bear children Wells voiced them explicitly, lengthily and with apparent approbation.[39]

Thus it would seem that although Wells overtly believed a scientific education to be the mark, perhaps even the *sine qua non* of the truly modern woman, he seems to have been as unable to realise fully what this would entail in his female characters as he was to sustain the characterisation of a male scientist devoted to his research through the full length of a novel. The most likely reason for such a failure in the work of a writer who genuinely believed in the validity of the scientist's role in society is the autobiographical one. Wells's first degree and later his doctoral thesis on what we should now call sociology, the science which was perhaps the least technically specialised of its time, were such as to fit him for an appreciation of the role of science in general without giving him the actual experience of sustained autonomous research, and thus his descriptions of such a pursuit are brief and obviously second-hand. Moreover, his second wife, although a science student at the time of her marriage, and later a graduate, found her vocation in assisting Wells in his writing, in managing his business affairs and in bearing children. She is in this respect perhaps the prototype for Ann Veronica and Marjorie Trafford.

Theoretically an alternative reason for Wells's failure to realise fully the figure of the scientist at work for a prolonged period might well have been a general inability to write about science for the layman since this is widely acknowledged to be an extremely difficult task and one in which only a small minority of writers have succeeded. It is therefore relevant to discuss and assess the general means whereby Wells attempted to make scientific data and theories, and in particular the concerns of scientists, real and comprehensible to readers who had little or no knowledge of the science of their time.

Part IV
Wells's Techniques and His Approach to Art

10 Techniques of Persuasion and Presentation

The increasing difficulty of communication between scientist and layman has been realised, perhaps with undue emphasis, in a generation familiar with the concept of 'two cultures' for, despite the growing popularity of science fiction as a *genre* in its own right, the number of scientific writers who can communicate with a general audience remains remarkably small. Hence it is not surprising that the majority of science fiction readers are those who have had some scientific training. Kingsley Amis writes that:

> Science fiction interests do not coincide with those of ordinary fiction, though on occasion the two sets will overlap very considerably. The sense of curiosity involved, for instance, is different in each case; Science Fiction's is more intellectual . . . and it will not always appeal to, though it need not actually deny, the human warmth which we are right to look for in ordinary literature.[1]

Yet, despite the fact that the vast majority of Wells's readers had no scientific training, his books were so immensely popular that it becomes important to ask how he contrived to make his scientific romances interesting, even fascinating, to the general reader at a time when the average level of background knowledge about science was in fact lower than it is today. If we compare *The Time Machine* or even 'The Plattner Story' with the pedestrian geometry of Charles Hinton's contemporary *Scientific Romances* [1886] and *The Fourth Dimension* [1904] it is easy to see not only how much better Wells understood the concept of a fourth dimension, but also how superior was his ability to make his readers envisage such a concept with him. All Hinton's technicolour plates of solid figures, and his pages of explanatory geometry, fail to make his ideas concrete realisations, while in two pages of *The Time Machine* Wells has swept the most sceptical reader along with him in his chain of causality.

Many of the techniques which Wells employed have since become standard devices in science fiction but at the turn of the century they were for the most part innovatory. Earlier writers had tended to omit technical details, largely through their own ignorance, but partly perhaps in the belief that their inclusion would destroy *rapport* with the non-scientific reader. Wells on the other hand realised that there were only two major prerequisites necessary to interest his reading public – firstly the need to 'domesticate the impossible', making it appear feasible, and secondly the need to render scientific data and explanations, or pseudo-explanations, both comprehensible and palatable to the lay reader. The techniques whereby these requirements were met are of interest both in their own right and in their implications for the role of literature in general, and deserve some detailed consideration.

It is often assumed that in the scientific romances Wells was writing about things which were clearly impossible, but this is because many readers do not realize the scope of the events upon which Wells was drawing. A close examination reveals that although he often dealt with the improbable, and occasionally added details that were frankly impossible, his line of reasoning never departed from scientific principles. His most usual focus of interest was the borderline between the improbable and the impossible, partly because he was fascinated with the potential for extrapolating from known facts into a penumbral region where it had not occurred to others to go. This preoccupation represents both Wells's emphasis on the adventure of the mind, and also his avowed mission to open people's eyes to a whole world beyond their present blinkered gaze but within their reach. In *The World Set Free* this is symbolised as power which may be had for the seeking, but which has remained untapped because no one thought of looking for it:

> Could anything be more emphatic than the appeal of electricity for attention? It thundered at man's ears, it signalled to him in blinding flashes; occasionally it killed him, and he could not see it as a thing that concerned him enough to merit study. It came into the house with the cat on any dry day, and crackled insinuatingly whenever he stroked her fur. It rotted his metals whenever he put them together . . . yet there is no single record that anyone questioned why the cat's fur crackles or why hair is so unruly to

brush on a frosty day, before the sixteenth century. For endless years man seems to have done his very successful best not to think about it at all; until this new spirit of the Seeker turned itself to these things. How often things must have been seen and dismissed as unimportant before the speculative eye and the moment of vision came.[2]

In choosing this speculative region as his subject matter, Wells greatly increased the scope and variety of his stories, while stepping but rarely into the realm of pure fantasy. The sense of reality in these stories is preserved chiefly by means of a meticulous attention to the laws of causality.

His usual procedure is to take a broad generalisation and then to describe a set of supporting circumstances, several of which may in isolation strain credulity, but which, taken together present a consistent argument. Then, having done his utmost to induce a suspension of disbelief in the reader, he attempts to work out the consequences in as logical a manner as possible, so that although the assertions may become progressively less credible *per se*, it is difficult for the reader to find a point where he may validly reject the argument. Here, as Wells himself explained, the technique is to trick the reader

. . . into an unwary concession to some plausible assumption and get on with his story while the illusion holds . . . and then as soon as the magic trick has been done the whole business of the fantasy writer is to keep everything else human and real.[3]

This device is highly effective in *The Invisible Man* and *The First Men in the Moon* at the end of which Wells unashamedly has Bedford say, 'I would like to see the man who could invent the story that would hold together like this one'[4]; but it is no less operative in 'The Land Ironclads' (which, it must be remembered, centred on a postulate so startlingly new in Wells's day as to seem virtually impossible), in 'The Country of the Blind', 'The Diamond-Maker', 'The Remarkable Case of Davidson's Eyes', 'The Plattner Story', 'The Truth about Pyecraft', 'The Man Who Could Work Miracles' and 'The New Accelerator'. The last two despite their apparent frivolity are especially fine examples of this technique; they show Wells at his light-hearted best, overturning the presuppositions of those who think an extraneous event may be introduced into a closed system without throwing the whole system into imbalance. When Fotheringay, the 'man who could work miracles', in blithe, unthinking imitation of Joshua, orders the earth to 'jest stop rotating, will you', he is completely unaware of the full sum of the consequences; but Wells is not. Having described the resultant chaos with great vivacity, he condescends to explain to the benighted reader the logical chain of events involved:

> You see, when Mr. Fotheringay had arrested the rotation of the solid globe, he had made no stipulation concerning the trifling movables upon its surface. And the earth spins so fast that the surface at its equator is travelling at rather more than a thousand miles an hour, and in these latitudes at more than half that pace. So that the village, and Mr. Maydig, and Mr. Fotheringay and everybody and everything had been jerked violently forward at about nine miles per second – that is to say, much more violently than if they had been fired out of a cannon. And every human being, every living creature, every house and every tree – all the world as we know it – had been so jerked and smashed and utterly destroyed. That was all. These things Mr. Fotheringay did not, of course, fully appreciate.[5]

'Under the Knife' contains a brilliant use of this strict attention to causality in the description of the narrator's soul released from its material body. Wells has taken the familiar Platonic doctrine of the soul and described what would in fact ensue from such a separation of soul from body. The result is both wholly surprising and yet, once the explanation is given, logically irrefutable. If the soul, freed from the restricting body, flies upward, the earth will not remain beneath it but will spin away in its orbit.

This fidelity to scientific fact becomes, in Wells's hands, not a liability but a unique and integral part of his plot. So far from neglecting or slurring over any awkward consequences of his original thesis, he incorporates these consequences into the very material of his story. The traditional writer of the marvellous tale dilated upon the adventures and advantages which invisibility rendered possible, and even if he bothered to consider the disadvantages, ignored them as inconveniences irrelevant to his plot. Wells, on the other hand, *makes* his story, *The Invisible Man*, out of these very disadvantages.

The conclusion of *The War of the Worlds*, in some ways Wells's most masterly ending, is both wholly unexpected at first reading and yet completely prepared for during the story. The ending may not have been Wells's own invention,[6] but if he did borrow the idea, he integrated it superbly into his novel. We are told, early in the novel, that the Martians have eliminated disease on their own planet, and later that they feed on injections of human blood; the ending follows with grim inevitability: they will be infected with diseases to which humans, through long exposure, carry immunity, but to which the Martians are highly susceptible.

Besides this stress on causality in the scientific romances, Wells frequently relied for an atmosphere of credibility on the character of his narrators. He was seldom content merely to narrate a short story *in propria persona* and usually created a narrator whose reliability is vouched for, either by some external authority or by a direct appeal of the narrator himself. Nearly half the short stories end with such a tag asserting them to be genuine experiences or true observations, while in the scientific romances there is frequently some reference to an external source, a journal, a newspaper article or some allegedly authoritative person ready to support the narrator's claims.

Besides being a guarantee of fidelity, the character of the narrator may become important as an excuse for omitting details which would make the fiction difficult to sustain. Thus in *The First Men in the Moon*, Wells is at pains to show, from the start, both the absent-mindedness of Cavor and the irresponsible nature of Bedford, who is incapable of concentrating his attention on anything for more than a few minutes. After this introduction it is scarcely surprising, we are made to feel, if some of the essential details concerning the construction of the cavorite sphere are lost or glossed over in the resultant report; Wells has sufficiently exonerated himself, and indeed Bedford continues to remind us to the end that 'my scientific attainments, I must admit, are not great, but . . .'.[7] The narrator of 'The Plattner Story' also claims to be ignorant of any details which might be required to substantiate his claims.

A variation on this device is that of the sceptical narrator who professes to disbelieve some unimportant detail of the events he has described, or to doubt the interpretation of them. This tends to reassure the reader by implying that the narrator is a clear-thinking sceptic and not a gullible dreamer who might have imagined the marvellous events he records. Thus the narrator of 'The Remarkable Case of Davidson's Eyes' declares himself from the beginning a somewhat reluctant recorder of the events of which he has been an eyewitness, and concludes with a claim to disbelieve the 'explanation' of Professor Wade, while reaffirming the truth of the actual events he has described:

> The whole of his theory seems fantastic to me. The facts concerning Davidson stand on an altogether different footing, and I can testify personally to the accuracy of every detail I have given.[8]

This device has the effect of supporting Wade's theory since its strongest opponent can offer no alternative explanation.

On the other hand, the narrator may doubt his own experiences, or fear that others will, as in 'The Story of the late Mr. Elvesham' and *The Time Machine*. The Time Traveller, after his penultimate journey, says to his audience: 'Treat my assertion of its [the narrative's] truth as a mere stroke of art to enhance its interest. And taking it as a story, what do you think of it?' The Editor, in this group, is duly sceptical: 'What a pity you're not a writer of stories!' And even the Time Traveller himself concedes: 'To tell you the truth . . . I hardly believe it myself. . . . And yet.'[9]

This effort to underbid the reader's scepticism and hence to gain his sympathy by an avowal of near-disbelief from the narrator, occurs in several of the stories. Bedford ends his narrative thus: 'So the story closes as finally and completely as a dream. . . . Indeed, there are moments when I do more than half believe myself that the whole thing was a dream.'[10] And the narrator of 'The Plattner Story' confesses: 'Frankly I believe there is something crooked about this business of Gottfried Plattner; but what that crooked factor is, I will admit as frankly, I do not know.'[11] Clearly a narrator who is forced to believe virtually against his own will gains more credence than one who indiscriminately accepts everything told to him. It is therefore necessary to provide some incontrovertible evidence in order to convince these honest sceptics. Such evidence, like Gulliver's souvenirs of Lilliput, is usually claimed to be of a tangible nature – Bedford possesses gold which he has never earned; the Time Traveller produces flowers of a hitherto unknown species which he claims are from the gardens of the Eloi; Plattner, who after his alleged journey into the fourth dimension has assumed a mirror-image form of his earlier self, has evidence of this in before-and-after photographs.

If a suspension of disbelief is to be achieved from the outset and maintained to the end, both the beginning and the conclusion of the story must be made particularly credible. Here Wells took considerable pains and used several devices to avoid the more obvious objections to his fantasies. In the shorter scientific romances where there is little time for a leisurely development of the plot, he concentrates all his powers of persuasion in the first chapters to induce a receptive attitude in his readers. One technique frequently used is that of the story within the story. Here the strongly realistic, even mundane outer envelope acts as a partial guarantee of the veracity of the inner story. Moreover the reader is thereby removed by one or two degrees from direct confrontation with the marvellous, and this automatically tempers his disbelief since he is able to identify with the demonstrably ordinary characters who actually experience the strange phenomena. The story may be found as a manuscript by the narrator as in *Dr. Moreau*, but more commonly Wells recreates in detail the atmosphere and the setting in which it is asserted that the events of the story occurred. He explained the superiority of *The Time Machine* over 'The Chronic Argonauts' partly in these terms:

I had realised that the more impossible the story I had to tell, the more ordinary must be the setting, and the circumstances in which I now set the Time Traveller were all that I could imagine of solid, upper-middle-class comfort.[12]

The conclusion of a scientific romance is perhaps the most difficult area in which to maintain the sympathy of the reader. Ideally, there should be some tangible evidence, rather than mere rumour, of the events recorded, but equally important, unless the scientific romance is set in the distant future, is the need to disguise the whereabouts of these physical evidences, lest they be proved non-existent. Thus the Aepyornis bones are alleged to have been sold to a dealer located vaguely 'near the British Museum'; Cavor's sphere, immune to gravity except when covered with special blinds, has conveniently flown off beyond recall since a small boy stepped inside and opened the blinds at the top; Cavor himself is left on the moon beyond hope of rescue or communication, while the Time Traveller has utterly disappeared, together with both his time machine and the model of it. Griffin's journals containing the formulae for achieving invisibility have been hidden by the tramp, Marvel, who cannot understand them yet will not allow anyone else to inspect them; Graham, the Sleeper, has long outlived the reader, while Moreau and Montgomery have died without trace on an island whose whereabouts can only be guessed.

Another concise and most ingenious conclusion occurs in the humorous tale, 'The Man Who Could Work Miracles', for in the midst of the havoc he has caused by ordering the earth to stand still, Fortheringay's last miracle, all-embracing in its terms, restores the *status quo* completely and thereby destroys all evidence:

> 'Let me be back just before the miracle began; let everything be just as it was before that blessed lamp turned up. . . . No more miracles, everything as it was.' . . .
>
> He opened his eyes. . . . He had a vague sense of some great thing forgotten that instantaneously passed. You see, except for the loss of his miraculous powers, everything was back as it had been; his mind and memory therefore were now just as they had been at the time when this story began. So that he knew absolutely nothing of all that is told here today. And, among other things, of course, he still did not believe in miracles.[13]

This device allows Wells the maximum scope for a panorama of earthly chaos and destruction without technically overstepping the bounds of realism. Obviously to ask why the narrator himself should remember the intervening occurrences destroys the illusion, but within the context of the humorous tale this device functions quite successfully; indeed Wells is quick to see how the very incompleteness of a story, a failure to explain all possible points and difficulties, may assist the illusion by simulating the fragmentary nature of a human document.

Valuable as these techniques are, Wells's major technique in creating a sense of verisimilitude lies in what an early reviewer perceptively defined as 'precision in the unessential and vagueness in the essential'.[14] The first and perhaps the most effective example of this occurs in *The Time Machine* when the narrator, having described with the utmost vagueness the model of the time machine as 'a glittering metallic framework, scarcely larger than a small clock, and very delicately made. There was ivory in it and some transparent crystalline substance' – a description which tells us nothing at all – proceeds with apparent earnestness: 'And now I must be explicit, for this that follows – unless his explanation is to be accepted – is an absolutely unaccountable thing.'[15] But the pro-

mised exactitude which follows certainly does not elucidate anything about the time machine. Instead Wells proceeds to describe in
minute detail the arrangement of the chairs, tables and candles in
the room, and the positions of the spectators relative to the Time
Traveller – factors which impress us as being important at the time
but which have no relevance at all to the demonstration of time-
travelling. Indeed, whenever the description of the time machine
becomes any more specific than a mention of crystal bars, it
becomes correspondingly less credible; it seems least real when
endowed with a part as concrete and imaginable as a 'saddle', for
this tends to suggest some kind of bicycle and to destroy its necessary
air of mystery.

Wells's vagueness in the essential is often skilfully concealed by
the excuse that either the reader or the supposed listener within the
story would not understand the technical details. Griffin begins to
explain his process for developing invisibility to Kemp, a doctor,
who might well be presumed to understand a simplified account but
to be ignorant of the finer points of the science of optics; these details
are therefore omitted, although allegedly a fuller explanation could
be given readily enough. This technique also functions successfully
in *Dr. Moreau* where Prendick explains that he was never allowed
into the laboratory when Moreau was actually at work on his
transformations. Bedford too reminds us that he cannot understand
or remember Cavor's instructions for making cavorite: all he recalls
is that the process involved helium and required heating.

Related to this technique is Wells's frequent assertion that he is
refraining from fuller explanations since such mundane details
would only bore the reader who, it is assumed, is more interested in
learning the 'facts' of the story. In 'The Crystal Egg' Wells intrudes
upon the narrative to remark:

It would be tedious and unnecessary to state all the phases of Mr.
Cave's discovery from this point. Suffice that the effect was this:
the crystal, being peered into at an angle of about 137 degrees
from the direction of the illuminating ray, gave a clear and
consistent picture of a wide and peculiar countryside.[16]

The technique involved in even such a brief interjection as this
should not be overlooked. Wells begins with the relatively dull fact
of the angle of observation and ends his sentence with the prospect of
a 'wide and peculiar countryside', so that we are only too ready to

dispense with technical exactitude and proceed to the more interesting reasons why the countryside is peculiar. By such a trick of construction Wells is able to insert a brief and virtually meaningless detail to assert his *bona fides*, and then pass swiftly on, with the reader's assent, to the purely fantastic crux of his story.

Alternatively there may be some alleged need for secrecy or haste, or some other apparently unavoidable reason why the explanation must be withheld or postponed. The Diamond-maker cannot divulge his procedures lest diamonds flood the market, thereby rendering his discovery worthless. Bedford, by his repeated references to what has been lost in transmission or is not reported in full, preserves throughout his account the fiction that Cavor's message comes from the moon. Griffin promises Kemp that he will describe his invisibility process in more detail later, but subsequent events render this impossible. Similarly, George Ponderevo affirms his attention to explain the finer points of his plane's construction later in the novel – 'But that I will write about later'[17] – but conveniently forgets to do so.

Perhaps the most ingenious variation on this technique is that used in *Men Like Gods*. The citizens of this highly advanced society communicate almost exclusively by telepathy which depends upon the common background of the parties concerned. Therefore the Earthlings can 'hear' only that part of discourse which they (and we) can understand, that is to say, only that part involving the background knowledge which they already possess. Hence when the utopian, Serpentine, attempts to describe the process of transmitting bodies through the F dimension, the Earthling visitors cannot receive this explanation, nor can it be formulated in words for the benefit of the reader.

But if Wells was vague about the essential facts of his marvellous stories, he was scrupulously explicit about the mundane details surrounding them. When Virginia Woolf wrote, in criticism of his social novels, that he would 'spend immense skill and immense industry making the trivial and the transitory appear the true and the enduring',[18] she was describing exactly the technique which had ensured the success of the scientific romances. The narrator of 'The New Accelerator' makes no attempt to be explicit about Gibberne's distillation which accelerates the pace of life several thousand times, except to make a vague mention of hyper-phosphates and a green phial, but he is careful to report that when he encountered Gibberne on the fateful day: 'I was going up the Sandgate Hill towards

Folkestone – I think I was going to get my hair cut. . . .'[19]

Subsidiary to these techniques, but adding substantially to their plausibility, is Wells's ability to incorporate scientific phrases into his descriptions as a tacit assurance that we should trust his judgment since his credentials clearly include an extensive background of science. This is particularly useful in supporting his 'precision in the unessential' and he seems to have discovered its usefulness quite early in his writing. It is already present, although with less naturalness than he was later to achieve, in 'The Chronic Argonauts', where the alleged author describes the sudden appearance of the time machine thus:

> The thing was not square as a machine ought to be, but all awry; it was twisted and seemed falling over, hanging in two directions as these queer crystals called triclinic hang.[20]

The simile of the triclinic crystals tells us virtually nothing about the machine, but it creates an illusion that the narrator is a scientifically-trained observer. The young Wells tended to flourish these somewhat self-conscious scientific testimonials, at times ill-advisedly. In 'A Tale of the Twentieth Century', an early essay published the year before 'The Chronic Argonauts', there is an unfortunate taint of the undergraduate determined to impress – as indeed Wells was in 1887. We are informed pompously: 'No longer were As_2O_3 and SO_2 to undermine the health of London. Ozone was to abound exceedingly.'[21] However the later works in general show this technique polished to a more sophisticated level so that the phrases fall in naturally with the character of the narrator. Even Bert Smallways has had sufficient grounding in rudimentary physics to explain credibly why champagne rushes out of a bottle at high altitudes.

> 'Atmospheric pressure,' said Bert, finding an application at last for the elementary physiography of his seventh-standard days.[22]

In the short story, 'Under the Knife', Wells casually introduces the simile of the galvanometer – not in order to compare it to something better known, but reducing it to the subsidiary relation within the simile and thus tacitly demonstrating his long familiarity with such an instrument as a normal appliance of life. This sense of familiarity with scientific concepts and phraseology is in evidence throughout

Wells's work, not merely in the scientific romances. Thus in describing the moment when Remington and Isabel recognise their mutual passion, Wells has Remington resort to a simile from physics: 'The quick leap of her mind evoked a flash of joy in mine, like the response of an induction wire.'[23]

Allied to this introduction of scientific terms is the recurrent mention of the names of well-known scientists as a supposed guarantee of the truth of the statement to follow. George Ponderevo establishes his credentials in aeronautics by such name-dropping: 'I was beginning to get keen upon the soaring experiments I had taken on from the results then to hand of Lilienthal, Pilcher and the Wright Brothers . . .'[24] and uses a similar technique to render credible the quap analysis. He remarks casually:

It was before the days of Capern's discovery of the value of canadium and his use of it in the Capern filament, but the cerium and thorium alone were worth the money he extracted from the gas-mantles then in vogue,[25]

a statement sufficiently close to the facts about tungsten filaments to produce a transferred credibility. Later the 'quap' episode is made more concrete by an apparently artless reference to a description of the ore in the *Geological Magazine* for October 1905, together with mention of 'pitch-blende, rutile, and the like' so that we tend, uncritically, to add quap to the list. It might almost seem that Wells was playfully testing himself by insisting on the improbable name 'quap', and then daring us to disbelieve in it. The short story 'The Moth' has well-documented footnote references to alleged publications by the two protagonists in journals, the titles of which appear to have a rock-like authenticity but are, in fact, fictitious. When, in *Tono-Bungay*, we are told that Uncle Ponderevo, having tried unsuccessfully to buy the *British Medical Journal* and the *Lancet* for the more effective promotion of Tono-Bungay, finally acquired *The Sacred Grove*, a literary magazine, we are almost disposed to believe its title as valid as those actual ones just mentioned. 'The New Accelerator' was first published in the *Strand Magazine* of December 1905, and on the title page Wells unblushingly states of Gibberne, the fictitious discoverer of a fictitious drug that:

Unless my memory plays me a trick his portrait at various ages has already appeared in the *Strand Magazine* – I think late in 1899;

but I am unable to look it up because I have lent that volume to someone who has never sent it back. The reader may recall the high forehead and the singularly long black eyebrows.[26]

There follow more details concerning Gibberne's places of study and field of research, introduced with suitable apology to all those who must be aware of such common knowledge.

One of the basic themes of the scientific romances was the onslaught on the world and on traditional assumptions by strange forces; whether physical objects like those of 'The Sea Raiders', 'The Empire of the Ants', 'The Star' and 'The War of the Worlds', or strange influences and experiences, as described in 'The Plattner Story' and 'The Remarkable Case of Davidson's Eyes'. Such themes are the traditional material for horror stories, yet in all these cases Wells was interested less in the opportunity for spine-chilling descriptions, than in devising a possible explanation for the alleged events, and always the explanation he favoured was the least occult one. If strange in itself, it is the more likely to be paired with another hypothesis still less scientifically respectable. Wells thus gains more credence for the less mystical explanation by comparison than he would have achieved had it been posited alone. Nearly always his technique is to affirm the truth of the alleged facts or occurrences and then to present alternative explanations between which the narrator, claiming to be a hard-headed sceptic, usually declines to choose but nevertheless indicates his bias. This bias may or may not indicate the view which the reader is intended to accept. In 'The Plattner Story' the narrator's view does seem to coincide with the one Wells wishes to suggest, and the technique in this case is combined with the use of an apparently sceptical narrator:

> On the one hand we have seven witnesses . . . and one unde-
> niable fact; and on the other we have – what is it? – prejudice,
> common sense, the inertia of opinion. . . .
> One other thing . . . I must insist upon lest I seem to favour
> the credulous, superstitious view. Plattner's absence from the
> world for nine days is, I think, proved. But that does not prove his
> story. It is quite conceivable that even outside space halluci-
> nations may be possible. That at least the reader must bear in
> mind.[27]

Here, by claiming to discount the report of Plattner's extra-spatial observations and to suggest that what he 'saw' was hallucinatory, he gains acceptance for the preliminary concept of going outside space, an implication at which the narrator does not baulk.

Although he always strains towards a less occult alternative, Wells's 'explanations' may sometimes seem less than successful to the modern reader because, in general, they are given in terms of the physical sciences, whereas we are now more accustomed to seek for explanations of extraordinary personal experiences, such as those described in 'The Remarkable Case of Davidson's Eyes', in the realm of psychology. Yet, with the exception of 'The Red Room' and 'The Moth', Wells almost completely ignored the psychological hypothesis, or rather, he contrived to make the story discount it by insisting upon the actuality of certain physical events or evidences. This is probably a further reflection of his preoccupation, at the time of writing the romances, with biological and physical sciences rather than with characterisation, and of his enduring scepticism about the merits of psychology.

Clearly, then, Wells mastered several valuable techniques for inducing a suspension of disbelief, not merely in stories of everyday circumstances, but in the relation of events which bordered on the impossible and which would normally evoke frank incredulity. Perhaps more important, however, are the techniques whereby he contrived to present actual scientific facts in a manner interesting to the lay reader. Wells himself was much concerned with this problem, not merely to ensure the success of his own stories, but also for the wider education of the general public. One of his earliest articles was an essay in *Nature* entitled 'Popularising Science', in which he attacked scientists who professed to write for a popular audience of non-scientists but whose labours effected more harm than good and who

> appear bent upon killing the interest that the generation of writers who are now passing the zenith of their fame created, wounding it with clumsy jests, painting it with patronage and suffocating it under their voluminous and amorphous emissions.[28]

His major attacks are directed against those who write exclusively in technical terms, forgetting that 'as a general principle, one may say that a book should be written in the language of its readers' and that technical jargon, 'from a literary standpoint must be called "slang" ";[29] against those who assume that because the general reader is ignorant of specialist terminology he is therefore an idiot and must be 'written down' to; and against those who resort to facetious jests and lumbering wit in a mistaken belief that this makes their subject palatable. Instead, Wells proposed two ways in which scientific facts may be presented honestly and plainly and yet be intrinsically interesting. The first involves the construction of the account and the second the emphasis which, he believed, should rest upon the philosophical end and purpose of the scientific knowledge being put forward, rather than on technical details which can interest only specialists in the field. It is worth examining briefly the ways in which Wells practised these principles to elicit and maintain his readers' interest. He wrote:

> A scientific paper for popular reading may and should have an orderly progression and development. . . . The fundamental principles of construction that underlie such stories as Poe's 'Murders in the Rue Morgue' or Conan Doyle's 'Sherlock Holmes' series, are precisely those that should guide a scientific writer. . . . First the problem, then the gradual piecing together of the solution.[30]

Like his models, Poe and Conan Doyle, he ensures that his short stories are compact, symmetrical in composition and economically written. The best of the longer romances are of similar expert construction. *The Invisible Man* and *The War of the Worlds* present and *just* exhaust their themes without ever overloading them or boring the reader by repetition. In a very real sense Wells's stress on causality, as discussed above, is the natural outcome not only of his appreciation of science but also of his enthusiasm for the mystery stories of Poe and Conan Doyle, with the difference that whereas mystery stories are intent upon tracing causal relationships backwards, from effect to source, Wells generally traces the results of some commonly-held assumption forward to their logical conclusion. One can see this procedure as the very basis of several of the short stories – 'The Man Who Could Work Miracles', 'The Truth about Pyecraft', 'The New Accelerator', as well as *The Invisible Man*. It also underlies his entertaining article, 'The Things that Live on Mars', which is virtually a detective story in a serious scientific vein, and demonstrates the close affinity between this latter genre and the inductive method of experimental science.

The other major point which Wells stressed in his article on popularising science was the need to concentrate upon the purpose, the metaphysical 'why' of events, for, seen in its widest context, any fact can become interesting, indeed of vital importance, to every reader. Thus Wells tends to examine not scientific principles *per se*, but their effect on individual characters and their causal implications for society or mankind as a whole. In discussing the possible distinctions between 'realism' and 'romanticism' in his work he maintained that the two could never be separated because 'the scientific episode which I am treating insists upon interesting me, and so I have to write about the effect of it upon the mind of some person'.[31] *The Invisible Man* is not primarily about a person whose only major characteristic is his invisibility; it is about the personality of Griffin, a brutal monomaniac. Certainly Wells is fascinated by the detailed physical results of such a concept – the visible footsteps, the visibility of newly eaten and as-yet-unassimilated food, the fact that dogs sniff at the heels of the invisible man because his scent is still perceptible, the inconvenience of traffic which does not stop for him when he tries to cross the road, the necessity of being naked and unencumbered by parcels, and the order in which visibility returns once the invisible man is dead – but he is also interested in the effect which such a discovery has upon the character of the man himself and on the others whom he encounters. Much of the novel is concerned with Griffin's desire for power and wealth from his discovery, and the ruthlessness which this arouses in him, but the most vivid picture of cruelty in the novel is the final description of the townsfolk, honest average citizens, who have come to hate what they fear until they are capable of unsuspected brutality:

Hardly a dozen yards off ran a huge navvy, cursing in fragments and slashing viciously with a spade, and hard behind him came the tram-conductor with his fists clenched. Up the street others followed these two, striking and shouting. . . . Kemp grasped the wrists, heard a cry of pain from his assailant, and then the spade of the navvy came whirling through the air above him and struck something with a dull thud. He felt a drop of moisture on his face. . . . He gripped the unseen elbows near the ground. 'I've got him!' screamed Kemp. 'Help! Help hold! He's down! Hold his feet!' . . . Kemp clung to him in front like a hound to a stag, and a dozen hands gripped, clutched and tore at the Unseen.[32]

Similarly, in *Dr. Moreau* Wells is less interested in Moreau's experiment *per se* than in what it has to teach about the dual nature of man and the impossibility of deriving a valid ethic from the study of evolution. Here too the character of Moreau is under scrutiny – not merely as an allegorical figure, but also as the type of the scientist who would carry out such researches.

Although Wells criticised those writers who 'wrote down' to their readers, he also realised that if the scientific romances were to make their full impact it was necessary that the more subtle principles underlying them should not be missed by a reader whose training in science was minimal. He therefore devised several methods of 'explaining' these basic principles to the reader without appearing to do so. His usual technique was the obvious one of having a non-scientific narrator describe, in layman's terms, what he sees to another character who then explains it more accurately in terms of the technical principles involved. In 'The Crystal Egg' Wace, 'Assistant Demonstrator at St. Catherine's Hospital', fulfils this latter function, writing down what Cave observes together with explanatory asides. Clearly this is a more satisfactory technique than repeated authorial intrusion. A variation of this device consists in having the narrator encounter other characters who ask or answer the questions which the reader would like to ask. In *The Invisible Man* Griffin's meeting with the tramp, Marvel, although chiefly the occasion for more tricks, also elicits some necessary explanation, as does his reunion with Kemp. In *The Sleeper Awakes* Graham is at first confused by the world to which he awakens, but he (and we) are enabled to fill in the necessary background knowledge when he questions those whom he meets.

Only rarely in the scientific romances does Wells interject to proffer explanations in *propria persona*, for such interpolations can easily become irritating or pedantic. In *War in the Air* Wells was concerned to show the effect of the war on individuals and therefore deliberately chose to follow the adventures of a limited individual, Bert Smallways, and to speak, for the most part, through him. However, he also wished to expound the causes and results of the war on the scale of world history and therefore from time to time he sketched in the background panorama as an external narrator; but these transitions are skilfully effected without effort or irrelevance.

A further important device for avoiding didacticism is Wells's use of humour in the scientific romances. Humour in science fiction is rare, and, when it does appear is a subordinate effect, but Wells uses it in several important ways. In *The First Men in the Moon* it functions both as part of the characterisation of the flippant Bedford and also as an excuse for deficiencies in the forthcoming explanation. When it is necessary to account for the unsuspected hazard of leaving a prepared sheet of cavorite indoors, Cavor explains that fortunately the cavorite was not pegged down so that, when it levitated violently, the only result was the explosion of his, Cavor's, house; the fact that Cavor, the dedicated scientist, sees the loss of his house as being of minor importance is humorous in itself, but the alternative possibility is also explained with a lightness of touch and fortuitous phrase which robs it of any effect of didacticism:

> If the cavorite itself hadn't been loose . . . the air would be rushing up and up over that infernal piece of stuff now. . . . It would have whipped the air off the world as one peels a banana, and flung it thousands of miles.[33]

When, as occasionally happens, the humour serves no purpose in the story beyond sheer lighthearted entertainment, it is often in danger of disrupting the unity of the construction. This is particularly true of the early work where Wells seems at first not to have realised that there is insufficient time in a short story for a complex interplay of interests to be developed. Thus, in 'The Stolen Bacillus' the comic scenes of the cab-drivers and Minnie's pursuit of her husband can only detract from the central theme in a story of less than 3000 words. However, in Wells's best stories the humour is situational, arising naturally and inevitably from the central theme. Thus, in 'The Truth about Pyecraft', Wells is objecting to the vague and inaccurate terminology of popular speech when he describes, with strict accuracy, the dire results of 'losing weight' as distinct from 'losing mass', but the humour arising from the consequences mitigates any suggestion of didacticism. In 'The New Accelerator' he finds an abundant source of humour in elaborating the unforeseen consequences of running at two or three miles per second – the frictional heat generated which scorches one's clothes, the unusually deep impressions of one's footprints, the highly undesirable experience of viewing a wink virtually frozen in time:

> Studied with such leisurely elaboration as we could afford, a wink is an unattractive thing . . . one remarks that the winking eyelid does not completely close, that under its dropping lid appears the

lower edge of an eyeball and a line of white. 'Heaven give me memory,' said I, 'and I will never wink again.'[34]

and the pattering noises in an otherwise silent world – the sounds of everyday life analysed into their component vibrations. 'The Man Who Could Work Miracles' satirises the popular concept of 'standing still', a theme repeated with minor variations in 'Under the Knife' when the narrator's soul ascends, weightless, while the earth rushes away from it through space.

Apart from this situational humour, there is also an element of dark humour to be found in the scientific romances. At one level it exploits the inadequacy of the ordinary individual, both physically and mentally, in the face of circumstances not, as is more usual, for the purposes of pathos, but for irony. Typically, in Wells's work, a limited character is drawn into a world catastrophe and shown to be hopelessly incapable of coping with events, even of comprehending them. Thus the curate of *The War of the Worlds* embroiled in the chaos of the Martian invasion, can only conclude that God does not appreciate the work he has done in organising the Sunday Schools, and the sole comment which Bert Smallways can utter on witnessing the destruction of New York is 'Gaw!'

A further level of dark comedy is provided in these same catastrophic scenes by the grim irony of man's pomp and pettiness in the face of overwhelming forces, and his determination to indulge in wishful thinking even in the midst of the most horrific reality. Prince Karl Albert, marooned on Goat Island and dependent on Bert for his only means of escape, still struts imperially and demands extravagant gestures of homage. A similar discrepancy exists between Griffin's dreams of world domination and the unsuspected handicap of invisibility which he painfully discovers.

Wells's other major device for gaining and retaining interest was his ability to make use of his reader's awareness of current scientific and technological discoveries (if, indeed, he did not anticipate them). He thereby gained a sense of immediacy and also exploited both the public interest in current affairs and his readers' background knowledge, however fragmentary, imbibed from the newspapers of the day. Wells displayed an amazing talent for seizing upon such news, realising at once the implications of the new discoveries and envisaging them as the basis for fiction. In 1893 Schiaparelli first propounded the theory of Martian canals; the following year Percival Lowell, from his observations in Arizona, surmised that the 'canals' might be the work of intelligent beings conserving water. By 1896, Wells, in an article for the *Saturday Review*, 'Intelligence on Mars', was theorising astutely about the probable nature of such hypothetical beings, and their evolution compared with that of man. He also made the point (before Lowell put the same argument to British astronomers) that since Mars was an older planet than Earth, and thus closer to becoming a cold and dreary wasteland, any intelligent inhabitants would attempt to leave the dying planet and colonise their more habitable neighbour, Earth. Two years later, he used this supposition to remarkable effect in *The War of the Worlds*. Again, *The War in the Air* was written only three years after the Wright brothers first flew a distance of thirty-six miles, thereby making aeronautics a practical proposition. It was not accidental that in this novel he described the excitement over the great names in the early history of flying; every reader enjoys seeing in fiction the names with which he is already familiar in real life.

Not only did Wells gain popularity by exploiting world news, but his work, in its time, also served a genuine function in educating a wide public to understand the contemporary news and its implications a little more intelligently. This mutual benefit system and sense of immediacy are, of course, forfeited by the majority of science fiction writers who disregard the present and insist upon the future as the only milieu capable of providing sufficient scope for invention.

11 Art, Science and Structure: the Debate with Henry James

Inevitably Wells's preoccupation with scientific principles as his criteria for judging life had a profound effect on his approach to art and on his literary style.

In scientific research the criteria of any theory are, firstly, that it should be the closest possible approximation to experimental truth, and secondly, that it should have pragmatic value. Thus it is scarcely surprising that Wells, trained in such a systematic approach to experience, came to propound a materialistic view of art which brought him into sharp conflict with the Establishment in aesthetics and literature, and in particular with Henry James. Wells could not accept beauty and art as self-justifying, as ends in themselves; yet in literary circles they were almost universally held to be so. This assumption (and to Wells it was an unwarranted assumption, being beyond demonstration) aroused him to a rebellion which found explicit expression in several of his works. The social criticism of *The First Men in the Moon* includes a passage of lighthearted mockery at the expense of the artist who is so completely absorbed in himself and his work. Phi-oo, one of Cavor's Selenite mentors, describes for him the lunar equivalent of the artist:

> 'M'm – M'm – he – if I may say – draw. Eat little – drink little – draw. Love draw. No other thing. Hate all who not draw like him. Angry. Hate all who draw like him better. Hate most people. Hate all who not think all world for to draw. Angry. M'm. All things mean nothing to him – only draw. He like you . . . if you understand. . . . New thing to draw. Ugly – striking.'[1]

Over the years this mild satire became increasingly vindictive. In

Mankind in the Making Wells speaks of 'the artist who lives angrily in a stuffy little corner of pure technique' and later Benham in *The Research Magnificent* examines the claims of art and finds them wanting.

Characteristically Wells considered the artistic imagination 'uneducated' (in his own specialised sense of the word), as the product of undisciplined training. In his autobiography he writes of the celebrated literary artists of his day that

> their abundant, luminous impressions were vastly more difficult
> to subdue to a disciplined, co-ordinating relationship than mine.
> They remained therefore abundant but uneducated brains.
> Instead of being based on a central philosophy, they started off at
> a dozen points; they were impulsive, unco-ordinated, wilful.
> Conrad, you see, I count uneducated, Stephen Crane, Henry
> James, the larger part of the world of literary artistry. . . . They
> lapsed – though retaining their distinctive scale and quality –
> towards the inner arbitrariness and unreality of the untrained
> common man.[2]

Whereas the artist takes the common facts of existence and recreates from them a new entity, Wells was an inveterate respecter of facts and the causal relations between them. Facts might be manipulated for purposes of education, politics or organisation, but they were not to be disregarded, passed over lightly, or transformed into something else. Similarly objects were assessed by Wells strictly in terms of their usefulness, and if they did not qualify on these grounds, then no aura of, or association with, the past, no aesthetic appeal, could render them precious for him.

His other principal criterion was, as we have seen, that of consistency with the body of existing knowledge. Theories which remained totally irreconcilable with the emerging picture of reality were *ipso facto* inefficient, disruptive and best discarded since they could have no significant meaning in themselves, but only in relation to the whole.

Thus Wells came to novel writing with aims which were almost exclusively functional. After the turn of the century his increasing preoccupation with plans for sociological and ethical reform led him to subordinate all stylistic considerations to his main purpose of propounding his views as pungently as possible, with decreasing regard for characterisation, construction, or the art of elegant literary expression. For Wells, as for Huxley, writing was an instrument, never an end. It meant the art of clear exposition, of controversy, and he cultivated it for much the same didactic purposes as the scientist and the philosopher. Consequently James found Wells too naïvely simple for an artist, while Wells considered James 'too devious and complicated for sense'. Indeed, the opposition between their ideas of literature was almost total. Whereas Wells tended to tailor his subject matter rigorously to his central theme, his style was often loose and haphazard while of James the converse was true – he treated his subject discursively while his style was formal and tightly-knit. This divergence was the natural outcome of the relative values ascribed by the two authors to objective and subjective levels of experience, to the realms of science and of art.

The notorious and often acrimonious debate between Wells and James concerning both the content and form of the novel began in earnest with James's criticism of *Marriage* and this, together with Wells's reply, are worth considering briefly since they exemplify the diametrically opposed assumptions and criteria of the two authors.

Wells had written *Marriage* explicitly as a problem-novel in which the incidents preceding the Traffords' marriage are reported only fragmentarily, a mere background sketched in for technical completeness. James, however, demanded to know all such details in full – to know, for example, what was said by Marjorie and Trafford during the three hours they spent in the lane with the donkey-carts before their open declaration of love. He insisted that Wells's omission of such material implied that he did not himself know, and could not envisage, what had passed between them, and that this, in turn, was because he was not fundamentally interested or absorbed in the two characters for their own sake.[3] Wells, in defence, claimed that James's criticism was true but irrelevant:

> Henry James was quite right in saying that I had not thought out these two people to the pitch of saturation and that they did not behave unconsciously and naturally. But my defence is that that did not matter, or at least that for the purposes of the book it did not matter very much.[4]

Wells is here reiterating one of the claims he had already made emphatically in his manifesto, 'The Contemporary Novel' – the claim that the novel is a means to an end and not an end in itself.

You see now the scope of the claim I am making for the novel; it is to be the social mediator, the vehicle of understanding, the instrument of self-examination, the parade of morals and the exchange of manners, the factory of customs, the criticism of laws and institutions and of social dogmas and ideas. It is to be the home confessional, the initiator of knowledge, the seed of fruitful self-questioning. . . . The novelist is going to be the most potent of artists, because he is going to present conduct, devise beautiful conduct, discuss conduct, analyse conduct, suggest conduct, illuminate it through and through. . . . And this being my view, you will be prepared for the demand I am now about to make for an absolutely free hand for the novelist in his choice of topic and incident and in his method of treatment.[5]

Thus for Wells the novel was basically an ethical and sociological enquiry, whereas for proponents of the formalistic approach it was primarily a rendering of impressions. Granted his point that the novel had an ethical purpose beyond itself, Wells was little disposed to care about the form in which the story was couched, whereas for James the form was of primary importance.

Conrad, who aligned himself with James on this question, further differed from Wells in the intrinsic value which he wished to ascribe to every object, every incident, as a thing in itself. Wells records a discussion between himself and Conrad which illuminates this point.

I remember a dispute we had one day as we lay on the Sandgate beach and looked out to sea. How, he demanded, would I describe how that boat out there sat or rode or danced or quivered on the water? I said that in nineteen cases out of twenty I would just let the boat be there in the commonest phrases possible. Unless I wanted the boat to be important, I would not give it an outstanding phrase, and if I wanted to make it important, then the phrase to use would depend on the angle at which the boat became significant. But it was all against Conrad's over-sensitized receptivity that a boat could ever just be a boat. He wanted to see it with a definite vividness of his own. But I wanted to see it and to see it only in relation to something else – a story, a thesis. And I suppose, if I had been pressed about it, I would have betrayed a disposition to link that story or thesis to something still more extensive and that to something still more extensive and so ultimately to link up to my philosophy and my world outlook.[6]

This diversity of opinion between Wells and Conrad is clearly the result of the basic differences in outlook between the scientifically trained mind and the artistic imagination. On the one hand there is the desire for a unified system in which each unit is subordinate to the whole and derives its meaning largely, if not entirely, from its relationship to the whole, and on the other hand the emphasis upon the uniqueness of each entity, its intrinsic importance when seen as far as possible in isolation.

Consequent upon this divergence of viewpoint are the two radically different modes of expression of science and literature. Fundamentally the scientist aims to say only one thing at a time, and to state it with the maximum clarity and objectivity. To this end he simplifies and evolves a technically precise jargon until, in its purest form, scientific language ceases to rely upon a medium as ambiguous as words, and confines itself to the symbols of mathematics. The literary artist, on the other hand, purifies language for a different purpose. Rather than attempting to say only one thing at a time, he endeavours to reflect the complexity of human experience which is perceived on many levels simultaneously.

James deals at some length with this process in 'The Art of Fiction':

> Humanity is immense, and reality has a myriad forms.
> . . . Experience is never limited, and it is never complete; it is
> an immense sensibility, a kind of huge spider-web of the finest
> silken threads suspended in the chamber of consciousness, and
> catching every air-borne particle in its tissue.[7]

Thus the scientist's rule of thumb, that in choosing between rival theories one should prefer the simpler explanation, may be a good criterion in science; but it involves a simplification which was unacceptable to the experiences treasured by James and Conrad. Wells assumed that to clarify an issue he must prune away the inessential or leave only as much as would lure his readers on to his main argument. James, on the other hand, aimed to clarify only in the sense of rendering the complexities of life most precisely and completely. To remove the nuances, the complexities, was, in his view, to produce a mere travesty of experience, a meaningless lump of flesh cut off arbitrarily from the living body.

Again, in scientific writing the content is the primary concern. Scientific wording can be changed, translated or amended and, provided clarity is not sacrificed, nothing is lost; but if the meaning is rendered obsolete by new facts, new experimental knowledge, the original paper loses all its scientific value and becomes of historical interest only. Of the arts, the converse holds: no change in expression can be made without affecting the whole work but neither can a great work of art be rendered obsolete by new facts.

For Wells the content was the all-important aspect of the novel. His belief that the cultivation of art for its own sake would lead eventually to the neglect of its original inspiration was allegorised in the early short story, 'The Pearl of Love'. Here the beloved wife, in whose memory the Prince began to construct a superb monument, is eventually forgotten. Preoccupied with art as an end in itself the lover eventually finds his wife's sarcophagus a disproportion, a flaw in the otherwise perfect piece of architecture and orders its removal. Wells's impatience with those who regarded form and style as ends in themselves clearly underlies his retaliation to James's criticism. In the light of later reflection he wrote of their relationship:

I bothered him and he bothered me. We were at cross-purposes based . . . on very fundamental differences not only of temperament, but training. He had no idea of the possible use of the novel as a help to conduct. His mind was turned away from any such idea. From his point of view there were not so much 'novels' as The Novel, and it was a very high and important achievement. He thought of it as an Art Form, and of novelists as artists of a very special and exalted type. He was concerned about their greatness and repute. . . . One could not be in a room with him for ten minutes without realising the importance he attached to the dignity of this art of his. I was by nature and education unsympathetic with this mental disposition. But I was disposed to regard a novel as about as much an art form as a market place or a boulevard. . . . That was entirely out of key with James's assumptions.[8]

During the heat of the debate he resorted to a more vigorous and satirical attack. A Jamesian novel, he wrote in *Boon*, is like a church lit, but without a congregation to distract you, and with every light and line focussed on the high altar, and on the altar, very reverently placed, intensely there, is a dead kitten, an eggshell, a bit of string . . . having first made sure that he has scarcely left anything to express, he then sets to work to express it with an industry, a wealth of intellectual stuff that dwarfs Newton. . . . He brings up every device of language to state and define. Bare verbs he rarely tolerates. He splits his infinitives and fills them up with adverbial stuffing. He presses the passing colloquialism into his service. His vast paragraphs sweat and struggle; they could not sweat and elbow and struggle more if God himself was the processional meaning to which they sought to come. And all for tales of nothingness. . . . It is a magnificent but painful hippopotamus resolved at any cost, even at the cost of its dignity, upon picking up a pea which has got into the corner of its den.[9]

As a gesture of reconciliation after this savage attack in *Boon*, Wells wrote to James suggesting that, although they supported two diverse approaches to art, perhaps both were valid:

There is, of course, a real and fundamental difference in our innate and developed attitudes towards life and literature. To you literature like painting is an end, to me literature like architecture is a means, it has a use.[10]

But James, in reply, categorically denied any distinction 'between a form that is [like] painting, and a form that is [like] architecture' and instead reasserted as strongly as possible his former position:

It is art that *makes* life, makes interest, makes importance, for our consideration and application of these things, and I know of no substitute whatever for the force and beauty of its process.[11]

Indeed Wells's deliberate disregard for style elicited criticism from many who genuinely admired other aspects of his work. Desmond MacCarthy remarked that:

Mr. Wells has always been set on believing that the value of a novel depends upon the amount of good stuff in it; that it is a hold-all into which you can cram anything you have ready. Had

patience been added to his cluster of extraordinary gifts he would
have been among the world's great novelists.[12]

Again, whereas Wells accused Arnold Bennett of being preoccupied
with mundane considerations Bennett reciprocated by charging
Wells with complete disregard for all 'surface values', because he
was intent only on his thesis of the moment, everything else being
rendered subsidiary to this:

> Like all great reformers you are inhuman and scornful of
> everything that doesn't interest you. Hence the complaint of the
> anti-Wellsites that in your scientific novels there is no individual
> interest, that the characters don't exist individually, a not unjust
> complaint. The pity of it is that these persons cannot perceive the
> 'concerted' effort of your 'scientific' novels. You are not really
> interested in individual humanity. And when you write a 'non-
> scientific' novel you always recur to a variation of the same type of
> hero, and you always will, because your curiosity, about
> individualities won't lead you further.[13]

Interestingly these criticisms have been least often levelled at the
scientific romances, not because the experiences described there are
any more subtly presented – rather the contrary – but because
Wells's aims, although more intellectually ambitious, are in other
ways more circumscribed, and less contentious. It was only when he
invaded the territory of the realistic novel that he fell foul of those
who saw the character novels of the nineteenth century as
representing the only valid line of development. Science fantasy was
acknowledged to be a peculiarly intellectual literary form, but *the
novel* was, for James, Conrad and Bennett, primarily an exploration
of sensuous and emotional levels of experience.

The early short stories and novels are also least open to the charge
of formlessness. Here Wells is still the zealous disciple of Poe and
Conan Doyle and the construction is, in most cases, sufficiently
tightly knit to further the theme. It is in the later sociological novels
that Wells seems most careless of form, the most notorious example
of apparent disorganisation being *Tono-Bungay*. Indeed, here we are
presented with a narrator who warns us in the first chapter:

> This book is going to be something of an agglomeration . . . I
> want to make it simply a hotch-potch of anecdotes and ex-

periences with my uncle swimming in the middle as the largest lump in the victual. I'll own that here, with the pen already started, I realize what a fermenting mass of things learnt and emotions experienced and theories formed I've got to deal with, and how, in a sense, hopeless my book must be from the outset. I suppose what I'm really trying to render is nothing more nor less than Life – as one man found it.[14]

This transparent excuse for chaos seems scarcely appropriate to the character of George. Had Uncle Ponderevo been the narrator we might be prepared to accept the lack of construction as a further element of characterisation, but George is the alleged author, and George is, we are told, a scientist – that is, in the Wellsian canon, the champion of disciplined thought and orderly procedures. Nevertheless it is possible to argue that this seeming flaw may in fact have been part of Wells's intention, and that if this is so it adds another level of meaning to the novel.

One of Wells's fundamental tenets was that nature itself is haphazard and chaotic, and that order is only imposed upon it by civilised man. George reflects, at the end of the novel, that 'One is in a world of accident and nature. . . . And amidst it all no plan appears, no intention, no comprehensive desire. That is the very key of it all.'[15] Wells himself had claimed that this predicament was a peculiarity of our species which was 'still, as a whole, unawakened to the possibilities which science indicated for the control of environmental chaos',[16] and for most of his life as described in the novel, George too is unawakened. He merely observes; he does not act with definition and strength, but is swept along by stronger personalities. The symbol of his groping is his glider which, without a skilful and determined commander, is tossed at the mercy of every air-current but if managed with concentration, self-denial and intelligence (it is stressed that George has to train rigorously in all these fields), this same glider soars and flies wherever the pilot dictates. So, too, George's later 'child', his destroyer, cleaves the water because of the perseverance, skill and enterprise of her designer. But George is only a novice in recognising this: virtually the whole of the novel deals with the adolescence of his will, and almost to the end he remains irresolute, thwarted by Beatrice. Thus if *Tono-Bungay* appears to be the worst constructed of all Wells's major novels, this is not necessarily the flaw it has generally been assumed to be. If it seems to weaken the conception of George *qua* scientist, it nevertheless elaborates the idea of what an aspiring scientist must first overcome before he can design 'the symbol of my destroyer, stark and swift, irrelevant to most human interests'.

Although such a case may be made for *Tono-Bungay*, widely considered to be one of the worst examples of Wells's 'carpet bag' construction, this clearly cannot serve as a general exoneration. Some of the short stories and most of the later novels could instantly be marshalled to show his lack of concern with form, and Wells himself was perfectly prepared to endorse James's criticisms:

> Tried by Henry James's standards I doubt if any of my novels can be taken in any other fashion [i.e. they can be read only uncritically]. . . . The main indictment is sound, that I sketch out scenes and individuals, often quite crudely, and resort even to conventional types and symbols, in order to get on to a discussion of relationships. The important point which I tried to argue with Henry James was that the novel of completely consistent characterization arranged beautifully in a story and painted deep and round and solid, no more exhausts the possibilities of the novel than the art of Velazquez exhausts the possibilities of the painted picture.[17]

Robert Bloom in his recent study of the later novels concludes that Wells's

> habit of calling himself a journalist rather than an artist is more a weary and gracious concession to the tireless aesthetic admonitions of James and his other nagging friends . . . than a fair statement of his position.[18]

In much of Wells's account there is certainly a sense of wishing to be rid of the whole tedious debate. But in the long run Wells did sincerely repudiate the narrow criteria of the James faction.

> All this talk that I had with Conrad and Hueffer and James about the just word, the perfect expression, about this or that being 'written' or not written, bothered me, set me interrogating myself, threw me into a heart-searching defensive attitude. . . . But in the end I revolted altogether and refused to play their game. 'I am a journalist,' I declared, 'I refuse to play the "artist".' If sometimes I am an artist it is a freak of the gods. I

am a journalist all the time and what I write *goes now* – and will presently die . . . I write as I walk because I want to get somewhere and I write as straight as I can, just as I walk as straight as I can, because that is the best way to get there. So I came down off the fence between Conrad and Wallas and I remain definitely on the side opposed to the aesthetic valuation of literature. That valuation is at best a personal response, a floating and indefinable judgment.[19]

Wells is surely justified in asserting the validity of his alternative aims. Even if his repeated remark about being a journalist is taken to imply a sense of impermanence about his writings, there are many aspects of his work which can be seen as an enduring legacy to literature as well as to Western thought.

Science fantasy, as perfected by Wells, not only issued in the proliferation of science fiction in later decades, but also influenced its development. Already in the 1970s the particular type of writing usually categorised as science fiction has passed into work which is preoccupied with sociological speculation about contemporary rather than future situations and which thus appears to be approaching a coalescence with the realistic social novel. Such a progression follows the sequence of Wells's own writings, as his earlier fantasies gave way to sociological speculation and finally to realistic social novels of contemporary life, and as the character of the scientist in his work passed from the alchemical figure of 'The Chronic Argonauts' into the less exotic character of the realistic novel, a character of moral depth and considerable sociological importance.

Wells's two greatest contributions, then, to the novel were firstly the introduction of several important new components and the re-introduction of at least one other major theme to literature, and secondly his role as an integrator of many apparently diverse disciplines and interests. In this latter realm the only other writer of this century who has attempted to combine such a range of concerns is the scientist-theologian, Teilhard de Chardin, who also found in evolutionary theory the great unifying vehicle for his thought. Yet, although there are still comparatively few explicit examples of interdisciplinary writing, it cannot be other than a hopeful sign that several of the finest modern writers have behind their work the strength of a scientific training, or a qualification in at least one branch of science or technology – Nabokov, the entomologist,

Solzhenitsyn, the engineer, Borgès, the mathematician. Their work points towards that unity of interest which Wells believed to be not only possible but essential for the sane development of society. More recently George Steiner also has eloquently revived Wells's plea:

> The gap between the literary imagination and the centres of feeling and moral debate in the sciences ought to be narrowed. . . . A tide of domestic trivia and erotic pretence has made much of the novel a soggy, routine pastime. At so many points the landscape of the imagination is meaner, more shop-worn than it need be. But the stakes are larger than literary.
>
> More than ever before the scientists themselves are conscious of the need to communicate 'outward', to translate into the common currency of speech and feeling that which is the core of their own existence. . . . Today the points of maximum pressure on individual and social life derive from biology and molecular chemistry. Work in these disciplines will soon alter the essential options for civilization. The scientists are saying: 'Come and meet us at least part-way, try and imagine with us, make some effort to get things right, even if in a simplified form'. The novelist is the eminent translator of the particular into the general: he imagines and senses ahead of us. And even for those who are neither writers nor scientists, the question should be one of simple pride: if we had lived in Florence during the Renaissance, would we not, on occasion, have sought to lunch with the painters?[20]

In Wells's work we see both this challenge and the first and most enthusiastic response to such a challenge.

Notes

INTRODUCTION

1. George Orwell, 'Wells, Hitler and the World State' in *Collected Essays* (London, 1961), p. 164.
2. George Steiner, 'Imagining science', *Listener*, LXXXVI, No. 2225 (18 Nov. 1971), p. 686.
3. M. R. Hillegas, *The Future as Nightmare* (New York, 1967), pp. 5, 34.
4. E. I. Zamyatin, *Herbert Wells* (St Petersburg, 1922), p. 54.
5. *Experiment in Autobiography*, Ch. 8, v, p. 623.

I. THE CONVERSION TO SCIENCE

1. Huxley, well known as an agnostic, if not an atheist, was highly amused at his title. He wrote to Sir John Donnelly, 'I am astonished that you don't know that a letter to a Dean ought to be addressed, "The Very Revd." I don't generally stand much upon etiquette, but when my sacred character is touched I draw the line.' Leonard Huxley, *Life and Letters of Thomas Henry Huxley* (New York, 1901), II, p. 38.
2. William Paley, *Evidences of Christianity* (1794) and *Natural Theology* (1802).
3. T. H. Huxley, 'Mr Darwin's critics', *Contemporary Review*, XVIII (Nov. 1871), 443.
4. H. G. Wells, 'Huxley', *Royal College of Science Magazine*, XIII (Apr. 1901), 211.
5. *Experiment in Autobiography*, Ch. 5, i, pp. 201, 204.
6. Ibid., Ch. 5, ii, p. 210.
7. Ibid., pp. 220–1.
8. Ibid., Ch. 6, vi, pp. 356–7.
9. Van Wyck Brooks, *The World of H. G. Wells* (London, 1915).
10. *Short Stories* (London, 1929), p. 1076.
11. *Marriage*, III, Ch. 4, vi, pp. 514–15.
12. *Short Stories*, vol. x, p. 570.
13. *Love and Mr. Lewisham*, Ch. 1, p. 241.
14. *The Food of the Gods*, Ch. 1, p. 4.
15. 'The discovery of the future', *Nature*, LXV, No. 1684 (6 Feb. 1902), 326.
16. Ibid., p. 330.
17. Ibid., p. 331.
18. A. G. N. Flew, *Evolutionary Ethics* (London, 1967), p. 31.
19. E.g. E. M. Forster, 'The Machine Stops' in *The Eternal Moment*; Aldous Huxley, *Brave New World*; George Orwell, 'Wells, Hitler and the World State' in *The Road to Wigan Pier*, Ch. XII.
20. Karl Marx, who wanted Darwin to accept dedication of at least part of *Das*

Kapital, sought support in theories of organic evolution for the kinds of processes he believed to occur in society: 'The course of history is a struggle of class as life itself is a struggle for existence.'

21. *A Modern Utopia*, Ch. 1, p. 7.
22. *The Open Conspiracy*, Ch. 12, pp. 163, 168.
23. *New Worlds for Old*, Ch. 2, pp. 23–4.
24. *Marriage*, Bk II, Ch. 3, xvii, p. 383.
25. C. Darwin, *The Descent of Man and Selection in Relation to Sex* (London, 1901), Ch. 21, p. 947.
26. B. Bergonzi, *The Early H. G. Wells* (Manchester, 1961), Ch. 1.
27. 'For his successful progress, man has been largely indebted to those qualities which he shares with the ape and the tiger.' T. H. Huxley, *Evidence as to Man's Place in Nature* (New York, 1897), p. 155.
28. T. H. Huxley, 'Evolution and Ethics' in J. S. Huxley and T. H. Huxley *Evolution and Ethics* (London, 1947), pp. 80, 82.
29. Ibid., p. 82.
30. *Men Like Gods*, I, Ch. 6, p. 107.
31. Introduction to *Works*, Atlantic Edition (London, 1924), II, p. ix.
32. 'Human evolution, an artificial process', *Fortnightly Review*, LXVI (1896), 590–5.
33. The Island of Dr. Moreau, Ch. 14, p. 91.
34. Ibid., Ch. 14, p. 91.
35. Ibid., Ch. 14, p. 97.
36. Ibid., Ch. 16, p. 123.
37. Ibid., Ch. 21, p. 167.
38. Charles Darwin, *The Life and Letters of Charles Darwin* (London, 1887), Vol. II, p. 312.
39. 'Consider for a moment the problem of evil. There are four possibilities with regard to evil. Either God is able but not willing to overcome it, or perchance he is not able, though he may be willing. It may be that he is neither able nor willing to overcome evil. Or it remains that he is both able and willing. Only the last would seem to be worthy of a good God, and it does not happen.' R. Cudworth, *The True Intellectual System of the Universe* (1678) (London, 1845).
40. J. Tyndall's address to the 1874 Meeting of the British Association, published as 'The Belfast Address' in *Fragments of Science* (New York, 1892), II, p. 201.
41. *Dr. Moreau*, Ch. 16, p. 123. In this case, unlike the passage quoted above, Moreau is represented, for the sake of realism, as being almost helplessly caught up in this process, rather than as directing it. In general, the only emotion he feels for wasted life is impatience at the delay it causes him.
42. Ibid., Ch. 14, pp. 44–5.
43. Ibid., Ch. 14, p. 93.
44. Ibid., Ch. 8, p. 45.
45. Ibid., Ch. 8, p. 45.
46. Ibid., Ch. 14, pp. 98–9.
47. Ibid., Ch. 12, p. 73.
48. Ibid., Ch. 14, p. 97.
49. Ibid., Ch. 18, pp. 132–3.
50. B. Bergonzi, op. cit., Ch. 4, p. 112.
51. Prendick, like Wells, has studied biology at the Royal College of Science under Huxley.

52. *The Times* (17 June 1896), p. 17; *The Athenaeum* (9 May 1896), pp. 615–16; *The Speaker* (18 Apr. 1896), p. 430, *The Saturday Review* (11 Apr. 1896), p. 368.
53. *The Island of Dr. Moreau*, Ch. 22, p. 170.
54. 'The Chronic Argonauts', Pt II, quoted by Bergonzi, op. cit., Appendix I, pp. 209–10.
55. 'The Rediscovery of the Unique', p. 111.

2. SCIENTIFIC METHOD AND WELLS'S CREDENTIALS

1. Letter from Wells to Bennett, 19 August 1901, reprinted in *Arnold Bennett and H. G. Wells* (ed. Harris Wilson) (London, 1960), p. 59.
2. E. R. Lankester, 'The present judged by the future', *Nature*, LXV. Supplement (13 Mar. 1902), iv–v.
3. 'A lunar romance', *Nature*, LXV, (9 Jan. 1902), 218.
4. Arnold Bennett, 'Herbert George Wells and his work', *Cosmopolitan Magazine*, XXXIII (Aug. 1902), 466.
5. L. Silberstein, *The Theory of Relativity* (London, 1914), p. 134.
6. L. Szilard, 'Reminiscences', *Perspectives in American History* (Cambridge, Mass., 1968), II, p. 99.
7. Ibid., p. 102.
8. J. S. Huxley, 'H. G. Wells', *The Spectator* CLXXVII (16 Aug. 1946), 161.
9. *The Work, Wealth and Happiness of Mankind*, Ch. II, ii, pp. 66–7.
10. Ibid., p. 67.
11. Thomas Hobbes, *Leviathan*, I, iv.
12. A. West, 'H. G. Wells', *Encounter*, VIII, No. 2 (Feb. 1957), 53.
13. *Experiment in Autobiography*, Ch. 5, ii, pp. 225–6.
14. 'The rediscovery of the unique', *Fortnightly Review*, L (July 1891), 106, 111.
15. B. Bergonzi, *The Early H. G. Wells* (Manchester, 1961), p. 168.
16. *The Work, Wealth and Happiness of Mankind*, Ch. II, ii, p. 67; iv, p. 76.
17. See Verne's contrasting of Wells's work with his own, as quoted by J. Kagarlitski, *The Life and Thought of H. G. Wells* (London, 1966), p. 113; V. Brome, *H. G. Wells, A Biography* (London, 1951), p. 70; G. Murray, 'Gilbert Murray's reminiscences of literary giants', *John O'London's*, II (14 Apr. 1960), 427–8; A. C. Ward, *Twentieth-Century Literature* (London, 1964), Ch. II, p. 34; I. Raknem, *H. G. Wells and His Critics* (Oslo, 1962), p. 206.
18. B. Bergonzi, op. cit., Ch. I, pp. 16–17.
19. *The Wonderful Visit*, Ch. 18, p. 172.
20. 'Human evolution, an artificial process', *Fortnightly Review*, LXVI (1896), 590.
21. 'The Door in the Wall', *Short Stories*, pp. 159–160.
22. Ibid., p. 161.
23. *Experiment in Autobiography*, Ch. 5, iii.
24. Letter to Arnold Bennett, October 1897, reprinted in *Arnold Bennett and H. G. Wells*, pp. 34–5.
25. Ibid., p. 35.
26. *The Invisible Man*, Ch. 20, p. 128.
27. B. Bergonzi, op. cit., Ch. 7, p. 166.
28. *Experiment in Autobiography*, Ch. 8, v, p. 624.
29. W. Heisenberg, *Physics and Philosophy* (New York, 1962).

30. J. Jeans, *The New Background of Science* (Michigan, 1959), p. 2.
31. *Experiment in Autobiography*, Ch. 6, ii, p. 309.
32. Ibid., Ch. 3, ii, p. 96.
33. Charles H. Hinton, *Scientific Romances* No. 1. 'What is the Fourth Dimension?' (London, 1884). Proceeding by analogies with 'Linelanders' and 'Flat-landers', Hinton proposes that either we exist in three dimensions only and hence, like the 'Linelanders' and 'Flatlanders' are mere abstractions in the mind of a being that conceives us, or else we have a four-dimensional existence. 'In this case, our proportions in it must be infinitely minute, or we should be conscious of them . . . it would probably be in the ultimate particles of matter that we should discover the fourth dimension.'
34. Raknem claims that 'The Canterville Ghost' makes use of time-travel, but it does not in fact suggest this, and speaks only of a fourth dimension of space, and that in the most casual terms without any allusion to the idea of time at all.
35. A. Einstein, 'Zur Elektrodynamik bewegter Körper', *Annalen der Physik*, XVII (1905), 891–921.
36. *The Time Machine*, p. 5.
37. Ibid., p. 13.
38. W. B. Pitkin, 'Time and pure activity', *Journal of Philosophy, Psychology and Scientific Method*, XI (1914), 524.
39. *The Time Machine*, pp. 13–14. It is, of course, an intentional irony that it should be the psychologist who raises the very objection to which he should know the answer. It is another example of that inability to apply what one knows in one situation in another less familiar context – a state of mind which Wells repeatedly satirised.
40. Ibid., pp. 25–6.
41. Ibid., p. 116.
42. W. B. Pitkin, op. cit., p. 523.
43. I. Zangwill, 'Without prejudice', *Pall Mall Gazette*, VII (Sep. 1895), 153.
44. Ibid., p. 155.
45. J. B. Burke, 'Mr Wells and modern science', *Dublin Review*, CLXIX (Oct. 1921), 233.
46. 'The transplantation of living tissues', *Natural Science*, VIII (May 1896), 291.
47. P. Chalmers Mitchell, 'Mr Wells's *Dr Moreau*', *Saturday Review*, LXXXI (11 Apr. 1896), 368.
48. Ibid., p. 369.
49. 'The limits of individual plasticity', *Saturday Review*, LXXIX (19 Jan. 1895), 90.
50. Ibid., 90. Several contemporary reviewers saw *Dr. Moreau* as an attack on vivisection. See, e.g. *The Critic*, XXVI (25 July 1896), 55; *Spectator*, LXXVI (11 Apr. 1896), 519.
51. *Experiment in Autobiography*, Ch. 1, ii, p. 20.
52. 'Popularizing science', *Nature*, L (26 July 1894), 301.
53. *Experiment in Autobiography*, Ch. 6, v, p. 349.
54. *Tono-Bungay*, Bk II, Ch. 1, vi, p. 165.
55. *The Science of Life*, Bk IX, Pt III, Ch. 59, iv, p. 1482.
56. Quoted by G. West, *H. G. Wells – A Sketch for a Portrait* (London, 1930), p. 156.

Notes

3. SCIENCE AND TECHNOLOGY

1. Dickens's *Hard Times* (1854), with its image of the machine as a mad elephant insensitive to human rhythms, constitutes the most vivid and sustained protest in the novel against the industrial age, but Charles Kingsley, Elizabeth Gaskell and Benjamin Disraeli also inveighed against specific social evils occasioned by a machine-oriented society.
2. H. G. Wells, 'Lord of the Dynamos', *Short Stories*, p. 352.
3. Ibid., pp. 352–3.
4. Ibid., p. 354.
5. Ibid., p. 363.
6. Review of *The Plattner Story and Others*, *The Critic* XXVIII (31 July 1897), 59.
7. I. Raknem, *H. G. Wells and His Critics* (Oslo, 1962), p. 361.
8. The metaphor of sleeping and awakening to find a new world in the future is a rich one in this context. It is no accident that it has provided the frame for several allegorical stories in a similar vein. Mercier's *Memoirs of the Year 2500* is couched in the form of a dream, and Edward Bellamy's *Looking Backward* (1888), the first genuine attempt to apply evolutionary theory to industrial organisation, also uses a pattern of sleeping and reawakening to transport Julian West to the year 2000.
9. Wells may have derived the idea for Ostrog, as well as the name, from M. Y. Ostrogorsky's book, *Democracy and Organization of Political Parties* which he mentions in his *Experiment in Autobiography* (Ch. 8, v, p. 599). Although the English translation of Ostrogorsky's book appeared in 1902, three years after the first edition of *The Sleeper*, it seems probable that Wells would have heard about this controversial book in conversation even if he had not read the earlier French edition.
10. The actual ending of the novel is ambiguous, but in the preface to the 1910 edition, Wells elucidated it: 'My Graham dies, as all his kind must die, with no certainty of either victory or defeat.' (*The Sleeper Awakes* (1910) p. ii).
11. Wells's comment, 'Graham dies, as all his kind must die' may be read as further support for this view, for it implies that in different circumstances Graham need not have died.
12. B. Bergonzi, *The Early H. G. Wells* (Manchester, 1961), p. 152.
13. P. Parrinder, *H. G. Wells* (Edinburgh, 1970) pp. 44–5.
14. H. G. Wells, *The First Men in the Moon* (London, 1924), Ch. 1, p. 21.
15. Ibid., Ch. 24, p. 258.
16. H. G. Wells, 'The Land Ironclads', *Short Stories* (London, 1925), p. 413.
17. H. L. Sussman, *Victorians and the Machine* (Cambridge, Mass., 1968), Ch. 6.
18. H. G. Wells, *A Modern Utopia* (London, 1925), Ch. 3, viii, pp. 99–100.
19. H. G. Wells, *The World Set Free* (London, 1925), Ch. 1, iii, p. 37.
20. Ibid., Ch. 1, iii, p. 40.
21. H. G. Wells, *The War in the Air* (London, 1925), Ch. 6, vi, p. 200 and Ch. 8, i, p. 243.
22. M. Schorer, 'Technique as Discovery' in *Critiques and Essays on Modern Fiction*, ed. J. W. Aldridge (New York, 1952), p. 73.
23. H. G. Wells, *The World Set Free* (London, 1925), Ch. 5, iv. p. 225.
24. H. G. Wells, *Tono-Bungay* (London, 1925), Bk IV, Ch. 3, iii, pp. 528–9.

4. SCIENCE AND GOVERNMENT – THE WELLSIAN UTOPIA

1. *Experiment in Autobiography*, Ch. 9, i, p. 651.
2. Ibid., Ch. 9, i, pp. 651–2.
3. *The Island of Dr. Moreau*, Ch. 14, p. 101.
4. M. R. Hillegas, *The Future as Nightmare* (New York, 1967), p. 39.
5. *Anticipations*, Ch. 9, p. 245.
6. Ibid., Ch. 8, p. 227.
7. Ibid., Ch. 9, p. 250.
8. *Experiment in Autobiography*, Ch. 9, i, pp. 652–3; cf. *Anticipations*, Ch. 5, p. 155, and Ch. 9, p. 258.
9. *A Modern Utopia*, Ch. 9, i, pp. 231–2.
10. *First and Last Things*, Bk III, xii, pp. 311–14.
11. *The New Machiavelli*, Bk I, Ch. 3, iii, pp. 66–9.
12. Letter of 8 February 1902, *Arnold Bennett and H. G. Wells*, ed. Harris Wilson (London, 1960), p. 74.
13. *Kipps*, Bk II, Ch. 3, i, p. 209.
14. Ibid., Bk II, Ch. 1, ii, pp. 169–70.
15. Ibid., Bk III, Ch. 2, i, p. 401–2.
16. *The War in the Air*, Ch. II, v., pp. 356–7.
17. Napoleonic imagery occurs frequently, always in a derogatory sense, throughout *Tono-Bungay*.
18. *A Modern Utopia*, Ch. 9, iii, p. 245.
19. *Men Like Gods*, Bk I, Ch. 5, vi, p. 80.
20. Ibid., Bk III, Ch. 2.
21. *New Worlds for Old*, Ch. 2, pp. 23–5.
22. *The World Set Free*, Ch. 3, iii, pp. 141–2.
23. T. H. Huxley, 'Evolution and Ethics' in J. S. Huxley and T. H. Huxley, *Evolution and Ethics* (London, 1947).
24. *A Modern Utopia*, Ch. 3, vi, p. 92.
25. *The War in the Air*, Ch. 4, i, p. 96.
26. *A Modern Utopia*, Ch. 1, p. 7.
27. T. H. Huxley, op. cit., p. 62.
28. *Men Like Gods*, Bk II, Ch. 1, ii, p. 171.
29. See, e.g. *The Outlook for Homo Sapiens*, p. 166.
30. *A Modern Utopia*, Ch. 2, ii, p. 34.
31. Ibid., p. 35.
32. Socrates, Plato and Campanella had all abolished the family unit in their utopian schemes, while More advocated that it be placed under State control.
33. *The Sleeper Awakes*, Ch. 20, p. 414. This idea may well have been inspired by Verne's description of similar mother-substitute devices in *Amiens in the Year 2000*.
34. *A Modern Utopia*, Ch. 3, iv, p. 80.
35. See, e.g. Robert Jungk, *Brighter than a Thousand Suns*, trans. J. Cleugh (London, 1958).
36. H. Rose and S. Rose, *Science and Society* (Harmondsworth, 1970), Ch. 9, p. 181.
37. Ibid., Ch. 9, pp. 181–2.
38. *A Modern Utopia*, Ch. 1, vi, p. 24.
39. Ibid., p. 10.

40. G. Connes, *Etude sur la Pensée de Wells* (Paris, 1926), p. 441.
41. L. Mumford, *The Story of Utopias* (London, 1923), p. 184.
42. B. Webb, *Our Partnership* (London, 1948), p. 226.
43. Ibid., pp. 230–1.
44. Held under the auspices of the Fabian Arts Group, 1907.
45. G. B. Shaw, in 'The First Public Conference on Mr. H. G. Wells's "Samurai"', *The New Age* (n.s.), 1 (2 May 1907), p. 10.
46. J. B. Crozier, 'Mr. Wells as a sociologist', *Fortnightly Review*, LXXVIII (Sep. 1905), 424.
47. M. Belgion, *H. G. Wells* (London, 1953), p. 21.
48. Quoted by J. Baines in *Joseph Conrad* (London, 1959), p. 232.
49. G. K. Chesterton, 'Mr. H. G. W. and the Giants' in *Heretics* (London, 1905), Ch. 5, p. 79.
50. *A Modern Utopia*, Ch. 1, i, p. 9.
51. *Experiment in Autobiography*, Ch. 9, i, p. 649.
52. *The Croquet Player*, Ch. 4, pp. 72–3.
53. *All Aboard for Ararat*, Ch. 2, pp. 75–6.
54. George Orwell, *The Road to Wigan Pier* (London, 1959), Ch. 12, pp. 192–3 and 225–6.
55. Similarly, in *Marriage*, Trafford and Marjorie, Stifled by the superficialities and ease of Edwardian London, embark for the wilds of Labrador to reassess their life and work in enforced solitude. Trafford, in particular, is seen as a forerunner of the Samurai.
56. *Experiment in Autobiography*, Ch. 9, ii, p. 660.
57. E.g. B. Bergonzi, op. cit., Ch. 7; V. Brome, op. cit., Appendix.
58. E. Shanks, 'The Work of Mr. H. G. Wells' in *First Essays in Literature* (London, 1923), pp. 162–3.
59. Wells acknowledges Heraclitus, Empedocles, Plato, More, Bacon, Campanella, Wordsworth, Spencer, Morris and Bellamy as sources of his utopian ideas.
60. J. B. Crozier, op. cit., pp. 424–5.
61. G. K. Chesterton, op. cit., Ch. 5.
62. *Anticipations*, Ch. 9, pp. 249–51.
63. *The Science of Life*, Bk IX, Pt 3, Ch. 59, vi, p. 1494.
64. *A Modern Utopia*, Ch. 4, ii, p. 116; Ch. 4, iii, p. 125.
65. *The World Set Free*, Ch. 4, x, p. 200.
66. T. H. Huxley, op. cit., p. 81.
67. J. Harris, 'H. G. Wells', *T. P.'s Weekly*, x (12 July 1907), 53.
68. *The Star Begotten*, p. 160.
69. E. Shanks, op. cit., pp. 150, 167–8.
70. *Anticipations*, Ch. 5, p. 130–1.
71. *Men Like Gods*, Bk III, Ch. 2, vi, p. 286.
72. *Guide to the New World*, Ch. 41, pp. 146–7; cf. also *The Fate of Homo Sapiens*, xxv, pp. 294–5.
73. 'World Encyclopaedia' in *World Brain* (London, 1938), p. 10.

5. WASTE AND DISORDER OR ORDER AND UNIFORMITY?

1. Cf. *Experiment in Autobiography*, Ch. 2.
2. *The New Machiavelli*, Bk I, Ch. 2, vi, p. 49.
3. *Experiment in Autobiography*, Ch. 2.
4. *Tono-Bungay*, Bk IV, Ch. 3, ii, pp. 525–6.
5. Ibid., Bk III, Ch. 3, i, pp. 374–5.
6. Ibid., Bk IV, Ch. 2, ii, p. 507.
7. Ibid., Bk III, Ch. 4, v, pp. 446–7.
8. Ibid., Bk IV, Ch. 3, i, p. 519.
9. *The New Machiavelli*, Bk I, Ch. 2, v, pp. 47–8.
10. Ibid., Bk I, Ch. 4, ix, p. 151.
11. Ibid., Bk II, Ch. 2, viii, pp. 250–1.
12. *The Passionate Friends*, Ch. 6, ix, p. 168.
13. *Marriage*, Bk III, Ch. 5, vii, p. 584.
14. *First and Last Things*, Bk III, iii, p. 277.
15. *Tono-Bungay*, Bk IV, Ch. 3, iii, pp. 528–9.
16. *The New Machiavelli*, Bk I, Ch. 2, v.
17. *Anticipations*, Ch. 9, pp. 243–4.
18. Ibid., Ch. 9, p. 245.
19. *A Modern Utopia*, Ch. 3, i, pp. 66–7.
20. Ibid., Ch. 7, iii, p. 203.
21. It was, ironically, their planned approach to Socialism which had first attracted Wells to their ranks because it appeared to him more constructive than either the resentment-based anarchism of the Marxists or the haphazard approach of the Liberals.
22. *The New Machiavelli*, Bk II, Ch. 2, iv, pp. 232–3.
23. Ibid., Bk II, Ch. 2, viii, p. 251.
24. *The Dream*, Pt I, Ch. 3, i, pp. 72–3.
25. Ibid., Pt I, Ch. 4, iii, p. 114.
26. 'The novels of Mr. George Gissing', *Contemporary Review*, LXXII (Aug. 1897), 200.
27. *Love and Mr. Lewisham*, Ch. 32, pp. 516–7.
28. *Marriage*, Bk II, Ch. 2, iv, p. 287.

6. FREE WILL AND PREDESTINATION: FREEDOM AND LIMITATION

1. Charles Darwin, letter to Asa Gray, 22 May 1860 in F. Darwin, *Life and Letters of Charles Darwin* (London, 1887), II, p. 312.
2. J. Tyndall, 'The Belfast Address', in *Fragments of Science* (New York, 1892), II, p. 201.
3. *The Time Machine*, *Short Stories*, p. 117.
4. *Anticipations*, Ch. 9, pp. 246–7.
5. *First and Last Things*, Bk II, iii, pp. 234–6.
6. Quoted by U. C. Knoepflmacher, *Religious Humanism and the Victorian Novel* (Princeton, N.J., 1965), p. 108.
7. *First and Last Things*, Bk II, i, pp. 231–2.
8. Ibid., Bk II, xii, p. 261.

9. *Kipps*, Bk I, Ch. 2, iii, p. 50.
10. *Love and Mr. Lewisham*, Ch. 32, pp. 514, 516.
11. *Tono-Bungay*, Bk IV, Ch. I, viii, pp. 498–9.
12. A. West, 'H. G. Wells', *Encounter*, VIII (No. 2) (Feb. 1957), 53, 56.
13. B. Bergonzi, op. cit., Ch. 1. It should be noted, however, that 'Zoological Retrogression' (1891) indicates Wells's familiarity with the concept of degeneration before Nordau's book (published 1894).
14. It was only at W. E. Henley's request that Wells extended the germinal idea of time-travelling to provide glimpses of the future. See *Experiment in Autobiography*, Ch. 8, i, p. 515.
15. Cf. 'Zoological Retrogression', *Anticipations*, and 'The things that live on Mars' for parallel procedures.
16. 'Mr. Wells explains himself', *T.P.'s Magazine* (Dec. 1911), 3.
17. *Experiment in Autobiography*, Ch. 8, vi, p. 638.
18. *The Fate of Homo Sapiens*, Ch. 10, pp. 107–8.
19. J. Kagarlitsky, op. cit., Ch. 1, p. 36.
20. *The Fate of Homo Sapiens*, Ch. 26, pp. 311–12.
21. *Mind at the End of its Tether*, i, p. 69.
22. *The World Set Free*, Ch. 5, iii, p. 223.

7. SCIENCE AS MYTH AND MYSTICISM

1. H. F. Jones, *Samuel Butler, Author of Erewhon* (London, 1919), I, p. 385.
2. See e.g. W. Archer, *God and Mr. Wells* (London, 1917) and Wells's own *Experiment in Autobiography*, Ch. 9, iv.
3. *Experiment in Autobiography*, Ch. 9, iv, p. 673.
4. *A Modern Utopia*, Ch. 11, v, p. 326.
5. *The Science of Life*, p. 386.
6. J. S. Huxley, *Evolution in Action* (London, 1953), p. 132.
7. *Anticipations*, Ch. 4, p. 93.
8. *New Worlds for Old*, Ch. 13, p. 301.
9. *The First Men in the Moon*, Ch. 23, pp. 237, 240.
10. *First and Last Things*, Bk II, ii, pp. 233–4.
11. Ibid., Bk II, viii, pp. 247–9.
12. Introduction to the 1914 edition of *Anticipations*, reprinted in the Atlantic edition, Vol. IV, pp. 281–2.
13. *First and Last Things*, Bk II, viii, p. 249.
14. Ibid., p. 250.
15. Ibid., Bk II, ix, p. 256.
16. Ibid., Bk II, viii, p. 249; Bk II, ix, pp. 255, 256.
17. Ibid., II, i, p. 232.
18. *The Open Conspiracy*, Ch. 12, p. 179.
19. *First and Last Things*, Bk II, viii, p. 250.
20. *The World Set Free*, Ch. 4, xii, pp. 211–12.
21. Ibid., Ch. 5, viii, p. 244; cf. Ch. 5, iv, p. 225.
22. Ibid., Ch. 5, ix, pp. 247–8.
23. *Boon*, Ch. 2, iii, p. 423.
24. *The Dream*, Ch. 8, i, pp. 314–16.

25. D. H. Lawrence, *Calendar*, III (Oct. 1926), 256.
26. C. Darwin, *Autobiography*, ed. N. Barlow (London, 1958), pp. 138–9.
27. Ironically, Lawrence's phrase 'blood consciousness' and the concepts which he implies thereby, are very close to Wells's 'great stream of the blood of the species', although neither author seems to have noticed any correlation.
28. *The Science of Life*, Bk IX, Pt III, Ch. 59, viii, p. 1497.
29. *The Work, Wealth and Happiness of Mankind*, Ch. 2, iv, p. 73.
30. *Experiment in Autobiography*, Ch. 9, x, pp. 824–6.
31. 'Religion and Science' in *Guide to the New World*, p. 103.
32. *Tono-Bungay*, Bk IV, Ch. 3, iii, p. 529.
33. 'On the quality of illusion in the continuity of individual life in the higher metazoa, with particular reference to *Homo sapiens*', *Nature*, CIII (1 April 1944), 395.
34. *Love and Mr. Lewisham*, Ch. 32, p. 516.
35. *The Food of the Gods*, Bk III, Ch. 5, iii, pp. 305–6.
36. 'The discovery of the future', *Nature*, LXV, No. 1684, (6 Feb. 1902), 331.
37. *Marriage*, Bk III, Ch. 4, x, pp. 529–30.
38. *The Outline of History*, Bk IX, Ch. 41, v, p. 759.
39. *Men Like Gods*, Bk III, Ch. 4, iii, p. 316.
40. Wells suggests this explicitly in *A Modern Utopia* when he speaks of the stars not escaping us in the end, for before the sun declines to its twilight and the earth becomes uninhabitable men will have discovered other homes in the universe. This was the first serious prediction of space-travel as a step necessary for man's survival.
41. A. Huxley, *Literature and Science* (London, 1963), III, pp. 11–12.
42. Ibid., xxv, p. 65.

8. WELLS'S CONCEPT OF THE INDIVIDUAL

1. E. Crispin, quoted by Kingsley Amis, *New Maps of Hell* (London, 1961), p. 128.
2. W. Cross, 'The mind of H. G. Wells', *Yale Review*, XVI (Jan. 1927), 314.
3. Ibid., Bk III, Ch. 1, i, pp. 279, 280.
4. Ibid., Bk IV, Ch. 1, viii, p. 498.
5. *The War in the Air*, Ch. 3, i, p. 66.
6. Henry James, letter to Wells (19 November 1905), quoted by L. Edel and G. N. Ray, *Henry James and H. G. Wells* (Urbana, 1958), p. 105.
7. *Experiment in Autobiography*, Ch. 7, iv, p. 477.
8. *The War of the Worlds*, Bk I, Ch. 1, p. 213.
9. *In the Days of the Comet*, Prologue, p. 3.
10. *The Star*, p. 570.
11. *Tono-Bungay*, Bk I, Ch. 1, iii, p. 9.
12. *Experiment in Autobiography*, Ch. 7, v, p. 503.
13. E. Zola, *The Experimental Novel*, reprinted in Becker (ed.), *Documents of Modern Literary Realism* (Princeton, 1963), p. 193.
14. *Athenaeum*, (Oct. 1910), 450; *Spectator*, CV (22 oct. 1910), 654–5; *Spectator*, CVII (Oct. 1911), 602.
15. *The Wheels of Change, Love and Mr. Lewisham, Kipps, In the Days of the Comet,*

Tono-Bungay, The New Machiavelli, The Wife of Sir Isaac Harman, The Undying Fire, Meanwhile and *The Dream.*

16. Voltaire, *Vathek, Rasselas,* Tom Paine, Plato's *Republic, Gulliver's Travels,* and later *The Free Thinker,* Shelley, Carlyle, William Morris. Cf. *Experiment in Autobiography,* Ch. 3, vi, p. 138, and Ch. 6, ii, p. 305.

17. 'The depressed school', *Saturday Review,* LXXIX (27 Apr. 1895), 531.

18. *Tono-Bungay,* Bk I, Ch. 1, i, p. 3.

19. See Chapter 6 above.

20. J. S. Huxley, 'H. G. Wells', *The Spectator,* CLXXVII (16 Aug. 1946), 161.

21. Odette Keun, 'H. G. Wells – the player', *Time and Tide,* XV, (13 Oct. 1934), 1250. Cf. R. C. K. Ensor, '*Experiment in Autobiography* – a review', *The Spectator,* CLIII (12 Oct. 1934), 529.

22. *Marriage,* Bk I, Ch. 3, vi, p. 149.

23. *Tono-Bungay,* Bk IV, Ch. 3, iii, p. 529.

24. *Mankind in the Making,* pp. 16, 47, 334; *A Modern Utopia,* p. 7.

25. Ibid., pp. 37, 41–51, 152, 294.

26. See e.g. *A Modern Utopia,* Ch. 6, v, p. 181 (note) which refers to Havelock Ellis's *Man and Woman.*

27. *Anticipations,* Ch. 7, p. 206.

28. *A Modern Utopia,* Ch. 3, iii, p. 75.

29. In the 1880s and 1890s, it was still widely regarded with suspicion as a quasi-magic art, practised by charlatans. Freud studied hypnotism as a means of psychotherapy in cases of hysteria under Charcot in Paris, 1885, but on his return to Vienna found that his reports of these techniques met only with ridicule and rebuffs from his colleagues. R. S. Woodworth, *Contemporary Schools of Psychology* (London, 1965), Ch. 9, p. 255.

30. *Experiment in Autobiography,* Ch. 1, ii, pp. 24–6.

31. *Kipps,* Bk II, Ch. 3, iii, p. 217.

32. Ibid., Bk III, Ch. 3, viii, pp. 449–50.

33. *The New Machiavelli,* Bk III, Ch. 1, i, pp. 311–12.

34. *Marriage,* Bk III, Ch. 1, v, p. 419.

35. *The Passionate Friends,* Ch. 7, v, pp. 221–2.

36. *A Modern Utopia,* Ch. 7, iii, p. 204.

37. *Marriage,* Bk III, Ch. 4, xiv, pp. 547–8.

38. *Ann Veronica,* Ch. 16, v, p. 367.

39. *Tono-Bungay,* Bk II, Ch. 4, iii, pp. 228–30.

40. *Marriage,* Bk I, Ch. 2, ii, p. 65.

41. *Ann Veronica,* Ch. 12, vii, p. 294.

42. *Tono-Bungay,* Bk III, Ch. 3, v, p. 402.

43. *Ann Veronica,* Ch. 8, v, pp. 191–2.

44. *Kipps,* Bk I, Ch. I, pp. 5–6.

45. *Experiment in Autobiography,* Ch. 2, v, p. 79.

46. *Ann Veronica,* Ch. 17, iii, p. 389.

47. Ibid., Ch. 16, i, pp. 357–8.

48. W. Cross, 'The mind of H. G. Wells', *Yale Review,* XVI (Jan. 1927), 315.

49. *Kipps,* Bk I, Ch. 3, ii, pp. 66–7.

50. *Tono-Bungay,* Bk IV, Ch. 1, iv, p. 477.

51. Ibid., Bk IV, Ch. 1, i, p. 465.

52. Ibid., Bk III, Ch. 2, i, p. 311.

53. Ibid., Bk III, Ch. 2, i, p. 313.
54. *Ann Veronica*, Ch. 17, i, pp. 380–1; Ch. 17, ii, p. 385.
55. C. G. Jung, *Collected Works*, Vol. VII, pp. 173, 178–9.
56. *The Wheels of Chance*, Ch. 13, p. 62.
57. *The Food of the Gods*, Bk I, Ch. 1, iv, p. 14.
58. 'The Moth', *Short Stories*, p. 378.
59. 'Under the Knife', *Short Stories*, p. 419.
60. Ibid., p. 422.
61. *Experiment in Autobiography*, Ch. 7, i, pp. 418–19.
62. Ibid., Ch. 7, iv, p. 467.
63. *Ann Veronica*, Ch. 8, vii, pp. 197–8.
64. Ibid., Ch. 8, viii, pp. 198–9.
65. Ibid., Ch. 11, i, p. 269.
66. *The New Machiavelli*, Bk IV, Ch. 2, ii, pp. 488–9.
67. *The World Set Free*, Ch. 5, vii, pp. 235–7.
68. *Experiment in Autobiography*, Ch. 7, ii, p. 425.
69. Ibid., Ch. 7, v, p. 498.
70. *The New Machiavelli*, Bk III, Ch. 1, viii, p. 344.
71. Wells quickly realised that Dorothy Richardson's novels marked 'an epoch in the technical development of the novelist's art, a real and successful thrust towards a new reality and intensity' (cf. *Experiment in Autobiography* Ch. 8, iii, p. 557). He also appreciated Joyce's work at a time when few others did. Arnold Bennett records that: 'The fame of James Joyce was founded in this country mainly by H. G. Wells, whose praise of *A Portrait of the Artist as a Young Man* had considerable influence upon the young. . . . Indeed he commanded me to read it and to admire it extremely'. E. A. Bennett, *Things that Have Interested Me*, No. 2 series (London, 1923), p. 191.
72. *Experiment in Autobiography*, Ch. 7, v, p. 497.
73. Ibid., Ch. 7, v, pp. 496–7.

9. THE SCIENTIST AS A LITERARY CHARACTER

1. The one outstanding exception is of course George Eliot's portrait of Lydgate in *Middlemarch*.
2. 'The chronic argonauts', reprinted in B. Bergonzi, op. cit., Appendix, p. 190.
3. B. Bergonzi, op. cit., p. 35.
4. 'Of a book unwritten', *Certain Personal Matters*, p. 167. This essay contains a modified description of 'The man of the year million' published in the *Pall Mall Gazette* LVII (6 Nov. 1893), 3.
5. *The Wonderful Visit*, xiii, pp. 150–1.
6. *Experiment in Autobiography*, Ch. 5, iii, p. 228.
7. 'The Moth', *Short Stories*, p. 368.
8. Alfred Tennyson, *In Memoriam*, LV.
9. *The Invisible Man*, Ch. 19, p. 124.
10. Ibid., Ch. 23, p. 166.
11. Ibid., Ch. 23, p. 164.
12. L. Huxley (ed.), *The Life of Thomas Henry Huxley* (New York, 1901), I, p. 239.
13. 'In one of his latest works, *Love and Mr. Lewisham*, Mr. Wells has . . . for the

first time given the Royal College of Science the dignity of literary recognition.' E. R. Lankester, *Nature*, LXV (No. 1689), Supplement (13 Mar. 1902), iii; cf. *Experiment in Autobiography*, Ch. 5, iii, pp. 232–3.
14. Cf. *Experiment in Autobiography*, Ch. 5, iii, pp. 232–3.
15. *Love and Mr. Lewisham*, Ch. 32, p. 517.
16. *The First Men in the Moon*, Ch. 2, p. 31.
17. Ibid., Ch. 18, p. 181.
18. Ibid., Ch. 23, p. 237.
19. Ibid., Ch. 23, p. 241.
20. *The Food of the Gods*, Bk I, Ch. 3, iii, p. 69.
21. Ibid., Bk III, Ch. 5, iii, p. 305.
22. *Tono-Bungay*, Bk II, Ch. 1, ii, p. 136.
23. Ibid., Bk II, Ch. 1, vi, p. 165.
24. Ibid., Bk III, Ch. 3, i, pp. 373–4.
25. Ibid., Bk IV, Ch. 3, iii, p. 539.
26. Ibid., p. 539.
27. *Marriage*, Bk II, Ch. 2, iii, pp. 285–7.
28. Ibid., Bk II, Ch. 3, i, p. 300.
29. *Ann Veronica*, Ch. 1, ii, p. 9.
30. Ibid., Ch. 5, v, p. 117.
31. Ibid., Ch. 13, i.
32. Ibid., Ch. 13, i, p. 297.
33. Ibid., Ch. 8, viii, p. 198.
34. *Marriage*, Bk I, Ch. 3, vi, pp. 148–51.
35. Ibid., Bk II, Ch. 3, iii, pp. 320–1.
36. Ibid., Bk III, Ch. 2, vii, p. 467.
37. *The Passionate Friends*, Ch. 10, iv, p. 334.
38. *Experiment in Autobiography*, Ch. 8, ii, p. 551.
39. *The New Machiavelli*, Bk IV, Ch. 2, i, pp. 486–8.

10. TECHNIQUES OF PERSUASION AND PRESENTATION

1. K. Amis, *New Maps of Hell* (London, 1961), pp. 147–8.
2. *The World Set Free*, Prelude, v, pp. 15–16.
3. *The Scientific Romances of H. G. Wells*, Preface to the Gollancz edition (London, 1933), p. viii.
4. *The First Men in the Moon*, Ch. 20, p. 209.
5. 'The Man Who Could Work Miracles', *Short Stories*, p. 373.
6. A similar situation occurs in Percy Greg's *Across the Zodiac*, (1880). Here rose cuttings, taken to Mars by the traveller, carry infecting bacteria to which the Martians have no resistance and Eunane, one of the narrator's wives, subsequently dies from the 'Turkish disease'.
7. *The First Men in the Moon*, Ch. 21, p. 213.
8. 'The Remarkable Case of Davidson's Eyes', *Short Stories*, p. 113.
9. *The Time Machine*, *Short Stories*, p. 113.
10. *The First Men in the Moon*, Ch. 20, p. 210.
11. 'The Plattner Story', *Short Stories*, p. 423.
12. *Experiment in Autobiography*, Ch. 8, i, p. 516.

13. 'The Man Who Could Work Miracles', *Short Stories*, pp. 374–5.
14. 'Review of *The Plattner Story and Others*', *Athenaeum*, No. 3635, (26 June 1897), 837.
15. *The Time Machine*, *Short Stories*, p. 10.
16. 'The Crystal Egg', *Short Stories*, p. 528.
17. *Tono-Bungay*, Bk III, Ch. I, ii, p. 289.
18. Virginia Woolf, 'Modern Fiction', *The Common Reader* (London, 1925), p. 187.
19. 'The New Accelerator', *Short Stories*, p. 440.
20. 'The chronic argonauts, (*Science Schools Journal*, 1888), reprinted by Bergonzi, op. cit., p. 201.
21. 'A tale of the twentieth century', reprinted by Bergonzi, op. cit., p. 182.
22. *The War in the Air*, Ch. 3, i, p. 70.
23. *The New Machiavelli*, Bk IV, Ch. I, iv, p. 463.
24. *Tono-Bungay*, Bk III, Ch. I, ii, pp. 288–9.
25. Ibid., Bk III, Ch. I, iv, p. 304.
26. 'The New Accelerator', *Short Stories*, p. 435.
27. 'The Plattner Story', *Short Stories*, pp. 423, 450.
28. 'Popularising science' *Nature*, L, NO. 1291 (26 July 1894), 301.
29. Ibid., p. 300.
30. Ibid., p. 301.
31. A.H.L., 'Realism versus romance', *Today*, xxv (11 Sep. 1897), 164.
32. *The Invisible Man*, Ch. 28, pp. 198–9.
33. *The First Men in the Moon*, Ch. 2, p. 30.
34. 'The New Accelerator', *Short Stories*, p. 447.

11. ART, SCIENCE AND STRUCTURE: THE DEBATE WITH HENRY JAMES

1. *The First Men in the Moon*, Ch. 23, p. 234.
2. *Experiment in Autobiography*, Ch. 8, v, p. 620.
3. Henry James, letter to H. G. Wells, 18 October 1912, reprinted in *Henry James and H. G. Wells*, ed. L. Edel and G. N. Ray (London, 1958), pp. 165–8.
4. *Experiment in Autobiography*, Ch. 7, v, p. 490.
5. 'The Contemporary Novel', an address to the Times Book Club, 1911, reprinted by L. Edel and G. N. Ray, op. cit., pp. 154–5.
6. *Experiment in Autobiography*, Ch. 8, v, p. 619.
7. H. James, 'The Art of Fiction' in *The House of Fiction*, ed. L. Edel (London, 1957), p. 31.
8. *Experiment in Autobiography*, Ch. 7, v, pp. 488–9.
9. *Boon*, Ch. 4, iii, pp. 455–6.
10. H. G. Wells, letter to Henry James, 8 July 1915, reprinted in Edel, op. cit., p. 264.
11. Letter from James to Wells, 10 July 1915, reprinted by Edel, op. cit., p. 267.
12. D. MacCarthy, a review of *The Bulpington of Blup*, *Sunday Times* (22 Jan. 1933), p. 8.
13. Arnold Bennett, letter to Wells, (30 Sep. 1905), reprinted in *Arnold Bennett and H. G. Wells*, ed. H. Wilson (London, 1960), pp. 124–5.
14. *Tono-Bungay*, Bk I, Ch. I, i, p. 6, and Ch. I, ii, p. 7.
15. Ibid., Bk IV, Ch. 3, ii, p. 526.

16. *First and Last Things*, Bk II, viii, p. 250.
17. *Experiment in Autobiography*, Ch. 7, v, pp. 492–3.
18. R. Bloom, *Anatomies of Egotism* (Lincoln, Nebraska, 1977), pp. 9–10.
19. *Experiment in Autobiography*, Ch. 8, v, p. 623.
20. George Steiner, 'Imagining science', *Listener*, LXXXVI, No. 2225 (18 Nov. 1971), 688.

Bibliography

Except where otherwise indicated the place of publication is London.

A. WELLS'S WRITINGS

Where possible the Atlantic Edition issued in 28 uniform volumes (Unwin, 1924–7) has been used, since the text for this edition was read and revised by Wells, who wrote a special preface for each volume. However, the Atlantic edition is not complete and where other editions have been consulted they are indicated. The date of original publication of novels is given in square brackets.

'A tale of the twentieth century', *Science Schools Journal*, I (May 1887), 187–91.
'The chronic argonauts', *Science Schools Journal*, I (April, May, June 1888), 312, 336, 367.
'The rediscovery of the unique', *Fortnightly Review*, L n.s. (July 1891), 106–11.
'Zoological retrogression', *Gentleman's Magazine*, CCLXXI (7 Sep. 1891), 246–53.
'On extinction', *Chamber's Journal*, X (30 Sep. 1893), 623–4.
'Popularising science', *Nature*, L (26 July 1894) 300–1.
'Fallacies of heredity', *Saturday Review*, LXXVIII (8 Dec. 1894) 617–18.
'The limits of individual plasticity', *Saturday Review*, LXXIX (11 Jan. 1895), 89–90.
'Excelsior', *Saturday Review*, LXXIX (13 Apr. 1895), 475.
'The depressed school', a review of *Eve's Ransom*, *Saturday Review*, LXXIX, No. 2061 (27 Apr. 1895), 531.
The Time Machine [1895].
The Wonderful Visit [1895].
The Stolen Bacillus and other Incidents [1895].

'Intelligence on Mars', *Saturday Review*, LXXXI (4 Apr. 1896), 345–6.
The Island of Dr. Moreau [1896].
The Wheels of Chance [1896].
'Human evolution. An artificial process', *Fortnightly Review*, LX
    (Oct. 1896), 590–5.
The Plattner Story and Others [1897].
The Invisible Man [1897].
'The novels of Mr George Gissing', *Contemporary Review*, LXXII (Aug.
    1897), 192–201.
'Realism versus romance' (an interview), *Today* (11 Sep. 1897), 164.
Certain Personal Matters (Lawrence & Bullen) [1897].
The War of the Worlds [1898].
'What I believe' (an interview by George Lynch), *The Puritan* I
    (Apr. 1899), 1–3.
When the Sleeper Wakes [1899].
Tales of Space and Time [1899].
Love and Mr. Lewisham [1900].
'Huxley', *Royal College of Science Magazine*, XIII (Apr. 1901), 109–11.
The First Men in the Moon [1901].
Anticipations [1901].
'The discovery of the future', *Nature*, LXV, No. 1684 (6 Feb. 1902),
    326–31.
The Sea Lady [1902].
'H. G. Wells, esq. B. Sc.' *Royal College of Science Magazine*, XV (Apr.
    1903), 221–4.
'Scepticism of the Instrument' (an address to the Oxford
    Philosophical Society, 8 November 1903) printed in *Mind*, XIII
    n.s., No. 51 (July 1904), 379–93.
Mankind in the Making [1903].
Twelve Stories and a Dream [1903].
The Food of the Gods [1904].
'George Gissing: an impression', *Monthly Review*, XVI (Aug. 1904),
    159–72.
A Modern Utopia [1905].
Kipps [1905].
In the Days of the Comet [1906].
The Future in America [1906].
New Worlds for Old [1908].
The War in the Air [1908].
First and Last Things [1908].
'The things that live on Mars', *Cosmopolitan Magazine*, XLIV, No. 4

(Mar. 1908), 335–42.

Tono-Bungay [1909].

Ann Veronica [1909].

The History of Mr. Polly [1910].

The New Machiavelli [1911].

The Country of the Blind and other Stories [1911].

'Mr Wells explains himself', *T.P's Magazine* (Dec. 1911), 3.

Marriage [1912].

The Passionate Friends [1913].

The World Set Free [1914].

The Wife of Sir Isaac Harman [1914].

Boon [1915].

The Research Magnificent [1915].

Mr Britling Sees It Through [1916].

God the Invisible King [1917].

The Soul of a Bishop [1917].

Joan and Peter [1918].

Natural Science and the Classical System in Education (ed. by E. R. Lankester), (Heinemann), 1918.

Report of the League for the Promotion of Science in Education 1916–1918 (Harrison), 1919.

The Undying Fire [1919].

The Outline of History [1920] (Newnes) 1920.

The Secret Places of the Heart [1922] (Odhams) n.d.

A Short History of the World [1922] (Collins), 1933.

Men Like Gods [1923].

The Dream [1924] (Jonathan Cape), 1926.

Christina Alberta's Father [1925] (Jonathan Cape), 1925.

The World of William Clissold [1926] (Benn), 1926.

The Open Conspiracy [1928] (Hogarth), 1930.

The Science of Life (with J. S. Huxley and G. P. Wells) [1931] (Cassell), 1938.

The Work, Wealth and Happiness of Mankind [1932] (Heinemann), 1932.

The Shape of Things to Come [1933] (Hutchinson), 1933.

Experiment in Autobiography [1934] (Jonathan Cape), 1969.

The Croquet Player [1936] (Chatto and Windus), 1936.

Star Begotten [1937] (Chatto and Windus), 1937.

World Brain [1938] (Methuen), 1938.

The Fate of Homo Sapiens [1939] (Secker & Warburg), 1939.

All Aboard for Ararat [1940] (Secker and Warburg), 1941.

Guide to the New World [1941] (Gollancz), 1941.
The Outlook for Homo Sapiens [1942] (Secker and Warburg), 1942.
'On the quality of illusion in the continuity of the individual life in the higher Metazoa, with particular reference to the species Home sapiens'. Thesis for the Doctor's Degree at London University 1944. Published in *Nature*, CLIII (1 Apr. 1944), 395–7.
Phoenix [1942] (Secker and Warburg), 1942.
I Came to a Happy Turning [1945], Tiptree Essex, (H. G. Wells Society) 1968.
Mind at the End of its Tether [1945], Tiptree Essex, (H. G. Wells Society) 1968.

Letters:

Henry James and H. G. Wells, ed. Leon Edel and Gordon N. Ray (Hart-Davis), 1958.
Arnold Bennett and H. G. Wells, ed. Harris Wilson (Hart-Davis), 1960.
George Gissing and H. G. Wells, ed. Royal A. Gettmann (Hart-Davis), 1961.

Bibliographies:

I. F. Bell and D. Baird, *The English Novel, 1578–1956*, Denver (Swallow), 1958.
H. G. Wells Society, *H. G. Wells, A Comprehensive Bibliography* (Lowe and Brydone), 1968.
Robert P. Weeks, 'Bibliography of criticism of H. G. Wells', *English Fiction in Transition* I (1957), 37 ff. and brought up to date in subsequent volumes.

B. BIOGRAPHY AND CRITICISM OF WELLS'S WORK

'A.D. 802, 701'. A review of *The Time Machine, Pall Mall Gazette*, LXI, No. 9504 (10 Sep. 1895), 4.
Allen, Waltcr, *The English Novel* (Phoenix House), 1954.
Archer, W., *God and Mr Wells* (Watts), 1917.
Bailey, John, 'Mr Wells's pacifist state', *The Nation* (London), xv (26 Sep. 1914), 887–8.
Belgion, M., *H. G. Wells*, British Council Series Writers and their

Work (Longman) 1953.

Bennett, E. Arnold, 'Herbert George Wells and his work', *Cosmopolitan Magazine*, XXXIII (Aug. 1902), 465–71.

Beresford, J. D., *H. G. Wells* (Nisbet), 1915.

Bergonzi, B., 'Another early Wells item', *Nineteenth Century Fiction*, XIII (1958), 72–3. *The Early H. G. Wells*, Manchester (University Press), 1961.

Bloom, R., *Anatomies of Egotism* (University of Nebraska Press) 1977.

Brome, V., *H. G. Wells, A Biography* (Longmans), 1951.

Brooks, Van Wyck, *The World of H. G. Wells* (Unwin), 1915.

Burke, J. B., 'Mr Wells and modern science', *Dublin Review*, CLXIX (Oct. 1921), 222–36.

Caudwell, Christopher, 'H. G. Wells' in *Studies in a Dying Culture* (John Lane), 1938, pp. 73–95.

Chaplin, F. K., *H. G. Wells, An Outline* (Macmillan), 1961.

Chesterton, G. K., 'Mr H. G. Wells and the giants', Chapter 5 of *Heretics* (Lane), 1905.

Connes, G., *Etude sur la Pensée de Wells*, Paris (Hachette) 1926.

Costa, R. H., *H. G. Wells*, New York (Twayne), 1967.

Craufurd, A. H., *The Religion of H. G. Wells and Other Essays* (Unwin), 1909.

Cross, W., 'The mind of H. G. Wells', *Yale Review* XVI (Jan. 1927), 298–315.

Crowley, C. P., 'Failure of nerve: H. G. Wells', *University of Windsor Review*, II, 2 (Spring, 1967), 1–8.

Crozier, J. B., 'H. G. W. as a sociologist', *Fortnightly Review*, LXXVIII (Sep. 1905), 417–26.

Dark, Sidney, *The Outline of H. G. Wells* (Leonard Parsons), 1922.

Dickson, L., *H. G. Wells: His Turbulent Life and Times* (Macmillan), 1969.

Ensor, R. C. K., '*Experiment in Autobiography*', *The Spectator*, CLIII (12 Oct. 1934), 529.

'First Public Conference on Mr H. G. Wells's "Samurai"', *New Age* I (n.s.) (2 May 1907), 9–11.

Garnett, David, 'The Scientific Romances of H. G. Wells', *New Statesman and Nation*, v No. 116 (n.s.) (13 May 1933), 602.

Haight, Gordon, 'H. G. Wells's "Man of the year million"', *Nineteenth-Century Fiction*, XII (Mar. 1958), 323–6.

Harris, J., 'H. G. Wells', *T. P's Weekly*, x (12 July 1907) 53.

Huxley, J. S., 'H. G. Wells', *The Spectator*, CLXXVII (16 Aug. 1946) 161.

James, Henry, 'The new novel', in *The Art of Fiction and Other Essays*, Oxford (University Press), 1948, pp. 181–214. 'The younger generation', *Times Literary Supplement* (19 Mar. 1914), 133–4 and (2 Apr. 1914) 137–158.

Kagarlitski, J., *The Life and Thought of H. G. Wells* (transl. from the Russian by Moura Budberg) (Sidgwick and Jackson), 1966.

Keith, A., 'Is Darwinism dead?', *Nature*, CXIX (15 Jan. 1927), 75–7.

Keun, Odette, 'H. G. Wells – the player', *Time and Tide*, XV (13 Oct. 1934), 1249–51; (20 Oct. 1934), 1307–9; (27 Oct. 1934), 1346–8.

Lankester, E. R., 'The present judged by the future', (a review of *Anticipations*), *Nature*, LXV, Supplement (13 Mar. 1902), iii–v.

Lawrence, D. H., 'Review of *William Clissold*', *The Calendar*, III, No. 3 (Oct. 1926), 254–7.

Lay, W., 'H. G. Wells and his mental hinterland', *The Bookman* (New York), XLV, No. 5 (July 1917), 461–8. 'The marriage ideas of H. G. Wells'. *The Bookman* (New York), XLV, No. 6 (Aug. 1917) 606–13.

Lemire, E. D., 'H. G. Wells and the world of science fiction', *University of Windsor Review*, II, No. 2 (Spring 1967), 59–66.

Levy, H., 'Science in literature; the short stories of H. G. Wells', *Nature*, CXX (8 Oct. 1927), 503–4.

Lodge, D., '*Tono-Bungay* and the condition of England', in *The Language of Fiction* (Routledge) 1966, pp. 214–42. 'Assessing H. G. Wells', *Encounter*, XXVIII, No. 1 (1967), 54–61.

'A lunar romance' (review of *The First Men in the Moon*), *Nature*, LXV (19 Jan. 1902), 218–9.

MacKenzie, N. and J., *The Time Traveller* (Weidenfeld and Nicolson), 1973.

MacCarthy, D., '*The Bulpington of Blup*', *Sunday Times* (22 Jan. 1933) 8.

McNamara, E., 'H. G. Wells as novelist', *University of Windsor Review*, II, No. 2 (Spring 1967), 21–30.

Mellersh, H. L., 'Shaw, Wells and creative evolution', *Fortnightly Review*, CXXV (Feb. 1926), 178–88.

Mitchell, P. Chalmers, 'Mr Wells's "Dr Moreau"', *Saturday Review*, LXXXI (11 Apr. 1896), 368–9.

'Mr Wells's War in the Air', *Westminster Gazette*, XXXII (24 Oct. 1908), 8.

Newell, K. B., 'The structure of H. G. Wells's *Tono-Bungay*', *English Fiction in Transition*, IV, No. 2 (1961), 1–8.

Newell, K. B., *Structure in Four Novels by H. G. Wells* The Hague (Mouton), 1968.

Nicholson, N., *H. G. Wells* (Arthur Barker), 1950.

Orwell, G., 'Wells, Hitler and the World State' in *Collected Essays* (Mercury), 1961, pp. 160 ff.

Parrinder, Patrick, *H. G. Wells*, Edinburgh (Oliver and Boyd), 1970.

Philmus, R. M., 'The Time Machine: or the fourth dimension as prophecy', *PMLA* LXXXIV, No. 3 (May 1969) 530–5. *Into the Unknown*, Berkeley (University of California Press), 1970.

'*The Plattner Story and Others*', *Daily Chronicle* (26 May 1897), 3.

'*The Plattner Story and Others*', *Athenaeum*, No. 3635 (26 June 1897), 837.

Pitkin, W. B., 'Time and pure activity', *Journal of Philosophy, Psychology and Scientific Method*, XI (1914), 521–6.

Poston, L., '*Tono-Bungay*, Wells's unconstructed tale', *College English*, XXVI (1965), 433–7.

Pritchett, V. S., 'Mr Wells's scientific romances', *New Statesman*, XXVI, No. 654 (4 Sep. 1943), 154–5. 'All about ourselves', *New Statesman*, LI, No. 1315 (26 May 1956), 601–2. 'The Scientific Romances' in *The Living Novel*, Dublin (Arrow), 1960, pp. 122–9.

Raknem, Ingvald, *H. G. Wells and His Critics*, Oslo (Allen and Unwin), 1962.

Randall, A. E., 'The two Machiavellis', *New Age*, VIII, No. 15 (9 Feb. 1911), 353–5.

Ray, Gordon, N., 'H. G. Wells Tries to be a Novelist' in *Edwardians and Late Victorians*, ed. R. Ellmann, New York (Columbia U. P.), 1960, pp. 106–159.

Russell, Bertrand, 'H. G. Wells: liberator of thought', *The Listener*, L, (10 Sep. 1953), 417–18.

Scheick, W. J., 'The thing that is and the speculative if', *English Literature in Transition*, XI, No. 2 (1968), 67–78. 'Reality and the word: the last books of H. G. Wells', *English Literature in Transition*, XII, No. 3 (1969), 151–4.

Scott James, R. A., '*Ann Veronica*', *The Daily News* (4 Oct. 1909), 3.

Shanks, Edward, 'The Work of Mr H. G. Wells' in *First Essays in Literature* (Collins), 1923, pp. 148–71.

Snow, C. P., 'H. G. Wells' in *Variety of Men* (Macmillan), 1967, pp. 47–64.

Spencer, S., 'H. G. Wells. Materialist and mystic', *Hibbert Journal*,

XLVI (July 1948), 358–61.
Steinberg, M. W., 'H. G. Wells as a social critic', *University of Windsor Review*, II, No. 2 (Spring 1967), 9–20.
'The Time Machine', *Nature*, LII (18 July 1895), 268.
'A tour de force: review of *The Outline of History*', *Nature*, CVI (30 Sep. 1920), 137–40.
'The transplantation of living tissues' – a review of *The Island of Dr. Moreau*, *Natural Science*, VIII (May 1896), 291.
Vidler, Alec R., *The Church in An Age of Revolution: 1789 to the Present Day*, Harmondsworth (Penguin), 1961.
Wagar, Warren, *H. G. Wells: Journalism and Prophecy, 1893–1946* (Bodley Head), 1964.
The Wellsian, The Journal of the H. G. Wells Society.
West, Anthony, 'H. G. Wells', *Encounter*, VIII, No. 2, (Feb. 1957), 52–9. 'The dark world of H. G. Wells', *Harper's*, CCXIV (May 1957), 68–73.
West, Geoffrey H., *H. G. Wells – A Sketch for a Portrait* (Gerald Howe), 1930.
West, Rebecca, *The Strange Necessity* (Cape), 1928, p. 199.
Zamiatin, E. I., *Herbert Wells*, St Petersberg (Epoch), 1922.
Zangwill, Israel, 'Without prejudice', *Pall Mall Magazine*, VII (Sep. 1895), 153–5.

C. OTHER SOURCES OF QUOTATION AND REFERENCE

Allott, K., *Jules Verne* (Cresset), 1940.
Amis, Kingsley, *New Maps of Hell* (Gollancz), 1961.
Bailey, J. O., *Pilgrims Through Space and Time*, New York (Argus), 1947.
Baines, Jocelyn, *Joseph Conrad* (Weidenfeld and Nicolson), 1959.
Barnett, L., *The Universe and Dr Einstein*, New York (Mentor), 1952.
Batho, E. C. and B. Dobrée, *The Victorians and After* (Cresset), 1962.
Bennett, E. Arnold, *Things That Have Interested Me*, Second Series (Chatto and Windus), 1923.
Blindermann, C. S., 'Huxley and Kingsley', *Victorian Newsletter*, XX (Fall 1961), 25–8.
Blyton, W. J., 'Brave New World planning' *Quarterly Review*, CDXXIV (Apr. 1940), 263–77.
Buckley, J. H., *The Victorian Temper* (Cass), 1966.
Butler, Samuel, *The Works*, ed. H. F. Jones and A. T. Bartholomew

(Jonathan Cape), 1923–4.

Campanella, Thomas, *City of the Sun* [1623], Washington (Dunne), 1901.

Cazamian, Madelaine L., *Le Roman et les Idées en Angleterre: l'influence de la Science 1860–1890*, Strasbourg (Librairie Istra), 1923.

Chapman, R., *The Victorian Debate: English Literature and Society, 1832–1901* (Weidenfeld and Nicolson), 1968.

Clarke, I. F., *Voices Prophesying War, 1763–1934*, Oxford (University Press), 1966.

Cleugh, M. F., *Time – And Its Importance in Modern Thought* (Methuen), 1937.

Coates, J. B., *Ten Modern Prophets* (Frederick Muller), 1944.

Conquest, Robert, 'Science fiction and literature', *Critical Quarterly*, v (1963), 355–67.

Crowther, J. G., *The Social Relations of Science* (Macmillan), 1941. *Scientific Types* (Barrie and Rockliff), 1968.

Crozier, J. B., *Civilization and Progress* (Longmans), 1885.

Dangerfeld, George, *The Strange Death of Liberal England* (Constable), 1936.

Darwin, Charles, *The Origin of Species* [1859] (Murray), 1906.

—— *The Descent of Man* [1871] (Murray), 1913.

—— *The Autobiography* (ed. N. Barlow) (Collins), 1958.

Darwin, Francis, *The Life and Letters of Charles Darwin* (Murray), 1887.

Decker, C. R., *The Victorian Conscience*, New York (Twayne), 1952.

Einstein, Albert, 'Uber einen die Erzeugung und Verwandling des Lichtes betreffenden heuristischen Gesichtspunkt', *Annalen der Physik*, xvii (1905), 132–8.

—— 'Uber die von der molekularkinetischen Theorie der Wärme geförderte Bewegung von in ruhenden Flüssigkeiten suspendlerten Teilchen' *Annalen der Physik*, xvii (1905), 549–60.

—— 'Zur Elektrodynamik bewegter Körper', *Annalen der Physik*, xvii (1905), 891–921.

Ellis, Havelock, *Man and Woman* [1894], (Heinemann), 1934. *The Nineteenth Century – a Dialogue in Utopia* (Grant Richards), 1900.

Evans, I. O., *Jules Verne and His Work* (Arco), 1965.

Flew, A. G. N., *Evolutionary Ethics* (Macmillan), 1967.

Frye, Northrop, 'Varieties of literary utopias', *Daedalus*, xciv (Spring 1965), 323–47.

Green, R. L., *Into Other Worlds – Space Flight in Fiction from Lucian to Lewis* (Abelard–Schuman), 1957.

Greg, Percy, *Across the Zodiac* (Trübner), 1880.

Gross, J., 'The road to Utopia', *New Statesman*, LXXVIII, n.s. (25 July 1969), 108–9.

Henkin, Leo J., *Darwinism in the English Novel 1860–1910*, New York (Russell and Russell), 1963.

Hertzler, J. O., *The History of Utopian Thought*, New York (Macmillan), 1923.

Hillegas, Mark R., *The Future as Nightmare*, Oxford (University Press), 1967.

Hinton, Charles H., *Scientific Romances* (Swan Sonnenschein), 1886.

—— *The Fourth Dimension* [1904], (Swan Sonnenschein), 1906.

Huxley, Aldous, *Brave New World* [1932], Harmondsworth (Penguin), 1971.

—— *Literature and Science* (Chatto and Windus), 1963.

Huxley, Julian S. and Thomas Henry Huxley, *Evolution and Ethics* (Pilot), 1947.

Huxley, Julian S., *Evolution in Action*, Indianapolis (Indiana University Press), 1953.

Huxley, Leonard, *The Life and Letters of Thomas Henry Huxley*, New York (Appleton), 1901.

Huxley, Thomas Henry, 'Mr Darwin's critics' *Contemporary Review*, XVIII (Nov. 1871), 443–76.

—— 'On the hypothesis that animals are automata, and its history', *Fortnightly Review*, XVI, n.s., No. XCV (1 Nov. 1874), 555–80.

—— *Science and Culture and Other Essays* (Macmillan), 1881.

—— 'Administrative Nihilism' in *Methods and Results*, New York (Appleton), 1896. *Science and Education*, New York (Appleton), 1897.

Hynes, S., *The Edwardian Turn of Mind*, Princeton (University Press), 1968.

Irvine, W., *Apes, Angels and Victorians*, New York (Meridian), 1955.

James, Henry, *The Art of Fiction and Other Essays*, Oxford (University Press), 1948.

James, William, *Principles of Psychology*, New York (Dover), 1950.

Jeans, James, *The New Background of Science*, Michigan (Ann Arbor), 1959.

Jones, Henry Festing, *Samuel Butler, Author of Erewhon* (Macmillan), 1920.

Jung, C. G., 'Two Essays on Analytical Psychology' in *Collected Works* (Routledge and Kegan Paul), 1953.

Jungk, R., *Brighter than a Thousand Suns* (transl. J. Cleugh)

(Gollancz), 1958.

Kaleb, G., *Utopia and its Enemies*, New York (Glencoe), 1963.

Keith, A., 'Is Darwinism dead?' *Nature*, CXIX (15 Jan. 1927), 75-7.

—— *Darwin Revalued* (Watts), 1955.

Knoepflmacher, U. C., *Religious Humanism in the Victorian Novel*, Princeton (University Press), 1965.

Lytton, S. Bulwer, *The Coming Race* [1871], (Blackwoods), 1872.

—— *Kenelm Chillingly: His Adventures and Opinions* [1873], (Blackwoods), 1875.

Maitland, L., *By and By: An Historical Romance of the Future* [1873] (Bentley), 1875.

Marder, L., *Time and the Space Traveller* (Allen and Unwin), 1971.

Marx, Leo, *The Machine in the Garden*, Oxford (University Press), 1964.

Mendilow, A. A., *Time and the Novel* (Nevill), 1952.

Mercier, L. S., *Memoirs of the Year 2500* [1772] (translated W. Hooper), 1772.

More, Sir Thomas, *Utopia* [1516] ed. J. Warrington (Everyman), 1965.

Morton, A. L., *The English Utopia* (Lawrence and Wishart), 1952.

Mumford, Lewis, *Art and Technics*, Oxford (University Press), 1952. *The Story of Utopias* (Harrap), 1923.

Nelson, William (ed.), *Twentieth Century Interpretations of Utopia*, Englewood Cliffs (Prentice Hall), 1968.

Oppenheimer, J. R., 'On science and culture' *Encounter*, XIX (Oct. 1962), 3-10.

Orwell, George, *The Road to Wigan Pier* (Secker and Warburg), 1959.

Rodwell, G. F., 'On space of four dimensions', *Nature*, VIII (1 May 1873), 8-9.

Roppen, G., *Evolution and Poetic belief*, Oslo (Allen and Unwin), 1956.

Rose, Hilary and Steven Rose, *Science and Society*, Harmondsworth (Penguin), 1970.

Routh, H. V., *English Literature and Ideas in the Twentieth Century* (Methuen), 1946.

'S', 'Four-dimensional space', *Nature*, XXXI (26 Mar. 1885), 481.

Schorer, Mark, 'Technique as Discovery' in *Critiques and Essays on Modern Fiction, 1920–1951*, ed. J. W. Aldridge, New York (Ronald), 1952.

Silberstein, L., *The Theory of Relativity* (Macmillan), 1914.

Snow, Charles P., *Science and Government*, Oxford (University Press), 1961.
—— *The Two Cultures and the Scientific Revolution*, Cambridge (University Press), 1961.
Steiner, George, 'Imagining science', *Listener*, LXXXVI (18 Nov. 1971), 686–8.
Sussman, H. L., *Victorians and the Machine*, Cambridge, Mass. (Harvard University Press), 1968.
Szilard, Leo, 'Reminiscences', *Perspectives in American History*, II Cambridge, Mass. (Harvard University Press), 1968.
Tillotson, Geoffrey, 'Morris and the machine', *Fortnightly Review*, CXXXV (Apr. 1934), 464–71.
Tyndall, J., 'The Belfast Address' in *Fragments of Science*, New York (Appleton), 1892. Vol. I, pp. 201 ff.
Webb, Beatrice, *Diaries 1912–24*, ed. M. Cole (Longmans), 1952.
—— *Diaries 1924–32*, ed. M. Cole (Longmans), 1956.
—— *My Apprenticeship* (Longmans), 1926.
—— *Our Partnership* (Longmans), 1948.
Whitehead, A. N., *Science and the Modern World*, Cambridge (University Press), 1936.
Whitrow, G. J. (ed.), *Einstein: The Man and his Achievement* (Longmans), 1967.
Wichler, G., *Charles Darwin: The Founder of the Theory of Evolution and Natural Selection*, Oxford (Pergamon), 1961.
Wilde, Oscar, 'The Canterville Ghost' [1887] in *Lord Arthur Saville's Crime and Other Prose Pieces* (Methuen), 1908.
Willey, Basil, *Nineteenth-Century Studies* Harmondsworth (Penguin), 1964.
Woolf, Virginia, 'Modern Fiction' in *The Common Reader* (Hogarth), 1925, pp. 184–95.
—— 'Mr Bennett and Mrs Brown' in *The Captain's Death Bed* (Hogarth), 1950, pp. 99–111.
Zamiatin, E. I., *We* [1920], New York (Dutton), 1952.

Index

Amis, K., 221
art, Wells's approach to, 241–50
authority, 37–8

Bennett, E. A., 41, 248
Bergonzi, B., 46, 47, 51, 55, 136, 198
biology, progress of in 19th century,
    12–13
Bromley, Kent, 11, 112
Butler, S., 81, 143–4

chance, 30–2
characterization, 7, 18–19, 163–96
    of the scientist, 7, 197–217
Chesterton, G. K., 100, 102, 105
Conrad, J., 100, 242, 244–5, 248, 251
Crane, S., 242
Crispin, E., 163
Crozier, J. B., 100, 104

Darwin, C., 14, 23, 31, 36
Darwinian theory, *see* Evolution, the-
    ory of,
Democracy, 85, 108, 119
determinism, (predestination), 6–7,
    58–9, 127–36, 140–1, 172
disorder, (*see* waste),
Doyle, A. Conan, 235

education, Wells's theories of, 63–5, 89
Eliot, G., 129
    Middlemarch, 214
Ellis, W. Havelock, 175
Essay on Population, 105
eugenics, 101, 105–6, 119
Evolution, theory of, 13, 16, 21–2, 27–
    9, 34, 127, 138, 151, 179

Fabian Society, 85, 88, 103, 146

fourth dimension, 54–6, 58–9, 221
free will, 127–36, 141
Freud, S., 176, 181, 185, 188, 191–2
future, Wells's thinking about, 2–5, 19–
    20, 108

Gaskell, E., 214
Gissing, G., 169

Hardy, T., 128–9
Heisenberg, W. K., 52, 158–9
Hinton, C., 54–5, 221
humour, in the scientific romances,
    237–9
Huxley, A., 81, 109–10, 158
    Brave New World, 4, 109
Huxley, J. S., 145, 172
Huxley, T. H., 12–16, 23, 25, 27, 33, 91,
    93, 107, 128, 131, 138, 144, 151,
    172, 204–5
    Administrative Nihilism, 25
    Evolution & Ethics, 25–6

immortality, 131–2
individualism, 94–5, 121, 125, 145
internationalism, 23, 92–3, 96–7

James, H., 166, 241–8, 250
James, W., 175
Jung, C. G., 175, 185

Keun, O., 172–3

Lamarckism, 29, 144–5
Lankester, E. R., 40
Lawrence, D. H., 152–3

Michelson-Morley experiment, 54–5
Mill, J. S., 129